INSIDE THE PUBLISHING REVOLUTION

||||||||||

THE ADOBE STORY

PAMELA PFIFFNER

INSIDE THE PUBLISHING REVOLUTION: THE ADOBE STORY
Pamela Pfiffner

This Adobe Press book is published by Peachpit Press.
For information on Adobe Press books, contact:
Peachpit Press
1249 Eighth Street
Berkeley, California 94710
510-524-2178 (tel), 510-524-2221 (fax)
http://www.peachpit.com

To report errors, please send a note to errata@peachpit.com
Peachpit Press is a division of Pearson Education
For the latest on Adobe Press books, go to
http://www.adobe.com/adobepress

Editor: Serena Herr
Production Manager: Kate Reber
Adobe Press Project Manager: Jeffrey Warnock
Book Design: Andrew Faulkner, Doug Beach, afstudio.com
Art Direction: Min Wang
Cover Design: Andrew Faulkner
Copyeditor: Karen Seriguchi
Permissions: Laurie Stewart
Composition: Andrew Faulkner, Doug Beach, Nathalie Valette
Graphics Preparation: Andrew Faulkner, Doug Beach

ISBN 0-321-11564-3
9 8 7 6 5 4 3 2 1

Printed and bound in the United States of America

In honor of two remarkable partnerships:

Chuck Geschke and John Warnock,
who gave birth to an industry

and

David and Patricia Pfiffner,
who gave birth to me

contents

FOREWORD

Adobe Systems is a company that came into being out of frustration. In 1982 we both had great jobs at one of the premier research facilities in the world. We were given state-of-the-art equipment. We worked alongside some of the world's best computer science minds, and we were allowed to work on problems of our own choosing. Our frustration grew out of a realization that none of our ideas were going to be used in products in the fast-changing world of personal computing. We either had to be content with research, or leave.

When we started the company, we had the hope of being successful but no great expectations. After all, we were proposing to solve problems in an entirely new way. We knew that if we failed, we could both get other jobs to support our families. What we did not know was that the world was ready for the inventions and ideas that we had to offer.

As our first product, PostScript, started to take hold during 1985, '86 and '87, we began to realize that the world of graphic arts, printing, and publishing was never going to be the same. The revolution that began as desktop publishing had fundamentally changed the cost, productivity, and efficiency of the entire industry. As Adobe grew, its influence expanded. The company had ceased to be a grand personal experiment and was now a force whose decisions affected the shape of publishing to come.

This unexpected success had a profound effect on us as individuals. We had been chosen, for better or worse, as primary influencers of an industry with 500 years of tradition, aesthetics, and values. We now had the responsibility to the industry to do the right thing. It became our goal to build a company whose culture and values reflected that responsibility. In less than two decades, Adobe helped transform the world of print communications from a manual, mechanical process to a fully digital workflow. Today, as all communication technologies are converting to digital, Adobe's products continue to expand the technological frontiers in photography, video production, animation, digital communication, and the World Wide Web.

Pamela Pfiffner, who has reported on our industry and has known Adobe since its inception, has combined her many interviews with former employees, people inside the company, and outside industry observers into a balanced, well-thought-out story.

This book, so ably written by Pfiffner, tells the story of the individuals that developed the technologies, marketed the products, and built Adobe Systems into the successful, vibrant, global organization it is today. As the founders of Adobe, we recognize that its accomplishments are based upon the efforts of thousands of past and current employees, the support of millions of customers around the world, and the cooperation of hundreds of business partners who assisted us in achieving this success. They are the real heroes of this story.

Finally, we acknowledge the constant loving support of the two most important people in our lives, Marva and Nan, to whom these words are dedicated.

John Warnock & Chuck Geschke

Los Altos, California

June 2002

INTRODUCTION

The history of Adobe Systems is so intertwined with the modern publishing revolution that it is hard to distinguish the two. Without Adobe and its products—PostScript, Photoshop, Acrobat, to name just a few—publishing as we know it today would not exist. On an ancillary note, without Adobe Systems, my career would have looked a whole lot different.

This book chronicles Adobe's history as it evolved alongside modern publishing, from print to Web, from systems to desktop applications, from independent graphic artists to collaborative workgroups. Adobe's story is remarkable because the company led by example. It developed a culture of design and engineering excellence that set standards for how we produce information. Other companies have contributed to the publishing revolution, but if there is one that links the entire story together—technology, design, communication, even computer operating systems—it is Adobe.

"With cheeky aplomb I hung out my shingle; I had few customers, but I still called myself a 'publisher.'"

The second, more personal point is woven into the words on these pages. Adobe has been a consistent note in my professional career—and in my personal life. That I've now written a book about a company that shaped my work is either a perverse metaphysical twist or an appropriate coda to one phase of my career.

My history with Adobe goes back to 1985, when I discovered the Apple LaserWriter. I'd been using a Macintosh and an ImageWriter dot-matrix printer for almost a year by then, thanks to my roommate, who bought an original 128 Kbyte Mac at the San Francisco Macy's department store in 1984. But the LaserWriter's ability to print crisp type was a revelation, although I didn't realize PostScript's role at the time. I made the connection when I started buying Adobe typefaces a year or so later. In 1986, I borrowed money from my father to buy a Macintosh SE and Aldus PageMaker 1.0. For my "good" printouts, I took a floppy disk down to a local Mac shop where, at the cost of $5 for 15 minutes of LaserWriter time, I printed my PageMaker files.

One of the files I printed (I remember it cost $20, so it must have taken an hour to print) was my application to the University of California at Berkeley Graduate School of Journalism, which I composed in PageMaker

Sumner Stone

Director of Typography at Adobe Systems
will talk on type design
in the age of digital machines

4 pm, Tuesday, 8 November
Conference Room, A+A Building,
Yale School of Art, 180 York St.

To encourage the acceptance of PostScript in the early 1990s, Adobe launched an educational campaign about digital type, aimed at the design community.

(styled type! two columns! 1-point rules!). After admission, I took advantage of the university's student purchasing program to buy my own LaserWriter (I had to petition Apple to do so, as the $7,000 printer wasn't offered then to students, on the basis that few could afford it). With cheeky aplomb I then hung out my shingle as Pixel Press, offering writing, design, and printing services. I had few customers, but I still called myself a "publisher." After I received my master's degree in 1988, my experience with the Mac and DTP landed me a job at MacWEEK, one of the first magazines to be produced digitally from start to finish, with an in-house Linotype imagesetter, its own infographic artist, and electronic file transfer to its printing plant in Wisconsin. As a cub reporter I had to work my way onto the graphics and publishing beat, but soon I was covering Adobe on a regular basis.

I've been doing this stuff ever since. Indeed my own career follows the evolution of publishing from print to Web and beyond. After running several print magazines, I gravitated toward the Internet and then linked the disciplines together in cross-media projects that involved print and Web, then Web and television. I currently run Creativepro.com, a Web site that reports on developments in the graphic design and publishing industries, in which Adobe is a driving force. Many years after my stint at MacWEEK, I'm still covering Adobe.

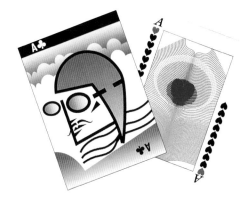

In researching and reporting this book, I found one recurring theme: that Adobe's products unleashed people's creativity in ways they hadn't thought possible. I can relate. My own discovery of PostScript fonts stirred an interest in typography and led me to explore its history and learn letterpress printing. I'm not a graphic designer by training, but thanks to Adobe software I can design and produce my own publication—whether it's a magazine prototype or a personal Web site or a playful experiment. Anytime the urge strikes me I can walk over to my computer and be creative. We take this for granted now, but think about it: Before Adobe, Apple, and Aldus gave birth to the desktop publishing revolution, computers were soulless, number-crunching machines. Today technology is a major form of personal expression. A large slice of the credit must be given to Adobe for that astonishing transformation.

I'm not alone in this creative conversion. The dozens of designers and artists interviewed for this book all credit Adobe products with changing their approach to work and, in some cases, with giving their careers focus. For instance, before he discovered Adobe Illustrator and Photoshop, Brad Johnson's vocation was carpentry. Now he runs the Web design firm Second Story Interactive. Brad's is just one of many stories I heard about Adobe's impact.

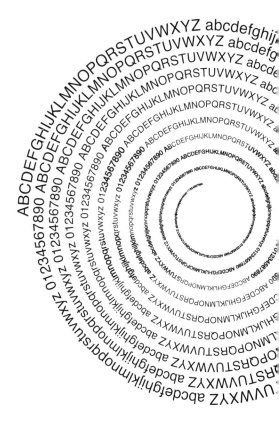

Had Adobe just developed a single clever piece of engineering, its story would be short. Instead, Adobe has grown to be one of the world's largest desktop software companies, second only to Microsoft. But what is fascinating to me as a journalist is how the company keeps evolving and how, in so doing, it shapes our expectations of what it means to communicate in the 21st century.

The next chapter in the Adobe story is still being written. After the successes of PostScript, Photoshop, and Acrobat, I wonder how the company will top itself. But I have no doubt that whatever happens will be interesting to watch.

Pamela Pfiffner

"We were prototypical scientists in that we wanted to have an impact. We weren't in it for financial gain."
— Chuck Geschke

Laying the Foundation

If the modern publishing era began when Johannes Gutenberg developed movable type in Germany in the 1450s, its successor was the transformation that took root in Silicon Valley in the 1980s, when John Warnock and Chuck Geschke formed Adobe Systems. Like Gutenberg's invention, Warnock and Geschke's PostScript technology created a radical new approach to printing marks on paper. And just as the modern press liberated publishing from the exclusive domain of educated scribes cloistered in monasteries, so too did PostScript expand publishing beyond printing presses and into the offices and homes of everyday people. Adobe is only one of several companies that created publishing as we know it today, but the company's influence is felt in every aspect of how we produce communications. It all began with PostScript.

1982

Intel 286 chip comes out

John Warnock and Chuck Geschke leave Xerox PARC to start Adobe Systems

Hewlett-Packard standardizes on 3.5-inch floppy drive, the first company to do so

Adobe Systems founded December 1982

ADOBE
SYSTEMS INCORPORATED

1983

First Adobe office on Marine Way in Mountain View

First PostScript licensing agreement signed with Apple Computer

PostScript developed

Adobe revenue: $83,000
Adobe employees: 13

First version of Microsoft Word released

THE EARLY YEARS

Like most revolutions, the one that changed publishing forever had its origins in an individual—in this case two individuals—who wanted to change the status quo. And like many other revolutionaries, these two men encountered each other in the right place at the right time, in this case California's Silicon Valley in the late 1970s, an era in which scientists and engineers found fertile soil for the seeds of a radically different future. The founders of Adobe Systems were not your typical radical subversives, however, although both sported the beards of the antiestablishment. They were thoughtful, almost conventional men who had a dream and the nerve to pursue it. When they met, it was like sparks igniting a flame.

Upon receiving his master's degree in 1964, mathematician John E. Warnock began teaching at the University of Utah. Simultaneously working on his Ph.D., Warnock studied under David Evans, founder of Utah's fabled computer science department. The school, then one of only 15 universities offering a computer science curriculum, educated such pioneers as Alan Kay (developer of the graphical user interface at Xerox PARC and later Apple), Jim Clark (a founder of Silicon Graphics and Netscape), Ed Catmull (cofounder of Pixar Animation Studios), Henri Gouraud (creator of the Gouraud 3D-shading method), and Bui-Tuong Phong (creator of the Phong computer-lighting effect).

The young teacher married in 1965 and quickly learned that an academic salary barely supported a growing family. When granted his doctorate in 1969, Warnock began a succession of computer-related jobs that took him through Vancouver, Toronto, and then Washington, D.C., where he worked at Computer Sciences Corporation in support of the Goddard

"Technology is like fish. If you don't cook it, it spoils."

— Chuck Geschke

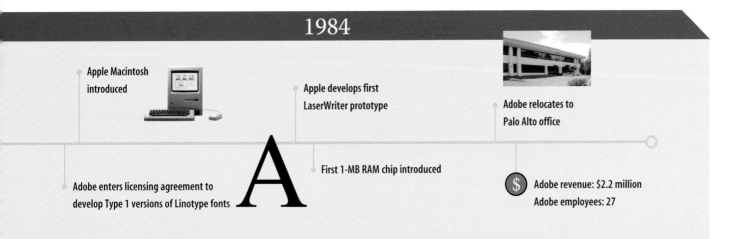

1984

Apple Macintosh introduced

Apple develops first LaserWriter prototype

Adobe relocates to Palo Alto office

First 1-MB RAM chip introduced

Adobe enters licensing agreement to develop Type 1 versions of Linotype fonts

Adobe revenue: $2.2 million
Adobe employees: 27

Space Flight Center. In 1972 David Evans, Warnock's mentor from Utah, invited him to join his firm, Evans & Sutherland, and to open an office at the Ames Research Center in the San Francisco Bay Area to work on the Illiac IV supercomputer. After two years Evans asked Warnock to leave Ames and begin work on flight simulators. In one 1976 project Warnock and colleague John Gaffney were asked to develop a ship simulator to train harbor pilots for New York harbor. Faced with the task of creating graphics that would provide realistic backgrounds of New York and New Jersey, they hit on the idea of an interpreted, stack-based graphics description language. Called the Design System, this device-independent language was the first precursor to PostScript.

The Best and the Brightest

In 1978 Evans & Sutherland asked Warnock to move back to Utah, where it was headquartered. But Warnock, ensconced in California with his family, decided instead to look for work in the Bay Area. He learned of an opportunity at the Xerox Palo Alto Research Center (PARC), a think tank and research lab supported by the company's skyrocketing sales of photocopying machines. Although it had been formed only eight years earlier, in 1970, Xerox PARC was already gaining a reputation as fertile ground for scientists and dreamers. One of those was Charles M. Geschke, known to everyone as "Chuck." It fell to Geschke, as a manager, to interview the prospect from Utah.

John Gaffney, seen here at an early Adobe party, coauthored the Design System with John Warnock while the two worked at Evans & Sutherland in the mid-'70s.

Geschke, like Warnock, was a mathematician. After considering the priesthood, Geschke studied classics and math at Xavier University in Cincinnati. With a young family, he too taught math to make ends meet. But teaching at John Carroll University, a Jesuit college in his hometown of Cleveland, wasn't fulfilling. After a former student, in a gesture of gratitude, taught him how to code, Geschke had become increasingly intrigued by computer programming. His wife, Nan, pointed out the obvious: he was happier writing programs. With his department head's blessing, Geschke quit John Carroll and entered Carnegie Mellon University's computer sciences program, one of the best in the country.

After earning his Ph.D. in 1972 from Carnegie Mellon, Geschke learned about the Xerox venture in California. Staffed with the brightest technology minds in the country, the research lab's mission was to develop technologies that could change the world. Indeed, Xerox PARC counts among its alumni such icons as Bob Metcalfe, David Liddle, Larry Tesler, Alan Kay, Gary Starkweather, and Charles Simonyi. The efforts of such men gave rise to the personal computer, the laser printer, the graphical user interface, the Ethernet, and other cornerstones of modern computing. As Geschke describes it, the goal at Xerox PARC was to develop computers that were used "not to calculate but to communicate."

The launch team of Adobe Systems cruised the San Francisco Bay during the first of the company's legendary parties. At left, Warnock with his wife, Marva Warnock.

Above, back row from left: Doug Brotz, Steve MacDonald, John Warnock, Chuck Geschke. In the front row, hardware engineer Dan Putman is third from left, next to Tom Boynton; engineer Carolyn Bell and employee number 1 Linda Garger are first and third from the right.

Xerox PARC

Geschke joined Xerox PARC as a principal scientist and researcher in its computer sciences lab, but with his leadership skills he soon found himself managing a loose confederation of geniuses.

"My concept of management was that you were a servant to the people who worked for you," Geschke says. "I wouldn't hire anyone I had to tell what to do." It's no wonder, then, that Warnock impressed Geschke during his interview. Today Geschke says simply: "Hiring John was my best hiring decision."

When Geschke met Warnock in 1978, the two felt an instant rapport. But over lunch they also discovered they had similar experiences and shared values. Both had their education funded by the U.S. Department of Defense's Advanced Research Project Agency (ARPA). Both were happily married to their first (and only) wives, an anomaly in the 1970s. Both had three children, two boys and a girl. Both had an interest in publishing and the graphic arts: Geschke's father was a color photoengraver, while Warnock's wife, Marva, was a graphic designer. Above all, both wanted to change the world.

POSTSCRIPT

In 1978 Scott Kim, then a research assistant at Xerox PARC, began working with John Warnock in the Imaging Sciences lab. Warnock helped Kim, a puzzle designer and mathematician, program this spiral in JaM, the precursor to PostScript. "John figured out the number of repetitions and handed it back to me," says Kim. The letters spell *infinity* both vertically and horizontally as the letters stack up on each other.

"We were prototypical scientists in that we wanted to have an impact," Geschke says. "We weren't in it for financial gain. It was more important to make a dramatic difference."

At Xerox PARC Geschke set Warnock on a path to investigate device-independent graphic systems. Such a breakthrough could have tremendous repercussions for Xerox, which dominated the photocopier market and viewed the laser printer market as a new and important revenue stream. But Xerox's technology for printing to those devices from its Star workstation was inelegant at best.

The Precursor to PostScript

Warnock partnered with Martin Newell to refine the concepts behind the Design System developed at E&S, adapting them for paper output rather than onscreen display. In 1979 the two unveiled "JaM." Abbreviated from their first names (John and Martin), JaM was the next iteration of what would become PostScript. Martin Newell later became Adobe's first technology fellow.

Like Gaffney's Design System, JaM was also device independent, but it differed from its precursor in that it incorporated raster graphics and bit-mapped fonts. Fueled by the promise of JaM, Warnock and Geschke continued to work on its development. In 1980 Geschke started the Imaging Sciences Laboratory at Xerox, a lab dedicated to exploring graphics and printing, among other disciplines.

In 1981 the team produced what became known as Interpress, a melding of JaM and Xerox's existing printing language, which was suitable for the office environment. In some respects Interpress was crippled by Xerox's insistence that it comply with all of Xerox's printing protocols. But in another respect it was quite advanced: Interpress was an early example of virtual designing. Its engineers were located in four towns and on two coasts; they communicated primarily through email.

After the unveiling, Xerox anointed Interpress its proprietary printing standard—at least internally. According to Geschke, Xerox PARC was ecstatic and congratulatory to the men on their breakthrough. Xerox Corporation was less so. Despite the engineers' lobbying, the company had no intention of including Interpress in commercial products or releasing it to the public. Some observers suspected that Xerox suffered a bout of corporate paranoia; others assumed an aversion to upsetting the status quo.

"Xerox said in effect, 'That's real nice, boys, we'll take it from here. Go back to your rooms,'" says Dan Putman, a founding scientist in Geschke's imaging lab.

Though untrained as businessmen, the two scientists sensed an opportunity and grew discouraged by Xerox's reluctance. Geschke and Warnock

"Xerox said, in effect, 'That's real nice, boys, we'll take it from here.'"

— Dan Putman

BizStats: 1982

No. of employees: 2

Revenue: none

>> John Warnock and Chuck Geschke found Adobe Systems with $2.5 million in seed money from Hambrecht & Quist. Company is named after a creek behind Warnock's home in Los Altos, California.

approached Putman in May 1982 and hinted they were up to something and that Putman should stay put for a while. Years later Geschke says: "It was obvious that it would take Xerox a long time to get this to market. But technology is like fish. If you don't cook it, it spoils."

Warnock later said that Xerox's history and PARC's vision were often incompatible: the former afraid to cannibalize existing products, the latter often too far ahead of the market. "Only some young company without a history could come out with a new technology," Warnock told the *San Jose Mercury News* in 1984.

So, in December 1982, Warnock and Geschke struck out on their own. Frustrated by Xerox's unwillingness to bring Interpress and other technologies to the office market, the two men formed a new company, naming it after the creek that ran behind Warnock's Los Altos, California, home.

They called it Adobe Systems.

CREATING ADOBE SYSTEMS

At its inception in December 1982, Adobe Systems had a staff of two: John Warnock and Chuck Geschke.

Starting up a new company was risky, especially for two fortysomething men with families to support. Warnock and Geschke were pragmatists, however. If Adobe failed, they knew they could find work elsewhere, given their pedigrees and the employment climate of Silicon Valley in the 1980s.

Besides, the two were confident in the technology. They knew that the software language they'd developed had natural applications for office environments in which dumb, noisy printers churned out page after page of poorly composed documents.

The programming language that became known as PostScript solved several problems. First, communications between PC and printer needed only one software language instead of a mishmash of specialized drivers and application protocols for each device. Second, the language could describe both text and graphics on one page, thus eliminating the need to literally cut and paste words and pictures onto paperboard. And this language would be hooked up to one of the new, quieter laser printers, sparing workers the clatter of dot-matrix and daisy-wheel models.

Preliminary Plans

But above all, PostScript was device independent, meaning that the files printed on a 300-dpi laser printer appeared the same when printed on a 1,200-dpi typesetter—only much better. The fonts were sharper, the graphics smoother, and the pictures more detailed, but the same piece of software spoke the same language to both devices. A file created once could be printed on many machines and look the same on every one. Warnock and Geschke excitedly debated the opportunities for products and services based on such a technology.

For advice on how to start a business, Warnock had flown to Salt Lake City in early 1982 to meet with his former teacher and employer David Evans, who in turn introduced the entrepreneurs to venture capitalist William Hambrecht. In their first meeting with Hambrecht, Warnock and Geschke unveiled their plan to open a series of printing shops at which businesses would drop off their files for output and pick them up later.

"Chuck would be the counterman, greeting customers, while John would be in the backroom mixing up his magic PostScript language that could

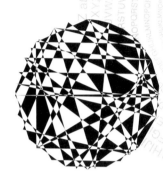

These early PostScript test files were coded by hand to demonstrate the language's versatility. The Adobe Systems Journal page was a milestone that assured continued funding from Hambrecht & Quist. It showed all the promised elements of PostScript: text, graphics, and images. The jagged ball was Warnock's killer test program, known as the "Death Star," that smoked out every last bug from the core graphics code.

J ohn Warnock and Chuck Geschke's partnership will go down as one of the great working relationships of Silicon Valley, along with that of legends Bill Hewlett and Dave Packard. The two men have distinct but complementary personalities, and they share personal values that have made them close friends outside work. Adobe's success and culture are directly attributable to their remarkable partnership.

On John and Chuck

Both are geniuses. But Chuck's genius shows through this company, while John's is right out there in front.

Tom Malloy, vice president, Advanced Technology Group (ATG)

People stereotype them: John's the technology guy and Chuck's the people guy. Chuck *is* very people oriented, and someone had to do the people and business stuff. But he was always very interested in technology; Chuck sacrificed his passion.

Janice Coley, Geschke's longtime assistant

They fit together nicely: Chuck was the calm one, John was the wild man.

Dick Sweet, Adobe scientist

Chuck is the polished seasoned statesman. John is the passionate mercurial inventor.

Linda Clarke, former vice president of applications marketing

On Chuck

Chuck is very logical and methodical. He was the implementer.

Steve MacDonald, original vice president of sales and marketing and former co-COO

Chuck was Mister Stability. He could do things like engineer the font cache in PostScript because it required extended work and attention to detail.

Doug Brotz, ATG principal scientist

Chuck is largely responsible for creating the culture that makes Adobe such a nice place to work.

Ed Taft, ATG scientist

Chuck has a calming influence on people. He grounds them. People would go into his office totally distraught and come out feeling much better.

John Warnock

We had this crazy public address system at the Charleston Road offices. On late Friday afternoons Chuck would get on the loudspeaker and say, "Well, I think it's time for a beer."

Jim King, ATG scientist

"John is like your brilliant older brother, while Chuck is like your dad."

— Bryan Lamkin

ON JOHN

John was notorious for his limited attention span. If we didn't get it figured out in a minute and a half, he's out of there.

Doug Brotz

Chuck and I had a saying: "You get the hammer and I'll get the nails." John's mind runs a mile a minute. You have to nail his feet to the floor if you want have a discussion with him.

Steve MacDonald

John is always full of ideas about opportunities for Adobe to solve problems in the graphic arts and publishing industries. He is also extremely effective at communicating his ideas to people and motivating them to turn the ideas into real products.

Ed Taft

ON MANAGEMENT STYLE

Chuck and John didn't tell us what to do. They gave us the rope to either succeed or fail.

Dave Pratt, former co-COO and general manager of applications division

John is rather excitable and emotional when speaking on things he is passionate about. Chuck is calmer and more reassuring, which makes him an effective spokesman during difficult situations.

Ed Taft

They're a great team. Chuck was such a good inside person—great with details and the day-to-day. John was the visionary. He always had ideas that may or may not be connected to market reality. It was that equilibrium that helped them succeed.

Paul Brainerd, Aldus Corporation founder

They project a persona that they're just a bunch of scientists and a couple of nice guys. But I had moments with John when he was not shy expressing his opinion about who had the upper hand. He could be a very aggressive businessman.

Gene Gable, president, Seybold Seminars and Publications

They were like indulgent fathers toward the engineers.

Bruce Nakao, former CFO

ON PARTNERSHIP

I don't think I've ever heard them argue, even though they've had plenty of opportunity to.

Doug Brotz

At one point they switched roles. Formerly, John was Adobe's primary public spokesman, while Chuck oversaw the day-to-day management of the company; in the mid-1990s, Chuck went on the road and John ran the company. They each had complete trust in the other's ability to run the company.

Ed Taft

All major decisions were talked about between themselves. You ask either one of them a question and the answer would be "I gotta talk to my buddy."

Steve MacDonald

ON RESPECT

It was remarkable and inspiring. Just the fact that they could carry off this partnership was pretty amazing. They reinforced and respected each other, and it percolated through the company.

Sumner Stone, Adobe's first director of type development

I can't think of any other two people who maintained that supportive a partnership over that long a period of time.

Jonathan Seybold, founder and former president, Seybold Seminars

ON EACH OTHER

John is the brother I never had.

Chuck Geschke

It has always been great to have a partner who is also my best friend.

John Warnock

Adobe's first logo was designed by Marva Warnock .

produce pages in 15 minutes," says Doug Brotz, a Xerox PARC alumnus and Adobe's fourth hire. Realizing the absurdity of such a scenario—they were scientists after all, not shopkeepers—Warnock and Geschke jettisoned that plan at Hambrecht's urging. Hambrecht then hired a consultant to assist the two men in writing a new business plan.

Warnock and Geschke hatched a revised plan to develop systems composed of high-powered workstations and printers and to sell them to large corporations like Boeing and Hughes Aircraft for in-house use. Leveraging PostScript's device-independent resolution, the workstation would be connected to a laser printer for draft copies and to a typesetter for camera-ready final output.

The plan to develop a new printing protocol for the office environment was good—so good that at least six other companies were trying to do approximately the same thing. Recognizing this competition as a healthy sign, Hambrecht gave them a personal check for $50,000 as an advance on startup costs when the pair departed Xerox in November 1982. The deal was sealed with a handshake. Later, the firm of Hambrecht & Quist invested $2.5 million in Adobe Systems—the only venture capital Adobe ever received. "Now they had the money to get out of John's bedroom," quips Dan Putman.

Everyone Sweeps the Floor

With the help of Clinton Nagy, a real estate broker who eventually joined the Adobe sales team, Adobe secured a 2,800-square-foot space on Marine Way in Mountain View, California. Warnock and Geschke leased computers and furniture. Friends and family were put to work—even Geschke's 80-year-old father stained the lumber for shelving. Graphic designer Marva Warnock, John's wife, designed the company logo.

The hands-on nature of the startup was communicated to everyone the company brought onboard. For years, Warnock and Geschke hand-delivered a bottle of champagne or cognac and a dozen roses to a new hire's house. The employee arrived at work to find hammer, ruler, and screwdriver on a desk, which were to be used for hanging up shelves, pictures, and so on.

"From the start we wanted them to have the mentality that everyone sweeps the floor around here," says Geschke, adding that while the hand tools may be gone, the ethic persists today.

The cofounders started compiling a team, drawing from a pool of friends and former coworkers from Xerox PARC that initially included Dan Putman, Tom Boynton, Doug Brotz, and Bill Paxton; over time they were joined by Ed Taft, Dick Sweet, and others. For some former PARC employees, the idea that business could be built around describing pages for laser printers was "goofy," says Brotz. "Of all the companies that came out of PARC I thought that this one was guaranteed to fail."

Nevertheless Brotz met with Warnock and Geschke over lunch for an interview. Brotz had worked on email systems at PARC and, compared to Warnock, had little experience with computer graphics. He expressed his reservations to the pair. Geschke replied: "You're a smart guy and you can learn. John will whisper everything he knows about graphics in your ear and you will build it." Brotz says today: "I said to myself, 'Even though this will fail, I will have the time of my life for five years.' Ultimately I chose the opportunity that had the least probability of success but the most opportunity for learning and having fun." He started at Adobe in March 1983; as of 2002, he is Adobe's longest-tenured employee.

Like any other startup, Adobe was a bit idiosyncratic. Hewlett-Packard veteran Steve MacDonald remembers going to meet Warnock and

Adobe's first office space was located on Marine Way in Mountain View, California.

BizStats: 1983

No. of employees: 13

Revenue: $83,000

Other:
>> Adobe incorporated in California

First OEM contract signed, with Apple Computer, to license PostScript driver and fonts for LaserWriter printers. Agreement includes an investment in the company.

Geschke for a lunchtime interview at a restaurant, only to find it closed—no one had called beforehand to check. Over lunch somewhere else, MacDonald was further perplexed to learn that Adobe didn't actually have a job for him—yet. Still he was intrigued and agreed to join the team in six months. He signed on as vice president of sales and marketing in May 1983.

The team swung into action, and a few months after Warnock and Geschke had struck out on their own, PostScript was born. Its authors were John Warnock, Chuck Geschke, Doug Brotz, Ed Taft, and Bill Paxton. PostScript bore little resemblance to Xerox's Interpress. Technically PostScript is much closer to JaM, but mindful of PostScript's origins as the Design System, Adobe entered into a licensing agreement with Warnock's old employer, Evans & Sutherland, to head off any entanglements over intellectual property.

Going Solo

Adobe borrowed a Xerox laser printer from fellow PARC alum Forest Baskett at Digital Equipment Corporation and used it to test its new printer controllers. By March 1983, Putman had a prototype PostScript laser printer up and running. "At that point the only question was what vehicle was going to take us to market," Putman says. Another early implementation of PostScript was developed for a top-secret, somewhat improbable high-resolution gravity-fed typesetter based on fluid mechanics. Putman, Adobe's second official employee and the designated "hardware guy," remarked that the scanning motion of the unusual device would have a smooth action: "All I said was 'Gravity is smooth.' That was the extent of my contribution."

Warnock and Geschke invited publishing consultant Jonathan Seybold to observe their progress. "The whole concept to describe pages in a device-independent way was a real breakthrough," Seybold says. "They took a radically different approach than anyone else. They invented a language and a way to interpret it in the output device so that as long as you had that engine it didn't matter what you put it into. It was exactly what was needed."

Word soon got out, and calls came in inquiring about what the PARC refugees were up to. One call came from Gordon Bell, then vice president of engineering at Digital Equipment Corporation (DEC). Bell told them that his company had spent years working to improve office printing and that while DEC had cracked the workstation and printer problems, it was struggling with the software communication between them. Perhaps Adobe would like to license its software to DEC?

Still intent on building and selling computers, the pair said no.

> "John had 50 flashes of brilliance a day. Maybe only one would pan out, but he's always thinking of something."
>
> — Doug Brotz

PostScript's breakthrough was the way it handled fonts. Instead of requiring hand-tuned bitmaps for each style and size of typeface, it could generate fonts of any size and shape from mathematical descriptions. Shown here: Linda Gass, with Chuck Geschke and John Warnock.

Ahead of the Curve

But Warnock and Geschke had another reason to decline Bell's offer. They had the solution to what had stymied their rivals and they weren't quite ready to share it. The key to PostScript's breakthrough was the way it handled fonts. Instead of requiring hand-tuned bitmaps to be generated for each style and size of typeface, PostScript was able to generate fonts of any size and shape from mathematical descriptions and do so automatically on the fly, thereby eliminating intensive manual labor. This method of building device-independent fonts is perhaps Warnock's crowning engineering achievement. To license the technology meant potentially giving up a competitive advantage.

"Technology is never created in a vacuum," Geschke says today. "If you're working on it, then someone else is too. The only way to succeed is to get there first."

In hindsight, although Adobe never built computers or opened storefronts, its original ideas were remarkably on target. The foundation of desktop publishing is PostScript's ability to connect PCs to output devices capable of any resolution, and the walk-in typesetting shops resembled what we now know as service bureaus.

But in 1983 Adobe's plans changed for good when Steve Jobs called.

STEPHEN JOHNSON

ANASAZI WHITE HOUSE ✦ STEPHEN JOHNSON
Adobe Photoshop

Stephen Johnson Photography

Photographer Stephen Johnson uses high-resolution digital cameras and Photoshop to capture the subtle tones and gradations that traditional film cannot. His work blends his friend Ansel Adams's eye for natural beauty with cutting-edge technology. In the course of making the film-based book *The Great Central Valley* (1993)—produced with Photoshop, PageMaker, and Illustrator—Johnson worked with Adobe to develop Photoshop's Duotone mode for the book's vintage photographs. Johnson is currently looking to publish his next work, *With a New Eye: The National Parks Project*, in which he embarked on a journey to photograph the country's national parks using all-digital technology. Adobe provided the initial funding for the project, which allowed Johnson to begin his 75,000-mile expedition. (www.sjphoto.com)

Stephen Johnson Photography

Stephen Johnson Photography

Stephen Johnson Photography

Stephen Johnson Photography

V
V

*"Film died an ugly
death for me in January
1994 because of Photo-
shop and the BetterLight
digital camera."*

Apple Computer president and CEO Steve Jobs (left), shown here shortly after the launch of the LaserWriter, backed PostScript from the moment he laid eyes on it. "I was simply blown away by what I saw," Jobs remembers.

Steve Jobs and the LaserWriter

When Apple Computer CEO Steve Jobs called Warnock in the spring of 1983, his company was already a success. The Apple II series of computers, which had been embraced by educators, and Apple's newest model, the Lisa, suggested that the graphical user interfaces developed at Xerox PARC could be adapted for personal computers in interesting ways. Unbeknownst to Warnock and Geschke, Jobs was already at work on his next innovation, the Macintosh, which displayed graphics, not just straight lines of ASCII text, onscreen.

Jonathan Seybold, founder of the influential conference Seybold Seminars, who had been had been following developments at Apple and Xerox PARC, says that when Jobs showed him the Macintosh he was convinced it was the future of not only computing but also publishing. "It was very clear to me that the distinction between computing and information science and graphics arts would just go away," he says.

Bob Belleville, an Apple employee and PARC alumnus who had caught wind of what Adobe was up to, advised Jobs to get in touch with Warnock. Jobs himself had glimpsed early examples of Warnock's work during a visit to Xerox PARC in 1979, when he also saw the first graphical user interface. Warnock and Geschke invited Jobs over for a visit.

Apple had a 72-dpi dot-matrix printer called the ImageWriter, but it was also working with printer-engine manufacturer Canon on a low-cost laser printer that produced crisp output for many thousands of dollars less than anything else available. But what Jobs didn't have was a way to tie the laser printer and the Macintosh together. As Jobs describes the scene: "John and Chuck were in their garage thinking about making laser printers, and we were in our garage working on ours."

Like Warnock and Geschke, Jobs knew that the key to the corporate market lay in improved office printing. Instead of high-end workstations, however, Jobs believed his easy-to-use personal computer with an onscreen point-and-click display could revolutionize office computing. IBM, which introduced its first PC in 1981, dominated corporate America, but its IBM 3800 laser printer cost hundreds of thousands of dollars. Jobs wanted to usurp Big Blue. High-quality printing, he knew, was the Trojan horse through which Apple could enter the steel-towered city.

PostScript wowed Jobs. "We were the first ones in the U.S. to have the Canon laser printer," Jobs recalls. "When we went over to see John and

"When we all saw that first sheet of paper come out of the LaserWriter, we knew we were going to hit it out of the park."

—Steve Jobs

Chuck, we could quickly see that our hardware was going to be better than theirs and that their software was more advanced than what we were working on. I was simply blown away by what I saw."

Over breakfast at a Cupertino health food restaurant, he proposed that Adobe license its technology to Apple for inclusion in a 300-dpi Canon-equipped laser printer driven by the Macintosh. According to Geschke, Jobs told them: "I don't need the computer. I don't need the printer. I need the software."

This time the duo took notice. "If someone keeps saying, 'You have a business here,' and it's not the business you're doing, then it's time to change your business," Geschke says now. Jobs says, simply, "I convinced them to drop plans to be a hardware company and be a software company instead."

They realized that by opting for a technology license, thus relieving themselves of the burden of manufacturing, they stood to profit handsomely from their software. In fact, Jobs offered them an advance of $1.5 million against PostScript royalties. He also invested $2.5 million in exchange for a 20 percent stake in the company, much to the dismay of Apple's new president, John Sculley, who questioned such an investment in an unproven company. Jobs insisted. When Apple cashed out six years later its stake was worth more than $87 milllion.

Jobs and Warnock hit it off immediately. "John and I liked each other and trusted each other. I would have trusted him with my life, and I think he trusted me," Jobs says today. "It was a good personal relationship even though we didn't always agree on everything."

The success of Apple and Adobe's partnership lay in more than just personal affection, however. Warnock and Jobs shared a deep and abiding belief that technology could transcend ordinary computing to achieve a higher aesthetic purpose. "We always felt that Apple should stand at the intersection of art and technology, and John felt the same way about Adobe," Jobs says. "The Mac was the first computer that was commercially available with a graphical user interface. We were doing typography on the screen, while with PostScript Adobe was doing type on the printed page. John had a developed aesthetic sense, too. We meshed together well."

During several negotiations in mid-1983, Jobs offered to buy Adobe outright. Over one meal at the Good Earth with Warnock, Geschke, Putman, and MacDonald, Jobs offered $5 million for the untested company. Having just emerged from the shadow of large corporations, they declined, preferring to go it alone.

 The Macintosh Office

Apple introduces
an alternative
to business as usual.

The PostScript-equipped
Apple LaserWriter was the
keystone of the Macintosh
office, in which office workers
were liberated from "dumb"
terminals and output devices.

The Appearance Problem

Adobe signed with Apple just one month before the Macintosh launched its opening salvo against soulless corporate computing (read: IBM) in the famous Ridley Scott–directed commercial that aired in January 1984. In the following months, Adobe aligned its sights to Apple's vision. Previously Adobe had been tuning PostScript for high-resolution devices. Printers such as the Canon engine that Apple was using were considered proof printers, and it was assumed the type would look terrible. But Jobs informed Adobe that the laser printer was now the only output device that mattered and that PostScript had to work flawlessly at 300 dpi. It was a challenging assignment.

"The Apple LaserWriter was just barely possible to achieve with the hardware technology available at the time," remembers Ed Taft, employee 16 and currently a principal scientist in Adobe's Advanced Technology Group. "The CPU was slow and memory was severely limited. It was a challenge to render a complex page of text and graphics at 300 dpi, all in software. Scan conversion of text from outline fonts was especially challenging; the conventional wisdom was that it couldn't be done in real time."

Dan Putman, Adobe's designated "hardware guy," was one of the principal architects of the PostScript controller board.

How the printer reproduced type was a big hurdle. Type had the propensity to appear thicker than intended at low resolutions, so thick that one type expert saw a 300-dpi PostScript-generated version of the regular-weight Souvenir font and mistook it for the bold weight. Warnock and Doug Brotz went to work on what they called "the appearance problem," while other type refinements such as hinting, which makes fonts look pleasing at small sizes, fell to Bill Paxton.

The appearance problem was solved when the stem width of letters scaled appropriately when printed at any resolution. It truly meant that letters of the same font size and style looked good whether printed on a 300-dpi laser printer or a 1,200-dpi typesetter. This capability was a major breakthrough for PostScript and for Adobe, so much so that Adobe has never filed a patent on it, as the patent-filing process requires the technique to be published, thereby exposing it to competitors.

Juggling Demands

Throughout the rest of 1984, Adobe engineers focused on porting PostScript to the Motorola 68000 chip used in the Canon laser printer's controller board. The Macintosh itself had limited processing power, so PostScript code was sent to the printer's controller board, which housed the software that interpreted the code and which had enough power to handle the necessary computations. Apple had planned to do its own engineering of the controller board, but that was before Adobe engineers fed Apple their ideas on the board's design. "We set up a meeting. Burrell Smith, Belleville's lead hardware designer, brought in Apple's controller design for the Macintosh and I brought in mine for the laser printer," says Putman. "What came out of it was the LaserWriter controller board."

Adobe was an exciting place to be. The company doubled in size, requiring a move to larger offices on Embarcadero Road in Palo Alto. The work was engaging and the engineers were confident. The teams enjoyed a great camaraderie and shared a work ethic carried over from the days at Xerox PARC. "John and Chuck brought in the best of Xerox PARC," says Tom Malloy, vice president and head of Adobe's Advanced Technology Group (ATG), the division in which most of Adobe's remaining PARC-era engineers work. "These are people who revel in state-of-the-art technology and who have a fervent commitment to have their products accepted." After the disillusionment of PARC, Adobe gave these engineers a public proving ground for their talent.

The work had its share of mishaps and light moments, however. Warnock's reputation as a mercurial thinker and fidgeter was well established. To work out his nervousness he often walked through the office juggling three plastic clubs. One day a juggling Warnock wandered into the hardware lab where engineers had laid out operational prototype con-

BizStats: 1984

No. of employees: 27

Revenue: $2.2 million

Other:
>> 68% of revenue comes from Apple royalty payments for use of PostScript in its printers

Adobe enters licensing agreement with Linotype to develop Type 1 versions of Linotype fonts

Adobe moves into Palo Alto office

ADOBE AND THE POWER OF POSTSCRIPT

John Warnock
John Warnock
Post Script
Post Script
Post Script

Adobe PostScript was a breakthrough on many fronts, but to technically inclined designers and printers, it was a revelation. As a programming language PostScript gave publishers the opportunity to customize code for specific needs. Because the interpreter resided in the printer, programming could seem like magic—type in code onscreen, push a button, and watch the page emerge from the printer with your intentions intact. It changed the way publishers regarded their output devices.

ON PERSONAL POWER

PostScript was revolutionary in that it had an interpreter running in a printer that you could access if you wanted to. In that sense the release of PostScript was almost as important as the release of the personal computer in terms of the control it gave us over printing.

> **Chuck Weger, president, Elara Systems, publishing consultant, and early PostScript user**

Scott Kim, one of the first people to design in PostScript, is known for his puzzles and art pieces. He designed this series of images in honor of PostScript's architect.

I got into writing PostScript because I bought a big expensive PostScript RIP from Linotype and I wanted to learn how to program this big expensive computer I'd bought.

> **Jim Birkenseer, cofounder with Peter Truskier of Premedia Systems, who learned PostScript at his father's prepress shop in 1989**

One of the best things I ever did was to write the PostScript code to gang multiple sheets on an imagesetter. I could save film, output more pages, and make more money. It gave me such a feeling of power to make this machine do my bidding.

> **Peter Truskier, who worked extensively with PostScript at prepress shop STAR Graphic Arts**

You wrote this code, then typed in "showpage" and out of the printer came your graphic. It was exciting, an earthshaking moment.

> **Chuck Weger**

ON PROGRAMMING POWER

PostScript did essentially two things. It gave the ordinary user with a Mac the ability to make whole pages of text and graphics. Second, it gave the technically sophisticated the opportunity to program pages. That's what created the genre of Stupid PostScript Tricks.

> **Chuck Weger**

Before Illustrator, we had to program all our designs in PostScript by hand. That helped me understand how PostScript and printers work. It taught me to think like a computer.

> **Luanne Seymour Cohen, who joined Adobe's creative department in 1986**

ON STAYING POWER

What's significant about PostScript is that they got it right. It's rare that a standard is set at the right time by the right people. From the beginning, PostScript was really well thought out and very stable.

> **Scott Kim, mathematician, programmer, and designer who studied under Donald Knuth at Stanford and apprenticed under John Warnock at Xerox PARC**

"People who think well in PostScript generally can't communicate with other human beings."

— Jim Birkenseer

I've got an original 1985 LaserWriter sitting in my basement—one of the first few hundred that came off the line. I can hitch it up right now and print from pretty much any modern program. It's incredibly slow by today's standards, and there's only enough memory for a couple of downloaded fonts, but it prints! How many pieces of software encoded into ROM in 1984 are still working today, eighteen years later?

> **Steve Roth, author of several books on PostScript and publishing, and editor of *Personal Publishing* magazine in the 1980s**

```
% Set each letter with stretching
(P) TwistAndStretch
(o) TwistAndStretch
(s) TwistAndStretch
(t) TwistAndStretch
(S) TwistAndStretch
(c) TwistAndStretch
(r) TwistAndStretch
(i) TwistAndStretch
(p) TwistAndStretch
(t) TwistAndStretch

% Set the "windstorm" caption
200 286 moveto
TimesItal10 setfont
(During a windstorm) show

showpage     % Print the page!
```

Publishing consultant Jim Birkenseer programmed this example of PostScript (right) to demonstrate the flexibility of the language. The payoff of such an exercise for any PostScript novice is the command "showpage," the final instructions before printing.

During an earthquake

During a windstorm

Starting with the "red book" in 1985, Adobe published a series of manuals that described how to program in PostScript. These volumes became bibles to technologically savvy publishers.

troller boards on workbenches. The engineers were worried that a club would land on a board, and a suggestion was made that they henceforth start charging admission to see executive acrobatics in the lab.

As 1984 progressed, the Apple-Adobe corporate strategy coalesced into "the Macintosh Office." Together the Apple Macintosh and PostScript-fueled laser printer would free office workers from the drudgery of document production (and the staid confines of an IBM workflow) by enabling them to create text- and graphics-rich documents on their computer screens and then print the pages exactly as they appeared. One key to the Macintosh Office was fonts.

Neither Apple nor Adobe had expertise in font design or production, although the principals at both companies appreciated fine typography. Fonts were the domain of the old-world printing industry and its photo-typesetting equipment. And therein lay the opportunity: The right partner would not only supply the needed fonts but also provide a high-resolution output platform for PostScript, using typesetters as the foundation.

Linotype's Leap of Faith

Adobe approached Compugraphic, at that time the United States' largest typesetting company. But Compugraphic had two strikes against it: The company wanted complete control over its fonts and over PostScript as well, which Adobe would not consider; and it had left bad feelings at Apple when an earlier deal over the Lisa computer soured.

Publishing consultant Jonathan Seybold once again played matchmaker. He advised Warnock to go see Allied Linotype, a 100-year-old printing firm with roots in metal typesetting. PostScript had the potential to undermine Linotype's business, but in what can only be described as a leap of faith, Linotype president Wolfgang Kummer licensed its treasured Times and Helvetica font families to Adobe and Apple. Plus, it agreed to work with Adobe to develop the first PostScript typesetter.

Although Linotype wasn't the country's largest typesetter manufacturer, it was the most established and most respected, so getting Linotype was something of a coup. Frank Romano, the Roger K. Fawcett professor of digital publishing at the Rochester Institute of Technology, asserts, "Once they got Linotype, PostScript was destined for success."

Adobe's engineers set about converting Times and Helvetica into four styles each (regular, bold, italic, and bold italic). Adobe also developed four styles of Courier, the ubiquitous face of the IBM Selectric typewriter (using oblique instead of italics to save valuable chip space), and a single version of Symbol, an assortment of letters and mathematical characters. Those 13 fonts, as the basis of the first LaserWriter, formed the Rosetta stone of modern digital type.

A test file showing PostScript's ability to create stencil-like effects with characters clipped through a self-intersecting geometric shape.

& * % $? : " { }

One of the first Adobe Originals typefaces, Trajan was created by designer Carol Twombly, who modeled it after characters found on an ancient Roman column. "Trajan was from the first century, the epitome of the capital-letter form, and it didn't exist in any digital format," says Twombly.

TRAJAN

ABCDEFGHIJKLMNOPQRSTUVWXYZ

1234567890

&

**Principal scientist Doug Brotz
with Warnock and Geschke.**

The Defining Moment

In the months leading up to the launch of the LaserWriter, Adobe laid the groundwork for its future. To make PostScript a standard, Adobe knew it needed more fonts. Liz Bond, a Xerox veteran and Adobe's first marketing person, approached Aaron Burns of International Typeface Corporation, the most important source of typefaces for New York's advertising and media communities. Adobe and ITC soon struck a deal to include ITC fonts in future iterations of PostScript.

In addition to securing Linotype as a provider of high-resolution output devices, Adobe signed with laser-printer manufacturer QMS. Based in Mobile, Alabama, QMS also used the Canon engine, so Adobe could quickly give it a PostScript controller board. In fact, QMS introduced a PostScript-based printer a month before Apple. But as the company had little sales or distribution prowess and lacked Apple's marketing muscle, QMS's printer will go down as a footnote to PostScript history.

In the summer of 1984, Jobs called Jonathan Seybold. "Steve wanted to see me urgently," Seybold recalls. "He said they had a deal with Adobe, they were signing a deal with Linotype, they had real fonts. I went to Cupertino and walked into this tiny room, and there stood Jobs and Warnock with a Mac and a LaserWriter. He showed me what they were up to. I turned to Steve and said, 'You've just turned publishing on its head. This is the watershed event.' When I turned to John, he had this look on his face. He was just so happy. I could tell he was thinking, 'This made the company. This is my validation.' It was a magic moment."

"When that first page came out of the LaserWriter, I was blown away," Jobs says today. "No one had seen anything like this before. I held this page up in my hand and said, 'Who will not want that?' I knew then, as did John, that this was going to have a profound impact."

It was the end of 1984, and the stage was set for the introduction of the Apple LaserWriter.

"I said, 'You've just turned publishing on its head. This is the watershed event.'"

—Jonathan Seybold

"All these technologies were converging. Had we been able to plan this, something would be wrong with the cosmos."

— John Warnock

Sparking the Revolution

When three upstart companies—Adobe Systems, Aldus Corporation, and Apple Computer—joined forces to create desktop publishing in 1985, shockwaves rumbled through the publishing world. Thanks to the combination of the Apple Macintosh, Aldus PageMaker, and the Adobe PostScript-equipped LaserWriter, publishing was liberated from the confines of proprietary typesetting and printing systems. Committed to advancing PostScript as an open standard, Adobe licensed PostScript to a broad spectrum of printer manufacturers in North America and abroad, particularly in Japan. The company also developed a robust digital font business that in turn inspired a typographic renaissance. But by the end of the decade, the backlash that had been brewing against Adobe boiled over, testing the company's mettle and ultimately forging another era of innovation for Adobe and the publishing business.

1985

Apple LaserWriter
released, costs $6,995

5th annual Seybold
Seminars show has
30 exhibitors

PostScript Level 1
released

Microsoft releases
Windows 1.0

Aldus PageMaker 1
(Mac) released

1986

Adobe Type Library
includes more than
100 fonts

Initial public offering
of Adobe stock

Adobe revenue:
$16 million

Radius introduces
8.5x11-inch Mac monitor

Sony introduces
the CD-ROM

1987

Adobe moves to Mountain View office

Illustrator
1.0 ships

PostScript licensed by
IBM and HP

QuarkXPress
debuts

THE DESKTOP PUBLISHING REVOLUTION BEGINS

The LaserWriter debuted to great fanfare at Apple's annual stockholder meeting on January 23, 1985, where Steve Jobs's legendary showmanship was on display. Onstage the Pointer Sisters belted out "I'm So Excited." In the audience were all 27 Adobe employees who had made the trip to Cupertino's Flint Center after toasting the culmination of their two-year effort at Adobe's office the evening before. The jubilant engineers who had toiled in obscurity were seeing their product in a forum where they could gauge the public's reaction to it.

"You couldn't walk out of there not feeling you were doing something great," says Dan Putman, Adobe employee number 2 and former senior vice president of the North American systems division.

The LaserWriter cost $6,995—steep by today's standards, yet astoundingly cheap compared with the IBM and Xerox laser printers of the day, which were priced three to ten times that. Plus, the LaserWriter had Adobe's special ingredient: PostScript. Almost immediately, analysts commented on the LaserWriter's output, praising its "near-typeset quality."

With the release of the LaserWriter, Adobe Systems was on the corporate map. The two soft-spoken scientists were thrust into the media spotlight, fielding interview requests to explain why the world's second-largest computer company had bet its future on an unknown startup.

"Like all revolutions, not that many people were involved. We just decided amongst ourselves."

— Jonathan Seybold

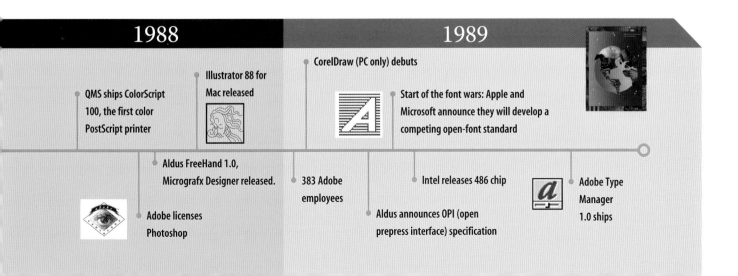

1988

QMS ships ColorScript 100, the first color PostScript printer

Illustrator 88 for Mac released

Aldus FreeHand 1.0, Micrografx Designer released.

Adobe licenses Photoshop

1989

CorelDraw (PC only) debuts

Start of the font wars: Apple and Microsoft announce they will develop a competing open-font standard

383 Adobe employees

Aldus announces OPI (open prepress interface) specification

Intel releases 486 chip

Adobe Type Manager 1.0 ships

Into the Limelight

Within days of the LaserWriter's public debut, Warnock flew east to introduce the Macintosh Office to the New York market. Flanked by Jobs, Linotype chairman Wolfgang Kummer, and ITC cofounder Aaron Burns, Warnock described PostScript as the glue that would hold the office publishing system together. At the press conference, Adobe announced two additional partnerships: one with Linotype to develop high-resolution PostScript typesetting devices, and another with ITC to license additional typefaces, including ITC Bookman, ITC Avant Garde Gothic, and ITC Zapf Chancery.

Thanks to the LaserWriter, the world's first PostScript printer, Apple became the largest printer company in the world, according to Jobs. But in the months after its high-flying introduction, the Macintosh Office stalled in midair. Although Adobe and the PostScript-equipped LaserWriter were turning heads, Apple and the Macintosh were under attack for the computer's lack of power and expandability. Sales of the Mac were sluggish, and they dipped perilously low by midsummer. Infighting at Apple between Jobs and Sculley took its toll, leading to Jobs's ouster. At one point Warnock and Geschke thought Apple would soon be out of business.

What was needed was a "killer app" that showed off both the Mac's graphical user interface and PostScript's printing capabilities. What was needed was PageMaker.

The Missing Piece

PageMaker was a new kind of program: part word processor, part graphics program, and more. Modeled after pagination programs used in newspaper production, PageMaker allowed users to lay out pages electronically—to combine text and graphics, put them in multiple columns, and incorporate type of various sizes—instead of using a drafting table and knife to splice together words and pictures mechanically.

Part word processor, part graphics program, Aldus PageMaker was the final piece of the desktop publishing puzzle.

PageMaker was the brainchild of Paul Brainerd, an ex-newspaperman who found himself adrift after newspaper computer-systems manufacturer Atex closed down the subsidiary company he operated near Seattle. Brainerd formed Aldus Corporation—named after the Renaissance printer who developed italic type and became a follower of Johannes Gutenberg, the inventor of movable type and hence the father of the modern printing industry—to put together a microcomputer-based pagination program for newspapers. Newspapers weren't interested in PageMaker, but publishing consultant Jonathan Seybold, who knew the Aldus founder from Brainerd's work at Atex, had an idea. He had already seen what the Macintosh and PostScript could do.

"When I saw what Paul had, I said, 'You have to talk to Apple,' and I put him in touch with the product managers for the Macintosh and the LaserWriter," says Seybold, who'd been hoping to see the confluence of personal computer and graphics-rich documents since the early 1970s. "The final missing piece of this puzzle was the software."

Brainerd made the rounds at Apple and then Adobe in mid-1984. He remembers the first time he walked into John Warnock's Palo Alto office. "The first thing I saw was that he had a page from the Gutenberg Bible hanging on his wall. I knew immediately that he had an appreciation of the art and craft of printing," Brainerd says.

Now all the tools were in place for a new way to publish: use PageMaker software to design and produce page layouts on the Macintosh, then print camera-ready pages on the LaserWriter. It was like having an entire publishing company on your desktop.

Brainerd dubbed the process and its tools "desktop publishing."

"At the time Aldus was writing the software, product manager John Scull showed me a list of five or so names of what to call this," says Seybold of the nascent industry, "and I said I liked the phrase 'desktop publishing.' Scull said Paul wanted to call it that, too. So that's what we called it."

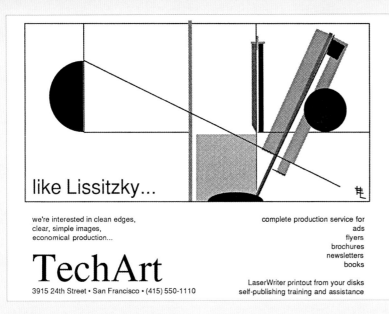

like Lissitzky...

we're interested in clean edges,
clear, simple images,
economical production...

TechArt
3915 24th Street • San Francisco • (415) 550-1110

complete production service for
ads
flyers
brochures
newsletters
books

LaserWriter printout from your disks
self-publishing training and assistance

This 1985 ad promotes TechArt, one of
the first walk-in shops providing PostScript
output from a LaserWriter and Macintosh.
Note the use of only two fonts—Times
and Helvetica.

When PostScript, the Apple Macintosh, and Aldus PageMaker came together in 1985, the landscape of publishing changed forever. Traditional methods of doing business vanished, replaced by new equipment and young upstart designers. Desktop publishing changed the way professional publishers worked and it inspired individuals to express themselves.

THE END OF AN ERA

I remember seeing a headline in a typesetters' magazine right after the PostScript output devices came out. The headline screamed "WAR!" Within five years there were no typesetters left.

> **Frank Romano, former publisher of**
> ***TypeWorld* and, later, *Electronic Publishing***

It was the Dark Ages. The technology seems so primitive now. You had to use a typositor to set headlines, then paste them up with rubber cement and X-Acto knives. All you had were black-and-white stats, so you comped color with marker overlays. If you went to work on a magazine

layout, you'd slice up your galleys and a couple of days later you'd get it back. Days intervened. It took weeks just to get type set and revisions back.

> **Louis Fishauf, illustrator and designer**

At a Seybold conference shortly after the LaserWriter was announced, I was cornered by a guy who made typesetting equipment. He almost assaulted me. "You have ruined my business," he shouted. "You pushed PostScript and you ruined my business."

> **Jonathan Seybold, founder,**
> **Seybold Seminars**

Typesetting and color separations were the biggest expenses at a publication. Phototype headlines were on the order of $2 per word. Color separations were so expensive that you couldn't afford to have color on every page. But when desktop systems and software came out, color became cheap. Every page went to color.

> **Roger Black, publication designer**
> **and chairman of Danilo Black USA**

APPLE'S CHANGING ROLE

When we all saw that first sheet of paper come out of the LaserWriter, we knew we were going to hit it out of the park. It was just a matter of how long it would take. You could sense the inevitability because it was so cool.

> **Steve Jobs, Apple CEO**

I had been working for Apple for a time. When I saw what this cute, clunky little thing could do, I had a flash that the Mac was where things were heading.

> **Luanne Seymour Cohen,**
> **author and designer**

In the beginning "desktop publishing" equaled "newsletter." If you drank the Kool-Aid, then DTP was good for office communications but not much else. The view inside Apple was that the software would sell Macs.

> **Clement Mok, former creative**
> **director at Apple**

In the fall of 1985 Apple was thinking about canceling the whole thing. What saved us was that we had negotiated the deal with Linotype.

John Warnock

CREATIVE FREEDOM

Adobe and Apple and PostScript and DTP created my whole career. I was moonlighting as a designer while working at the *New York Times* and *Newsweek*. What prevented me from opening a studio was money. I'd need a stat machine, a typesetting machine, and so on. Desktop publishing allowed me to open my own place.

Roger Black

I started my own company with a color Mac, a LaserWriter and layout software. I could compete with larger studios with better finished comps in less time. And for a lot less.

Clement Mok

DESIGN IMPACT

PageMaker and QuarkXPress automated production but they didn't automate design.

Roger Black

Typesetting shops used to be the keeper of the standards. Now there's a lot more bad typesetting. Digital type and desktop systems put more responsibility on the graphic communicator to maintain high quality.

Allan Haley, formerly of ITC, now with Agfa Monotype

The mainstreaming of graphics and type has given design a broader audience. That's a good thing. But design is a commodity because the practitioners are not well trained and the work can be mediocre. The highs aren't as high and the lows are still low.

Clement Mok

"I knew that bad design would happen. Look, if you give people 13 or 35 fonts, they'll use all of them on every page. New technology brings down design. The typesetters were horrified."

— John Warnock

Adobe and Apple changed the landscape entirely. Today's design and publishing are built on PostScript. I can't imagine a designer working in North America or Europe without a computer or an Adobe product. The methodology has changed. It's much more fluid. Everything is accessible to you. Control is in the hands of the designers.

Louis Fishauf

The best thing this revolution brought about is the change in the way the graphic designer does his work. Adobe brought design into the modern world. You could argue whether better stuff is being done today. Certainly more stuff is created and it's easier to create it.

Russell Brown, Adobe senior creative director

It created a new group of people who aspired to be like designers. They bought the whole nine yards.

Clement Mok

THE POWER OF THE PRESS

After the launch of the LaserWriter we started getting unsolicited testimonials from people. I had a vision of people publishing about noble acts, like Greenpeace. The first note we got was from these ladies who told us how excited they were to be able to publish their magazine. It was a lesbian newsletter, kind of pornographic in nature. The second newsletter that arrived was from a fundamentalist Christian sect. It wasn't exactly what we had in mind, but we gave them the voice to present their point of view.

Dan Putman, Adobe employee number 2

During the coup in Moscow all the presses had been shut down. Boris Yeltsin commandeered an HP printer, a PC, and a copy machine. There were pictures of Yeltsin surrounded by people with their hands outreached, trying to get copies of documents that were all produced in PageMaker. It's really a powerful image. It made me very proud.

Paul Brainerd, former Aldus CEO

Democracy? Hell, we're talking revolution. From 1985 to 1990, the typesetting market virtually disappeared. The creative professional became the driver of the printing process. America needed freedom before it could have democracy. Adobe technology gave us freedom.

Frank Romano

No customer had asked for PostScript. The market we were going after had five entrenched companies. There were 250,000 graphic artists then. Now there are at least 6 million.

John Warnock

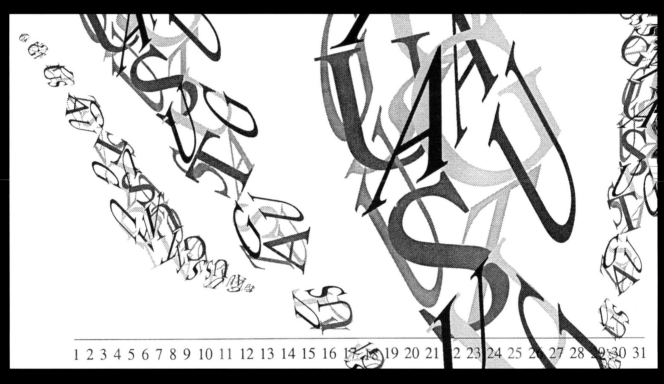

1 2 3 4 5 6 7 8 9 10 11 12 13 14 15 16 17 18 19 20 21 22 23 24 25 26 27 28 29 30 31

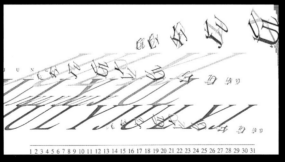

1 2 3 4 5 6 7 8 9 10 11 12 13 14 15 16 17 18 19 20 21 22 23 24 25 26 27 28 29 30 31

1985

This calendar was created with
Adobe's page description language POSTSCRIPT
and the master printed on a
300 dot per inch
laser printer

Adobe sent this 1985 calendar, printed
entirely on the new LaserWriter, to
Diane Burns at TechArt, one of the first
shops specializing in PostScript output
in San Francisco.

"That's how these things were decided in those days," he adds. "Like all revolutions, not that many people were involved. We just decided amongst ourselves."

Now Apple had a marketable concept. But according to Brainerd, Apple under the leadership of Sculley was reluctant to put significant money behind the LaserWriter, claiming the printer was too hard to sell and too expensive compared with Hewlett-Packard's new LaserJet printer. (The LaserJet, although it lacked much of PostScript's functionality, was positioned by HP as a competitor to the LaserWriter and priced at several thousand dollars less.) Plus, Apple saw publishing as a limited, and risky, business opportunity that it couldn't afford to focus on at the time. It would soon be proven wrong.

The Sum of Its Parts

PageMaker was the perfect application to show off the potential of the Macintosh as a publishing tool and the power of PostScript as a new printing paradigm. Using PageMaker, a designer could enter text and graphics, immediately see the results on the Macintosh screen, then hit the Print button and see the same document come out of the LaserWriter as an entire page, with all the text and graphics in place as designed. It made for a compelling story, especially with PostScript.

Prior to the LaserWriter, printers were passive machines, simply doing what the host computer told them to do. Because computers had limited memory and power, lines of text were all it could handle. Graphics were too big and too memory intensive for any computer except computer-graphic workstations to process, so photographs and line art were reproduced conventionally with stat cameras.

But PostScript made printers smart. Instead of dumb printers that had to accept simple lines of type, PostScript put intelligence into the printer itself, so that complicated files containing both text and graphics could be printed on a single page. Effectively, it viewed the printer as a companion computer and offloaded the burden of computation from the terminal to the printer itself. Adobe accomplished this by designing computer controller boards (for the printer) that contained chipsets embedded with PostScript software. These "brains" interpreted instructions on the fly, transforming code into type, lines, and circles, and executing instructions to scale a font or rotate a graphic. Handling so many computations required a robust processor. In fact the LaserWriter was so powerful that for a time it had more computing muscle than the Macintosh.

Finally, Apple agreed to piece together a $1 million budget to promote the concept of desktop publishing. In early 1985, Warnock, Geschke, and Brainerd hit the road to proselytize on behalf of PageMaker, the

Clement Mok, former creative director at Apple, designed this early guide to desktop publishing.

BizStats: **1985**

No. of employees: 44

Revenue: $4.6 million

Product releases:
    PostScript Level 1

Other:
>> Red book (PostScript Language Reference Manual) published

First PostScript LaserWriter introduced, for $6,995

Macintosh, and PostScript. Because the software was still in development, pages were carefully cobbled together in MacPaint and MacDraw to show analysts, the media, and prospective clients what a PageMaker layout looked like.

PageMaker was released to the public in July 1985. Overnight, an industry was born—with Aldus as a major player—breathing new life into Apple and placing Adobe clearly at the forefront of a revolution. Two years later the desktop publishing industry was a multimillion-dollar business.

"We never expected it," Warnock says. "This was a matter of being in the right place at the right time. All these technologies were converging. Had we been able to plan this, then something would be wrong with the cosmos."

"It took some interesting people to do this: It took John and Chuck, because PostScript was a tremendous breakthrough; it took Steve Jobs, who has an aesthetic vision; and it took someone like Paul, who could see a radically different way of doing things," says Seybold, who now consults on converging-media projects. "As a result, we transformed the way people communicate and we transformed the whole visual part of communication. With PostScript, raster output devices, and programs like PageMaker, you could do things you had never done before, not just duplicate what you had done with knives and wax. It very quickly moved beyond that."

Getting Good

Even as sales of PageMaker and the LaserWriter took off, however, commercial printers and publishers scoffed. The Macintosh wasn't powerful enough, the print quality not good enough. The LaserWriter's output was deemed adequate for comps or drafts—ironically, what Adobe had planned in the first place—but its quality was certainly not "near typeset" or "camera ready." Nor did the new desktop systems offer the variety of typefaces readily available in the world of professional printing.

The sobriquet "church newsletter" was used frequently by those who disparaged the caliber of early desktop publications. But several events silenced the detractors.

Adobe's partnership with Linotype came to fruition in the spring of 1985 with the introduction of the PostScript-based Linotronic 100 and 300 typesetters, which offered resolutions of 1,270 dpi and 2,540 dpi, respectively. Now output fidelity compared favorably with that of existing typesetting technology.

That early ability to compete with traditional typesetting was key to Adobe's success, believes Frank Romano, an industry observer and now

One of the first to recognize the impact desktop publishing would have on the industry, Jonathan Seybold launched what has become digital publishing's best-known trade show and seminar series.

the Roger K. Fawcett professor of digital publishing at RIT. "What made Adobe successful was that it operated on the high end, and once you control the high end you control everything below it," Romano says. "When you're on the low end, it's much harder to go up."

PostScript's impact on commercial printing was as revolutionary as its impact on office or personal laser printing, if not more so. The typesetting business was an entrenched, closed industry in which a few vendors jealously guarded their technologies. Their proprietary systems consisted of dedicated terminals into which operators entered strings of binary code. Each typesetter manufacturer had its own typeface library specific to that machine. Equipment from one vendor did not work with that of another. A client bought into a system and stuck with it. To upgrade a typesetting device meant buying a new and expensive workstation that controlled it.

It was a lucrative and fiercely competitive business with its roots in hundreds of years of tradition, and Adobe was a threat to the status quo. "The majority of typesetter manufacturers didn't want to pay attention to us," says former Adobe sales and marketing vice president Steve MacDonald. "Linotype saw the vision and took the risk."

Opening Closed Doors

The PostScript-equipped Linotronic blew the doors off a closed industry. Because of PostScript's ability to print text and graphics on the same page, the machines were no longer called typesetters but imagesetters. A raster image processor (RIP)—the brains of the imagesetter—turned bitmapped, or rasterized, information into curves, acting like a giant printer controller board. And like its desktop sibling, an imagesetter was connected to a Macintosh, not a proprietary workstation terminal. Over time, such a setup meant that customers could mix and match computers and imagesetters. Upgrading systems meant downloading new software to the RIP, not buying a whole new machine.

These open systems, coupled with device-independent output, formed the backbone of the desktop publishing revolution. The Macintosh represented the idea of using computers for communicating, not just calculating, and PageMaker allowed the creation of visually rich documents, but PostScript held it all together. It was, as Warnock and Geschke frequently described it, the "glue" of desktop publishing. "PostScript without the others would have been the right thing to do anyway," says Seybold. "But PostScript was necessary for the other two."

But high-resolution printing was only one avenue through which Adobe made its case that PostScript could match or even outdo traditional publishing systems. Adobe was in the process of building a type library that would soon rival that of any font foundry in the world.

"With PostScript, raster output devices, and PageMaker, you could do more than just duplicate what you had done with knives and wax. You could do things you had never done before."

— Jonathan Seybold

Bringing Type to Market

One knock against the new phenomenon of desktop publishing was its paucity of fonts. The LaserWriter offerings paled in comparison with what was available in traditional typesetting systems. But PostScript's device-independent font handling was the key to Adobe's unique accomplishment. Warnock and Geschke knew that to sell PostScript, they needed more PostScript type. So, concurrent with its work on the LaserWriter in 1984, Adobe began compiling a type library, first through licensing and then through original type development. In time, Adobe's type library would become the largest of its kind anywhere.

The agreement with Linotype for the first LaserWriter fonts laid the foundation of Adobe's type efforts. But Adobe soon brought in type designer Sumner Stone. "John and Chuck had already lined up Linotype by the time I got there, which impressed me," Stone says of his arrival in the summer of 1984. "Lino was so difficult to deal with that it must have been very impressed with what Adobe showed it."

Times and Helvetica had already been digitized—several times—by the time Stone went to Adobe's Palo Alto offices. "At first John and Chuck thought they would hire the wives of friends to digitize the typefaces," Stone remembers, chuckling. "They thought digitizing was a relatively minor issue that could be done by intelligent people who didn't have training in typography." Early results soon disabused them of that idea.

Adobe also entered into negotiations with the International Typeface Corporation (ITC), the primary type supplier to the New York advertising and media communities. According to Allan Haley, ITC's executive vice president at the time, ITC had also been searching for inroads into the lucrative business market. When Adobe came looking for fonts for its next laser printer, ITC was happy to oblige. At the time it was a gamble for ITC, as 90 percent of the company's sales were for proprietary typesetting systems like those from Linotype and Compugraphic. By the 1990s, however, 99 percent of ITC revenues came from digital fonts.

"It was all very low key," Haley remembers of the 1984 negotiations between Adobe and ITC. "No one knew this was going to go anywhere."

A Legacy of 35 Fonts

The second laser printer from Apple, the LaserWriter Plus introduced in 1986, contained more fonts from Linotype and ITC, bringing the number of core PostScript fonts to 35—the standard for PostScript printers ever

> *"We had the idea of fonts not as derivatives of what had gone before, but as something fresh and new designed just for this technology."*
>
> — Carol Twombly

Members of the Adobe type
team, from left: Jim Wasco,
Robert Slimbach, Carol Twombly,
and Fred Brady.

Adobe Garamond

ABCDEFGHI

JKLMONPQ

RSTUVWXYZ

abcdefghij

klmnopq

rstuvwxyz

1 2 3 4 5 6 7 8 9 0

Designed as the first Adobe Originals typeface by Robert Slimbach in 1989, Adobe Garamond proved that PostScript fonts could honor tradition even as it turned typesetting on its head. "My hope was that PostScript fonts would take off and be important works that stood the test of time," says Slimbach, who researched Claude Garamond's designs at the Plantin-Moretus Museum in Belgium.

since. The "LaserWriter 35," as the set is sometimes known, added 22 fonts to the original 13; the typefaces included ITC's Avant Garde Gothic, Bookman, and Zapf Chancery as well as Linotype's Palatino. Both Palatino and ITC Zapf Chancery were designed by the legendary Hermann Zapf, whose association with the undertaking lent PostScript fonts legitimacy in the type and publishing communities.

Given that the 35 fonts are a major element in the era of PostScript type, the choice of those typefaces was curious. The decisions were arbitrary and political rather than made with an eye toward defining late-20th-century typography. "No one knew how important this decision was going to be," says Stone.

According to Haley and Stone, Steve Jobs handpicked some of the typefaces under the guidance of ITC's Aaron Burns, who took a fatherly interest in the young Jobs. At one point Jobs wanted ITC Gorilla, a rounded serif that looked a bit like a bolder, rougher ITC Souvenir, a wildly popular font at the time. "It was a free-for-all," Stone says today. "When Jobs got involved, he had his opinions. He wanted to include Gorilla, but instead we wound up with Zapf Chancery, which was considered to be a 'fun' typeface. Bookman was a political compromise, as was Avant Garde, both of which were pushed by ITC as something they wanted for another serif and sans serif" to supplement Linotype's Times and Helvetica. Stone himself lobbied for Palatino, which he considered more modern than the other offerings. Helvetica Narrow, like Courier, was a software construct rather than a digitized typeface, done to save precious memory.

The quickest way to build a type library, of course, was to take existing designs and convert them. Adobe first deepened its relationship with Linotype and ITC. The companies sent Adobe its fonts as digital data, which Adobe converted to PostScript. PostScript fonts consisted of two pieces: a bitmap screen representation for display and a PostScript outline version for printing. Adobe's Bill Paxton developed a tool that converted the digital data to PostScript outlines and applied technical attributes unique to PostScript, such as hinting, which makes typefaces look good at small sizes and lower resolutions. The data from some font foundries wasn't necessarily precise, so Adobe's staff had the peculiar role of acting as "an interpreter between computer scientists and type designers," as Stone describes it. "There was a lot of handwork in the beginning."

The Stone Age

But Stone had made it clear when he signed on as director of typography that he was to be able to do original design. "Both Chuck and John placed a high value on innovation and creativity, so they were fine with that," he says. To signal to the rest of the company that typeface development was more art than science, he installed a drafting table in his office.

BizStats: **1986**

No. of employees: 87

Revenue: $16 million

Stock price range: $11 (IPO)

Other:
>> IPO on August 20 (Nasdaq: ADBE)

   84% of Adobe revenues from Apple

   Digital Equipment licenses PostScript for
   its printers

   Adobe Type Library includes more than
   100 fonts

Fonts were key to the early success of PostScript. Not only did fonts demonstrate the technical accomplishment that was PostScript, but they also signaled the end of typesetting with proprietary systems. Along the way PostScript fonts created new opportunities for hundreds of young designers who can now create their own typefaces. Today, everywhere you look—from magazines to billboards—you see a PostScript font in use.

THE BEGINNING

Adobe had the tiger by the tail. They thought they had a pussycat, when in fact they had the whole goddamn typesetting industry.

> **Matthew Carter, type designer, cofounder of Bitstream**

Getting the fonts from Linotype was the most important part of it. Had it only been Geneva and the Apple look-alike fonts, the graphics arts markets wouldn't have accepted it.

> **John Warnock**

Warnock knew that licensing ITC fonts would help establish Adobe's credibility. He saw the value in the intellectual property.

> **Allan Haley, formerly of ITC, now with Agfa Monotype**

The Mac taught people the word *font*.

> **Scott Kim, designer**

It's possible that on your Mac today the oldest file date is 1986, and that would be a font.

> **Roger Black, chairman, Danilo Black USA**

Type has supported the PostScript religion. Adobe wouldn't have had the success it had without the type program.

> **Matthew Carter**

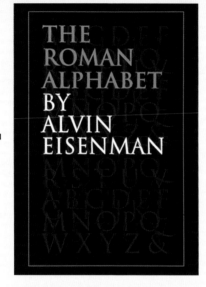

TYPOPHILES

John loved books and typography, so as type became a business for him, it was an enabler for his love of type. We were all romantics at that time. We would do dumb things for the love of it.

> **Allan Haley**

John is an avid book collector. Periodically he'd bring in an acquisition and show it to those of us in the type department. One day he brought in a Kelmscott Chaucer, which was pretty amazing. We pored over it for hours.

> **David Lemon, manager of type development**

John and Chuck are very conscious of quality. They're very proud people who won't accept anything shoddy. One reason John went into the world of computer graphics because his wife was a designer. That personal interest was a positive force about keeping this on track.

> **Sumner Stone, Adobe's first director of typography**

Min Wang designed this book jacket using Carol Twombly's Trajan, a premier example of the clean design for which Adobe became known.

> *"By 1990 it felt like we had all the fonts. By 1993 there were 10,000 PostScript fonts. By now it must be 100,000."*
>
> — Roger Black

DESIGN CHALLENGES

Adobe was new to type-making, so their fonts were not of the best quality in the beginning—especially their digitizations of Times and Helvetica.

> **Matthew Carter**

Adobe had to cross-check fonts on every application, every printer, every platform. They had to sandpaper the Béziers—smooth out the curves—to keep the control points down so the fonts would print.

> **Roger Black**

Making the design work on a bunch of different output devices was a requirement we had to keep in mind. It was a serious challenge.

> **Carol Twombly, Adobe type designer**

The Type Department

So many talented type designers got together at Adobe. We were isolated from the rest of the organization. It was a great think tank for type ideas and design.

Min Wang, graphic artist

It was an exciting time. We had the resources, and Adobe type was a big hit.

Sumner Stone

Of course then this huge company grew up around us. The oak tree got dwarfed by the redwoods.

Dan Mills, former type development director

We were the weird type people in the corner.

Robert Slimbach

Type was Adobe's great gift to the publishing world. We sold it too cheaply. Why were all fonts the same price? We didn't have a well-thought-out strategy on pricing.

Sumner Stone

Designing Originals

Robert and Carol are two of the best designers of the '90s. They made designs that we consider timeless. People will still want to use Myriad and Minion and Adobe Caslon 20 years from now. People will use the other foundries when they want to achieve a '90s look.

David Lemon

We've stuck to our guns, sticking to classical principles of legibility and functionality of design. We haven't got wrapped up in outrageous design.

Robert Slimbach

Adobe's fonts were too intellectual. As a designer it was immensely frustrating: the fonts were too good, it took too long to make them, and the results were too nice. They never looked rough

and ready. Designers wanted a Target division, not just Neiman Marcus.

Roger Black

Birth of an Industry

PostScript laid the foundation for the democratization of type design.

David Lemon

When the Type 1 format was released and Altsys revised Fontographer, the playing field was leveled for other foundries. There developed a fascination with typography that led to tabletop type foundries. Everyone got interested in fonts.

Matthew Carter

With the success of Adobe many new foundries have sprung up. The computer has given designers the opportunity to digitize their alphabets. There's been a flood of type in the past decade.

Robert Slimbach

Our attitude toward other foundries was, "That's great." The stranglehold of a few companies making type was loosened.

Sumner Stone

Robert Slimbach and Fred Brady at the Plantin–Moretus Museum in Belgium.

Adobe was seen as the establishment by the new designers, which is ironic given its short history. But we weren't a bunch of graybeards running around in tweed jackets. We just weren't as postmodern and avant-garde as they were.

Dan Mills

The Impact of PostScript Type

In the early '90s there was a new enthusiasm for type design. It's always been the most arcane of professions, with painful initiations and monastic orders. There had been a priesthood, but now there was a laity as well.

Matthew Carter

Adobe's impact is incalculable. I studied graphic design. When I told my adviser I wanted to design fonts, he told me that no one made a living that way. Thanks to Adobe that is now untrue.

David Lemon

For most of type's history, the people who designed and made type were the same—they were called punchcutters. That changed in the 1860s, when type was manufactured in factories, and the making and the designing of type were separated. PostScript put them back together. That reuniting is hugely important to me.

Matthew Carter

Type is always important. It has a significant position in the history of communication. There will always be people who understand that and those who don't see it. I knew we'd take out Letraset and that Monotype and Linotype's typesetting business would go down. But we had a responsibility to replace that with something better and to keep the values high.

John Warnock

Sumner Stone, Adobe's first director of typography, at his drafting table in 1986.

∨
∨

"Our aim was to give digital type design more credibility to professional typographers. Many purists had a wait-and-see attitude."

— Robert Slimbach

Almost immediately he began working on the eponymous Stone, the first commercial typeface created from scratch in PostScript. Published in 1987, Stone consisted of three designs—Serif, Sans, and Informal—and was later licensed back to ITC. A hallmark of ITC Stone, which was designed to take advantage of PostScript's device independence, was that it held up well at low resolutions and small sizes. Above all, it was a shot across the bow for old-school type foundries.

"It was a new typeface for the computer world, designed for a new environment, not just the digitizing of old faces," Stone says. It was also one of Adobe's first typefaces sold not as part of a printer or an operating system but as a stand-alone retail package (other fonts in the package were the 22 added to the LaserWriter Plus). On its own, one Stone design with six styles sold for $275. Compared with traditional typesetting, in which a single font weight cost $180, PostScript was a bargain. But for desktop publishers used to getting their fonts as part of a computer or printer, buying a typeface on its own was a new experience.

"We had a pretty strong awareness that we had to do education about type. We had to promote that this was a craft and that craftsmanship was important," says Stone. Adobe produced posters and pamphlets about type, supplemented by a quarterly catalog called *Font & Function* and elaborate type-specimen books. The campaigns worked. "We were surprised by how quickly the fonts sold. They sold like hotcakes," Stone says.

Fresh New Faces

Spurred by this success, Stone amassed a team of designers and technicians to develop original typefaces. Among them were Robert Slimbach, with whom he had worked at Autologic, and Carol Twombly, a graduate of Charles Bigelow's type program at Stanford. Slimbach and Twombly began as freelance digitizers in 1987 and 1988, respectively, and went on to design some of the most popular typefaces in the Adobe Originals program, under Fred Brady. Adobe also commissioned outside designers to create Adobe Originals. One of them, David Siegel, designed the popular Tekton, basing it on the lettering in architectural blueprints.

"We had the idea of fonts not as derivatives of what had gone before but as something fresh and new designed just for this technology," says Twombly, whose designs include Adobe Caslon, Trajan, Lithos, Chapparal, and (with Slimbach) Myriad, the last of which is now one of Adobe's corporate typefaces.

"Our aim was to give digital type design credibility to professional typographers," says Slimbach, who designed Adobe Garamond, Utopia, Minion, Jenson, and others. "At the time there were purist typographers who were still setting type by hand. Many had a wait-and-see attitude."

To strengthen Adobe's stance as a serious type foundry, Stone also convened a type advisory board that included publication designer Roger Black, Yale University Design School chair Alvin Eisenman, stone carver and letterer Stephen Harvard, and letterpress printer Jack Stauffacher. International type designers such as Gerard Unger and Erik Spiekermann often joined in. Adobe even produced packages of type for different uses, chosen by Black, Haley, Spiekermann, and others.

Barbarians at the Gates

As PostScript fonts took off, Adobe scrambled to get more typefaces into the marketplace, eventually licensing type-creation tools to font suppliers so they could digitize and convert their own fonts under Adobe's watchful eye. Old-world type foundries that had dismissed PostScript realized that they needed to adapt. Soon typesetters like Agfa, Monotype, and Berthold agreed to convert their formidable libraries to PostScript.

"PostScript was like the barbarians at the gate," says David Lemon, who joined Adobe in 1986 and who still works as Adobe's manager of type development. "It was the end of the exclusive type market. They had to join in or get out of business."

Not only did established type foundries join in, but a new breed of small independent type houses also sprang up. The release of a third-party product called Altsys Fontographer (now owned by Macromedia) enabled even laypeople to design PostScript fonts. An international boom in PostScript type design and development ensued.

Not since the age of metal type had there been such a prolific period of type development—and the digital-type era quickly surpassed even that in terms of the number of fonts produced and the number of people designing them. Adobe's library alone contains more than 3,000 typefaces.

Coming Full Circle

Adobe's dominant position soon came under attack as upstart designers produced edgier, less refined faces and as a raft of knockoff fonts appeared on the market and pushed down prices. Lax copyright laws governing typeface design allowed small companies to digitize entire font libraries and to sell the imposter fonts for pennies a typeface. (Adobe was able to secure protection for PostScript fonts as software programs through a 1999 court case.) Prices eroded further when Apple and Microsoft flooded the market with their rival font format, TrueType.

While demand for PostScript fonts had never been higher, type as a sustainable business was waning. In 1992 Adobe, continuing to look for ways to promote PostScript fonts, developed an innovative format called Multiple Master. Multiple Masters gave users more control over the appearance of their typefaces and revived such honored typographic

Advisory board member Stephen Harvard provided an important early critique of Robert Slimbach's Adobe Garamond typeface.

BizStats: **1987**

No. of employees: 172

Revenue: $39 million

Stock price range: $2 to $15 (2-for-1 split in March)

Product release:
Illustrator 1.0, Adobe's first desktop application

Other:
>> IBM and HP license PostScript for their laser printers

49% of Adobe revenues from Apple

400 applications support PostScript

Linotype licenses PostScript to develop Type 1 versions of its Mergenthaler Type Library, which contains more than 1,700 typefaces

Adobe moves into Charleston Road offices in Mountain View

JEFF SCHEWE

Jeff Schewe is an advertising photographer whose early advocacy of Photoshop made him a pioneer in digital imaging. His experiments with Photoshop have led to the development of several key features in the program. It was Schewe's work on the image "Hands and Globe," seen here, that inspired Mark Hamburg to create the History palette. Schewe was then asked to design the splash screen for Photoshop 5.0, code-named "Strange Cargo," below (note the Photoshop "eye" in the sun, which came from a portrait Schewe did of Hamburg). "Bird Lady" (1993) exemplifies one of the first uses of Schewe's cloning from "Snapshot and Saved," which eventually led to the "Hands and Globe" technique and the History feature. (www.schewephoto.com)

Adobe's Type Advisory Board circa 1988: from top right, clockwise, Stephen Harvard, Alvin Eisenman, Sumner Stone, Jack Stauffacher, Lance Hidy, and Roger Black.

techniques as optical scaling. The fonts were awkward to create and relied heavily on host applications, however. "Multiple Master never had good support in applications," admits David Lemon, who helped write the specifications for the format. "You had to manually adjust it. It looked too scary to people."

In 1996 Adobe joined with Microsoft to develop a next-generation font technology. Called OpenType, the format combines aspects of PostScript and TrueType to create fonts that can be used in print and on the Web and that can support extended character sets such as those in non-Latin alphabets. Adobe plans to convert its entire library to the OpenType format and all Adobe applications support OpenType fonts.

"We've come full circle," says Lemon, who spearheads the OpenType conversion. "In the beginning type development at Adobe started as a way to explain the value of PostScript. Now the focus is on how type can add value to the Adobe story. Just as fonts showed off what PostScript can do, so are they a way to show off what the applications can do."

Today it's difficult to comprehend the impact of PostScript fonts on modern publishing and on Adobe's success. Throughout the late 1980s and early 1990s, type drove the sales of PostScript printers to individuals. But Adobe had its sights set on a bigger target: the printer manufacturers themselves. Adobe's sales team hit the road to persuade those manufacturers to license PostScript for their output devices.

MIN WANG

Yale University graphic design student Min Wang went to Adobe as an intern in 1986 to draw kanji characters for Adobe's new Japanese type library. He soon alternated his time between lecturing at Yale and working at Adobe, where he designed pieces for the type department. Later senior art director and design manager at Adobe, Wang is now design director at Square Two Design. Shown here are posters designed to promote Adobe Originals typefaces, for which he created the logo based on the "a" from Robert Slimbach's Adobe Garamond. (www.square2.com)

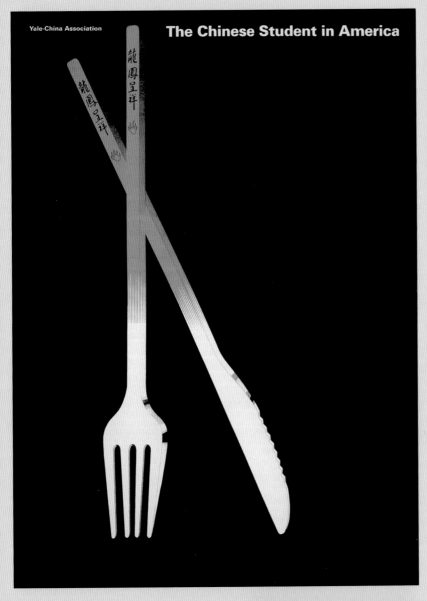

Yale-China Association

The Chinese Student in America

V
V

"Adobe was a great think tank for type ideas and design."

PostScript software engineer Bob
Chansler presses ROM chips into
a Linotronic controller board.

Forging Alliances

Before the LaserWriter was introduced, Adobe made the rounds of printer manufacturers and software developers, trying to persuade them to adopt PostScript. Contractually prohibited from talking about the deal with Apple, the team of Geschke, Warnock, and Steve MacDonald could do little more than promote the technology on its own merits. But that approach had two strikes against it: putting computer intelligence inside a printer was a foreign concept, and there was no proof of market acceptance.

"The software developers wanted to know what printers supported it, and the printer developers wanted to know which software products would support it," says MacDonald. "It was a chicken-and-egg thing. And as there were no printers, there was no hurry to sign."

Once the LaserWriter shipped and Adobe could talk about its relationships with Apple and Linotype, the company vigorously pursued licenses with other printer manufacturers. "When the LaserWriter came out, it was a lot easier to get those meetings," MacDonald says. "There was a shift from talking about the technology to talking about the business."

The deal with Apple gave Adobe a strong financial foundation. Adobe was paid 5 percent of the $6,995 list price of the LaserWriter, or $350, for each unit sold. In 1984 and 1985 almost all of Adobe's revenues were royalties from Apple (Apple later renegotiated the deal so that fees were paid on volume shipped). Apple's precipitous midyear fall in 1985 would have been enough impetus for Adobe to expand its client base. But more than revenue diversification was behind Adobe's drive to broaden its base of licensees. The company wanted to position PostScript as the standard for printing across the board and around the world.

Steve Jobs, for one, applauded Adobe's efforts to branch out, even though it might undermine Apple's lock on the PostScript printer market. "When I asked John to be a software company instead of a whole printer company, his retort to that was, 'Well, OK, as long we can make it an industry standard,'" Jobs says. "He convinced me it was in our best interest to make it an industry standard, because then we would see PostScript in typesetters and in all sorts of other printers that Apple would never make. Our customers would benefit from that more than we would lose from having some competition with the printers we did make. I bought in to that. For every printer that was competing with us, we would have three or so that were things we would never do that were great for us."

"John convinced me that it was in our best interest to make PostScript an industry standard."

— Steve Jobs

Stalking the OEM

Adobe went hunting for bigger game, setting its sights on IBM and Hewlett-Packard, both of which had robust printer businesses. It also eyed the Japanese market. "Apple and IBM had their devices manufactured in Japan. We knew that either we signed them up with PostScript or they'd come up with a solution themselves," says Geschke. The risk was not only that Adobe would lose the Japanese market but also that it would be just a matter of time before the Japanese sold that technology back to the U.S., thus cutting Adobe out of the loop.

Two companies were already attempting to siphon off business in North America: Imagen, which itself licensed technology to Hewlett-Packard for use as the printing protocol in HP's LaserJet printers; and Xerox, which ironically dusted off Warnock and Geschke's old program Interpress to position it as a competitor to PostScript. Xerox even threatened Adobe with legal action, claiming that PostScript was actually Interpress and that Warnock and Geschke had appropriated it when they left PARC. Adobe, which had its license for the Design System from Evans & Sutherland, quickly convinced Xerox otherwise.

Adobe knew that its technology was superior, but it didn't take the competition lightly. Warnock and Geschke viewed it as a challenge. The pair set up a friendly wager with MacDonald. As MacDonald had worked at HP, and the cofounders at Xerox, the bet was to see who could first sign up their former employer as a licensee. "It took me 57 meetings over seven years to sign HP as a vendor, but I did it," says MacDonald, who won a sports car for his efforts.

But other technologies weren't Adobe's only competition. Against the backdrop of the desktop publishing boom, printing was now a lucrative business. Companies who didn't want to pay Adobe's licensing fees but who wanted a piece of the action began developing PostScript imitations. These so-called clone manufacturers used Adobe's published specifications as well as some reverse-engineering savvy in an effort to duplicate PostScript. "At one point in 1986 I drew up a list of 40 companies that were already developing or were planning to develop PostScript clones," says MacDonald. While some companies achieved success with their imposter languages, few could match the elegance of Adobe's implementation. "Adobe PostScript was the gold standard. No one else could measure up," says Dan Putman. "We helped a lot of startups go out of business."

Even as Adobe compiled a growing list of printer-vendor clients, the young company had to work hard to prove it had legs. As a condition of some deals, more-established companies asked for "source escrow," in which a third party held on to the pertinent source code as insurance against Adobe's going out of business. That way, if Adobe failed, the client

Adobe's 1987 deal with IBM was a turning point. It not only gave Adobe clout in the market but also gave PC users access to Adobe PostScript Type 1 fonts.

THE EVOLUTION OF POSTSCRIPT

PostScript set the publishing world on its head in 1985, and it formed a basis for PDF in 1993. In between, it continued to evolve. And while Adobe's attention was increasingly focused on breakthrough products like Photoshop, PostScript remained critical to Adobe's technological and financial strength.

PostScript put Adobe on the map because it allowed output devices of all resolutions to use the same data to render a page. Professional publishers in particular benefited from being able to print a draft on an Apple LaserWriter—or, by 1988, on a composite thermal-transfer printer, the QMS ColorScript 100—and then send the same file to an Agfa or Linotronic imagesetter to produce black-and-white film of the cyan, magenta, yellow, and black plates for a four-color press run.

"PostScript is one of the few examples where thoughtful computer science has turned into a significant product line," says Jim King, a principal scientist in the Advanced Technology Group.

A MAJOR LEAP FORWARD

PostScript Level 2, which came out in 1990, offered several advances. The two most important features worked hand in glove: First, Adobe built in support for advanced color management. Second, it supported four-color separations inside the final PostScript output device. A PostScript interpreter could receive a composite color file, such as an Adobe Illustrator file, separate it into the four process-color components, and apply screening parameters. Separations no longer had to be created independently as an extra step in the production workflow.

In addition, Adobe improved PostScript's speed and reliability by optimizing the code, improving its memory management, and introducing

compression/decompression filters to enable files containing large images to be smaller, thus reducing transmission time. There were other new features as well, but the support for separations and the improved performance are what set PostScript Level 2 ahead.

Those advances, combined with a critical mass of applications that supported PostScript by the early 1990s and the ongoing speed and processing improvements in hardware CPUs, led to another dramatic change for publishers: The so-called black boxes—dedicated, hardware-based raster image processors (RIPs) that crunched PostScript code—gave way to software-based RIPs that were less expensive and were more flexible. So while PostScript 1 was revolutionary in how it brought the processing of pages to the actual output device, PostScript Level 2 brought the processing out into the open, into software.

FURTHER REFINEMENTS

In 1998 Adobe released PostScript 3—dropping the word *Level* from the technology's name. Adobe expanded PostScript's color space so that it could create separations for special orders like duotones or spot-color blends; enhanced PostScript's font capabilities; offered more gray levels and smooth shading to reduce banding in high-resolution out-

put devices; and added support for in-RIP trapping to complement in-RIP separations.

In a sense, PostScript 3 was icing on the cake—after all, PostScript Level 2 had already become an industry-standard page-description language, and the core technology of PostScript formed the foundation on which Acrobat, Adobe PDF, and Adobe's entire e-paper initiative was based.

"The Adobe imaging model is the bedrock of both PDF and PostScript, but there are many more things in PDF than in PostScript," says Tom Malloy, head of the Advanced Technology Group. "PostScript was developed to describe printed pages, while PDF was developed as electronic paper, with all that goes along with it."

> *"PostScript is one of the few examples where thoughtful computer science has turned into a significant product line."*
>
> —Jim King

Those last six words carry weight. Adobe is betting that "all that goes along with" PDF—including digital signatures, online annotations, and e-forms and e-transactions—will drive the company well into the 21st century. The technology that brought Geschke and Warnock 20 years of success appears to be the kernel for Adobe's future achievements.

In 1987, Adobe sent a team to Japan to persuade Japanese typesetting companies to adopt PostScript technology for their fonts. Its contract with Morisawa not only allowed Adobe to create PostScript versions of Japanese fonts (most of which contain 10,000 or more characters) but also opened the door for PostScript printer licenses.

JAPANESE FONTS

あ 安 才 於

あいうえおかき

安以宇衣於加幾

had access to the technical information it needed to update its products. Clinton Nagy, who helped negotiate most of Adobe's North American contracts, says it wasn't until Adobe's revenue exceeded $40 million that the requests for source escrow ceased.

The endless meetings, too, seemed designed to test the spirit of the young company. "During the meetings with Xerox, I'd have the feeling that if I got up to take a restroom break and came back seven years later, it would be the same meeting," says Putman, who attended negotiations to answer any hardware questions that came up. Nagy recalls one meeting with IBM held in the windowless room typical of many security-conscious industry giants. Halfway through the meeting, the IBM negotiators called for a 20-minute break—and didn't return for three hours. The IBM representatives had been waylaid by an internal debate, but to Nagy and Geschke their departure was unsettling.

The signing of IBM in March 1987 was to become a major catalyst for Adobe in securing additional licensees. "The IBM deal gave us the strength to carry on," says Nagy, who helped to negotiate it. On the day the agreement was to be signed, Nagy was supposed to meet Geschke at IBM's Colorado offices, but a snowstorm prevented Geschke's arrival. Nagy was left to fend for himself. After both parties signed the contract, he flew to California and then drove straight to the Adobe offices, arriving well after 5 p.m. "I walked down the hallway and everybody crowded around me, saying, 'Let me see it, let me see it,'" Nagy says. The signed IBM contract had talismanic power.

With Big Blue backing PostScript, it was hard for other companies to say no. "Less than 24 hours after IBM signed, HP called," MacDonald remembers, although it would take another couple of years for the terms of HP's agreement to be hammered out and products released into the field. "The battle had been won," Nagy adds. "Gradually it became more that if you wanted to be in the printer business, you had to have PostScript."

An ad for Adobe in the November 4, 1987, *Wall Street Journal* crowed about the company's licensing successes. After acknowledging Apple's role as PostScript's first licensee, the ad continued: "One by one the rest of the industry adopted PostScript, making it the first and only standard endorsed by virtually every major company in the computer industry." The roster of licensees included Agfa-Gevaert, Apple, Apollo Computing, AST Research, Dataproducts, Diconix, Digital (DEC), IBM, Linotype, Mass Micro Systems, NBI, NEC, NeXT, Quadran, QMS, Qume, Texas Instruments, Varityper, and Wang.

(The ad concluded by saying, "What's next? Display PostScript. We created the one and only standard in the industry and it's just the start." Display PostScript, which was intended to bring the device-independent model to monitors, never achieved the success of its printer sibling, and its development was eventually scuttled.)

A Foothold in Japan

Adobe's success with original equipment manufacturers (OEMs) wasn't limited to North America. Making PostScript a worldwide standard required an expansion into Japan and Europe. As most printer engines were made in Japan, that was the place to start.

In 1987, typography director Sumner Stone made the first foray in Adobe's effort to establish PostScript licenses for Japanese fonts. With each font containing 10,000 characters or more, the Japanese market for type held huge potential. The Japanese typesetting industry was ruled by two dynasties: Shaken in Tokyo and Morisawa in Osaka. Shaken would not be persuaded, but Morisawa could.

BEST WISHES FOR 1989 AND THE BEGINNING OF THE NEW ERA.

Sumner Stone created this new year's card for his Japanese colleagues. The text refers to the fact that there was a new emperor and therefore a new era, suggesting that the acceptance of PostScript might grow in Japan.

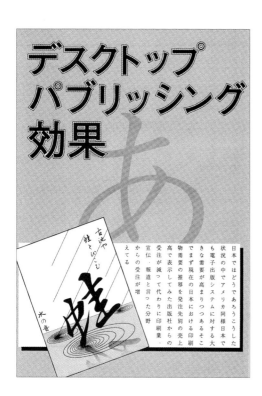

あ

デスクトップ
パブリッシング
効果

日本ではどうであろうこうした状況の中でアメリカ同様日本でも電子出版システムに対する大きな需要が高まりつつあるそこでまず現在の日本における印刷物需要の推移を発注先別の売上高で表示してみた代わりに印刷業・宣伝・報道と言った分野からの受注が増えてる

Diane Burns, cofounder of TechArt, went to Japan in 1987 on behalf of Apple. Her Japanese students called her *DTP no haha* (mother of desktop publishing). This page was produced on one of the first PostScript LaserWriters for the Japanese market.

Adobe licensed Morisawa's typefaces and in return gave Morisawa the tools to digitize the fonts. PostScript was designed to hold only 256 characters, so modifications to the code were necessary. "It was a big engineering addition to PostScript to accommodate so many glyphs," Stone acknowledges.

The Morisawa contract opened the door for PostScript and set the stage for print-engine licenses. "Fonts helped drive the adoption of PostScript in Japan," says Stone. Geschke, Warnock, MacDonald, Doug Brotz, and others trekked to Japan to line up printer-engine manufacturers, including Canon, Epson, Fujitsu, NEC, Panasonic, Ricoh, and Sony. Many of their Japanese counterparts were already familiar with Adobe when the Californians arrived. They had seen the desktop publishing explosion on their business trips to North America.

Business at Banquets

For the men from Adobe, negotiating Japanese style was an unusual experience in the 1980s. Meetings followed the same two-day pattern: one day of speech-making by company functionaries in an overheated room, punctuated by an elaborate meal washed down with plenty of beer and sake. The next day, camaraderie having been established over numerous toasts the night before, deal-making began in earnest.

Each Japanese company tried to outdo the other in hospitality, especially regarding food unfamiliar to American palates. "We wanted to show them we were tough, that we could take whatever they threw at us," says Brotz, who went along to provide input on PostScript technology. Geschke, as company president, was particularly honored. He was fed such delicacies as fish heads and sake infused with turtle blood. "What we wouldn't do to get a deal signed," Geschke says now, shaking his head.

Courtesy and cast-iron stomachs paid off. "We inked every deal," Brotz says. A high point came in 1987 when NEC and Fujitsu announced their support for PostScript. That the two largest computer makers in Japan should simultaneously adopt PostScript—and make a joint announcement—was unprecedented. It was the culmination of two solid weeks of negotiating for Adobe.

With Adobe's contracts, Apple's Japanese-language Macintosh, and a localized version of PageMaker, desktop publishing came to Japan in 1987, although PostScript printers didn't materialize for another year or so. Adobe could claim upwards of 50 PostScript OEM printer licensees by the 1990s, but the period of 1985 through 1987 secured Adobe's most important contracts and set the stage for the company's public debut in the stock market.

Adobe commissioned graphics to
showcase the potential of PostScript
in Japan. The kimono was drawn in
Illustrator 88 by David Smith.

Post-IPO, Adobe hired its first
bona fide sales force.

Becoming a Public Company

Adobe's initial public stock offering in 1986 in many ways reflected the strategy of the company itself: start small, keep focused, produce a good product, then watch it take off. What had begun as a relatively limited offering underwritten by one firm very soon attracted hordes of investors, both institutional and individual. The company's stock gathered momentum so quickly that it quadrupled its value in less than 18 months, making a lot of investors and Adobe employees very happy.

Adobe's IPO wasn't typical of many young startups. With the success of the LaserWriter and the significant revenue stream it produced, Adobe didn't need to raise capital to keep going. But in order to project a financial stability that would enable it to secure additional licenses both at home and abroad, the company decided to go public.

Earlier that year, Warnock and Geschke had reviewed what was required to take the company public. The finance department at the time consisted of an accounting manager plus the two founders, who hand-wrote the company checks themselves. A publicly held company clearly needed a more structured financial operation.

"In the first week I was there, the accounting manager went on maternity leave, the beta accounting software we were using died, and the Macintosh computer on which it ran lost its hard drive," remembers Bruce Nakao, who was hired in May 1986 as chief financial officer to shepherd the IPO process. Nakao didn't know much about fonts or graphics, but he was impressed by how down-to-earth and honest the Adobe employees seemed to be—and he interviewed with all 40 or so on staff at the time. "There was a lot of stuff for me to learn. We had to put in the financial infrastructure for a much larger company."

Developing that infrastructure would have to wait, however, as the very real demands of the IPO took precedence.

Wooing Investors

The IPO process had been put in motion by the time Nakao arrived. Hambrecht & Quist, the venture capital firm that gave Adobe its first $2.5 million, was the offering's sole underwriter, which spared Adobe the ritual courting of investment bankers. But as part of the normal IPO process, Warnock, Geschke, and Nakao hit the road, going from boardroom to boardroom to tell the Adobe story to mutual fund managers, financial analysts, and other institutional investors.

"The initial public offering was a wonderful stamp of approval from the industry that we were a viable entity."

— Clinton Nagy

Bruce Nakao, Adobe's first chief financial officer, took the company through its initial public offering.

Nakao laid out the financial opportunity while Warnock talked about the technology and future developments. While by now they were accustomed to selling the technology to printer vendors, explaining the value of PostScript to the investment community wasn't easy at first. "When John started talking, he seemed slightly nervous and his voice wavered. But as he warmed to his subject, his passion and enthusiasm surfaced, and investors loved his story. He just had a tremendous amount of credibility when talking about the company and the technology," Nakao says.

The Adobe story struck a chord with investors. Within five days, the book of interested investors was oversubscribed, indicating that the IPO was going to meet, if not surpass, expectations.

Although the IPO process went smoothly in general, there were a few bumps in the road. At one point Adobe came under SEC scrutiny as one of the first companies to be hit by a ruling regarding the issue of cheap stock before an IPO. "Adobe had been very generous to its employees with its options, including those granted within a few months before the IPO," says Colleen Pouliot. (Adobe's attorney at the time, Pouliot served as its in-house counsel from 1988 to 2001.) "The SEC thought we were giving employees cheap stock while charging more to the public." An agreement was reached in which Adobe amended its financial statements to reflect compensation charges for some of the pre-IPO options issued.

"The IPO was an exciting time," Pouliot says. "I got to come to the company and tell them what their obligations were when they held options. Engineers were really excited. People had worked very hard and this was the payoff."

Public Approval

Finally, on August 20, 1986, Adobe Systems issued 550,000 shares of stock, representing just 10 percent of the company and a market capitalization of approximately $6 million. Trading for the first time as ADBE on the Nasdaq stock exchange, the stock opened at $11. Demand for the available shares was high and the price climbed throughout the day. Steve Jobs and Bill Gates reportedly wanted to buy all outstanding shares. The stock closed at $14 and change.

Champagne corks popped at the Palo Alto offices. The hard work had paid off—literally. Adobe employees, many of whom had been issued options at $1 per share, ended the day financially much better off than when they began it. But the market's enthusiastic reception meant more than extra change in the pocket.

"The initial public offering was a wonderful stamp of approval from the industry that we were a viable entity," says Clinton Nagy. "Remember, we were simple technologists. This wasn't the heady dot-com era."

Keeping Their Feet on the Ground

In March 1987, on the heels of Adobe's deal with IBM and just seven months after the IPO, the stock had its first two-for-one split. Ten months later, in January 1988, it split again. That was just the beginning: In its first four years, Adobe roughly doubled its business each year, from $2.5 million in 1984 to $4.4 million in 1985, $16 million in 1986, $39 million in 1987, and $80 million in 1988.

"Being a newly public company was exciting and frustrating at the same time, as the company came under the very demanding scrutiny of investors," reflects Nakao on Adobe's meteoric rise. "But while we were excited about how the stock acted, we worked hard to keep our heads down and concentrate on the business. This could be difficult at times because there were days when I had to field 25 to 50 phone calls from sometimes worried or, at the least, inquisitive analysts and investors from Wall Street."

There was no doubt that the company and its founders had arrived. But even as Adobe was on its way to becoming a modern success story, Warnock for one didn't succumb to the excesses of the newly prosperous. For a long time he was perfectly content to drive an aging Alfa Romeo. Nakao recalls that not long after the IPO, John came into his office. "He was really excited and said, 'You have to come see my car!' I thought, 'Great, he finally got rid of that piece of junk.' I went outside to the parking lot and he said, 'Look, I painted the hood!'"

Adobe's reception in the halls of finance not only validated the company's mission but sparked new innovation as well as expansion. In less than a year Adobe relocated again, this time to more generous quarters on Charleston Road in Mountain View. The company was growing and the company hustled to keep pace with its own success. In the absence of a dedicated IT staff, Adobe's brilliant and opinionated engineers stepped in. "The engineers were our IT staff," Nakao says, remembering arguments over the twisted-pair wiring and coaxial cables running down the halls. "It was a belt-and-suspenders strategy."

But the quarter in which Adobe went public was a period of great productivity, and it set the stage for new directions. In a few short months the company released a product that changed its course forever: Adobe Illustrator.

After its successful IPO, Adobe expanded into new office space in Mountain View. Software engineers helped run the wiring.

Introducing Illustrator

The product that launched a new era for Adobe began as a labor of love. Over the years Warnock had watched as his wife, Marva, a graphic artist, worked with pen, curve, and knife. He saw parallels between what she drew with pen on paper and what PostScript printed with dots on paper. Existing computer graphics and drawing applications were clumsy, and they produced jagged lines when printed. Warnock saw in PostScript's Bézier curves the sinuous lines and precise corners required in expert illustration. Why not create an application to bring PostScript out of the printer and onto the screen?

Warnock nabbed PostScript consulting engineer Mike Schuster to work on a drawing package he called Illustrator. Not only was it an interesting intellectual problem, but such an application could also help sell more printers by making the magic of PostScript visible. Like fonts before it, this new application would make a connection between what users did onscreen and what came out of the printer.

Schuster worked alone—but with plenty of engineering assistance from Warnock and design input from the in-house creative team. "John was very influential in the design of Illustrator," says Russell Preston Brown, Adobe's first art director and now its senior creative director. But Warnock's approach was that of a scientist. Brown and his team quickly exerted their own influence.

> "Using the Pen tool
>
> was something only
>
> John could do."
>
> — Chuck Geschke

Drawing with Code

Brown had first been exposed to PostScript when as a freelance designer at Apple he printed a MacDraft file on a LaserWriter. "I was stunned and thrown on the floor by this," he says. "I could draw a circle, and when it printed it didn't have jagged edges. It was whole new era." Brown went to work as Adobe's only in-house designer in April 1985.

Brown's job was to come up with interesting graphics that promoted PostScript's capabilities. "I had to create pages that showed off PostScript: text, images, and graphics all on one page," Brown says. Because this was pre-Illustrator, all text and graphics were coded by hand. Brown produced Adobe's first marketing piece this way. "I programmed *Colophon* line for line in PostScript and printed it on a Linotype machine. It took days and days," he says.

The first *Colophon,* an eight-page tabloid dated October 1986, is a remarkable document. It contains bitmap images, line art, multiple

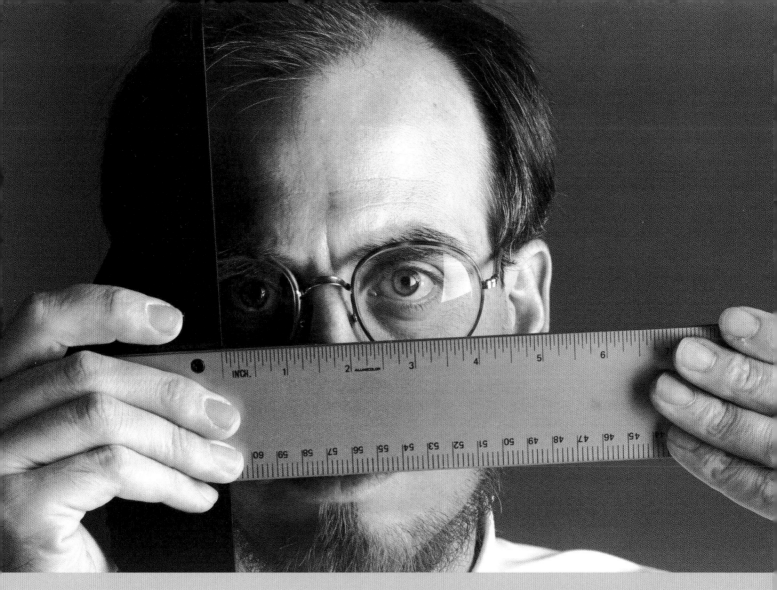

Russell Preston Brown, Adobe's
first art director.

PostScript fonts, colored type, rotated graphics, and individual page elements from PageMaker, Microsoft Word, and other applications—all merged into one PostScript file. "I'd use a scanner the size of a football field to bring in images, take the raw data, and encapsulate it in PostScript," Brown says. "You had to type in operators for shading, scaling, etc. You never got to see what you'd produced until you said Print. And if you printed it and it was too dark, then you had to go back and reenter the operators, and print again."

But if Brown and his small team of designers could produce complex pages using raw PostScript, the idea of making an application that allowed designers to create PostScript graphics more intuitively seemed a natural extension of Adobe's technology.

Warnock worked on all aspects of the program, including its color components. As an engineer, he had a scientist's view of color, which didn't always translate to the way designers and illustrators work. One day, he showed graphic designer Luanne Seymour Cohen how to specify color. "You had to type in this long string of numbers, like to the sixth decimal point," she remembers. "I told him no designer worked that way. We use

CMYK and Pantone percentages." Today Cohen shakes her head at her audacity—she was talking back to the head of the company, after all—but Warnock, always sensitive to the needs of graphic designers, changed it. (Color did not make it into the first version of Illustrator, however.)

That byplay between engineer and designer, Warnock and staff, was an important part of the Adobe culture. Brown remembers asking Warnock if the corporate logo could be redone, forgetting that it had been designed by John's wife, Marva Warnock. Warnock replied by asking whether Brown liked working at Adobe, Brown recalls. "When I replied yes, he said, 'You need to work at Adobe, and I need to live with her.' I didn't redesign the logo."

As work on Illustrator progressed, the program grew from a programming challenge to a product with public appeal. If customers bought PostScript fonts, why wouldn't they buy a truly unique product like Illustrator? From a business perspective, branching out into retail software also gave the company another revenue stream. Prospective customers included map-makers, manufacturers, scientific illustrators—anyone with a need for precise drawing. Fred Mitchell, in charge of product management, operations, and sales for the young company and now vice president for Adobe Ventures, recalls that the events leading up the launch of Illustrator were full of "Eureka!" moments as the team hit product milestones. "Being part of the Illustrator effort was just incredibly stimulating," he says.

Making a Splash

Adobe showed off Illustrator at the January 1987 Macworld Expo in San Francisco. It was the buzz of the show, astounding designers and illustrators previously skeptical of computer graphics and fueling the demand for desktop publishing software and, of course, PostScript printers.

The first version of Illustrator was a spare black-and-white program. The ability to do color was embedded in the program, though it was not yet available to the end user. But it was the Pen tool that turned heads. With the Pen tool an illustrator could draw Bézier curves onscreen, then scale and transform drawn objects into myriad sizes and shapes. There were some limitations—one had to draw each piece separately and then click Preview to see the complete illustration—but a single leaf turned into a thicket with a few clicks of the mouse.

Adobe shipped Illustrator on March 1, 1987. It cost $495, thousands of dollars less than the technical-drawing software previously available. The product package showed a lissome Botticelli Venus rendered in PostScript against a pixelated ground, putting in stark relief the transition from old-style computer graphics to PostScript's new world. Package designer Cohen says she chose an image whose classical, timeless quality resonated

Russell Brown programmed early marketing materials by hand in PostScript.

The tools of the illustration artists' trade could be instruments of torture in the wrong hands. Knives, overlays, inks, and brushes had to be wielded with consummate skill lest wasted hours be spent at the drawing board.

With Illustrator, Adobe gave artists the freedom to express themselves onscreen, unencumbered by mechanics. By harnessing the power of PostScript and its Bézier curves, Illustrator changed drawing and line art forever.

FIRST IMPRESSIONS

When I first saw Illustrator, I thought, "It looks like an illustrator designed this."

David Biedny, author, consultant, teacher

The Pen tool scared the hell out of me.

Sandee Cohen, author, teacher, and Illustrator expert

Illustrator blew my mind when I saw my first output. I was impressed with the cool Bézier curves onscreen, but when I saw my first Illustrator piece on Linotronic output—the crisp lines, the hairline rules—it just blew me away.

Louis Fishauf, illustrator and designer

EARLY DAYS

They took me into this corner room where they were working on a drawing program in PostScript. I thought it was a very clean design program. You saw it had the potential to do some pretty great things. But it was only black and white, and Undo wasn't working.

Ron Chan, illustrator and early beta tester

I upgraded to Illustrator 88 but I only had a black-and-white Mac, so I used printed color charts to apply color values. I had to take my disk down to the local Mac shop to see what it looked like on a color monitor.

Sharon Steuer, digital artist and author

The dumbest thing they did was to name it Illustrator 88 instead of 2.0.

Frank Romano, Rochester Institute of Technology

REPLACING RUBYLITH

Illustrator gave me the ability to create the clean vectors I used to draw with a Rapidograph and clean up with Pro-White. It was so much faster to use Illustrator. I could create as much detail as I wanted and then shrink it down as much as I wanted, yet preserve the detail and integrity. I once made a drawing of a Mac Plus into a tiny dot. It added 20 minutes to the processing time on a Linotronic 300—but to able to do that!

Bert Monroy, digital artist

No marketing person would believe in it. With Illustrator we set out to replace technical pens and Rubylith and French curves. At the time maybe 20,000 people did illustrations. A teeny market.

John Warnock

Art departments were not receptive to computer illustrations. Older guys thought it was a flash in the pan, that it wasn't real art.

Gordon Studer, illustrator

Find a designer who doesn't use Illustrator.

Frank Romano

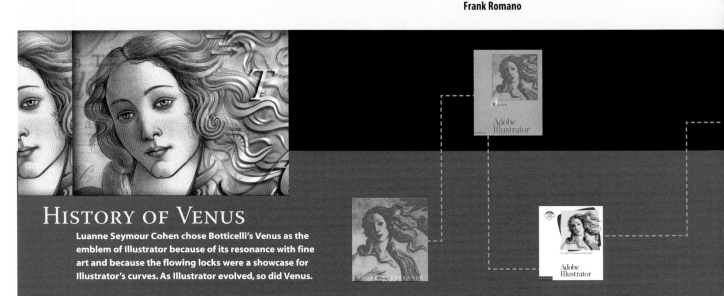

HISTORY OF VENUS

Luanne Seymour Cohen chose Botticelli's Venus as the emblem of Illustrator because of its resonance with fine art and because the flowing locks were a showcase for Illustrator's curves. As Illustrator evolved, so did Venus.

My evolution from art directing and designing to illustration comes from those tools. I never considered myself an illustrator in those days. Maybe I'd do a logo, but if I needed an illustration I called someone in. Suddenly I had those tools available to me. I had the capability to create illustrations myself.

Louis Fishauf

BYE-BYE, PIXELS

At the *San Francisco Chronicle* we were using PixelPaint. Drawing smooth lines in Illustrator was a pretty big revelation because everything else was chunky pixels.

Ron Chan

Illustrator changed everything. Before then everything was made of dots. Illustrator gave us beautiful curves. When Illustrator came out it never occurred to anybody that books and magazines and posters were going to come out of the Macintosh. You didn't think you could do anything professional-looking out of that little box on your desk.

Sharon Steuer

"Béziers revolutionized my drawing. That's when I broke away from pixels."

— Bert Monroy

Illustrator is crystal clear, precise, and mathematical. At *Newsweek* we used to scan things in and then trace them in Illustrator. The scanner had no halftones, so we'd trace over stock photos in Illustrator. We very quickly understood that we could use it to make logos.

Roger Black, publication designer

THE CREATIVE FLOW

If the computer and Illustrator didn't exist, you couldn't put down two flat panes of color. It was literally impossible to put color down without getting out the paintbrush or doing overlays. Then it became more about your skill with the X-Acto blade than about drawing. Now you don't feel bound by the process or the technical aspect of it.

Ron Chan

I don't touch traditional media anymore. With Photoshop and Illustrator I can get more detail, I can change my mind, I can change colors. It's enhanced my workflow. I don't have to clean tools and mix paints. My imagination just flows; it's not hindered by tools. I would lose the feeling for an image after changing colors and cleaning tools. But here, onscreen, mixing paint is limitless. Here, paint is forever. I won't run out of paint.

Bert Monroy

With Illustrator I worry about how things look instead of how to get there.

Ron Chan

Illustrator 6 was the most feature-rich upgrade I'd ever seen, with filters and pathfinders. The upgrade to 6 is the gold standard.

Sandee Cohen

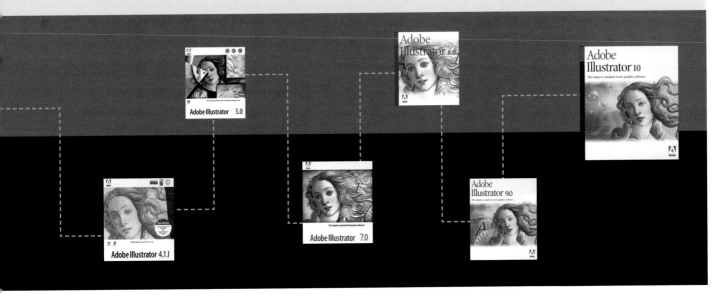

When Illustrator shipped in 1987, the package included a videotape of John Warnock demonstrating how to use Illustrator and its innovative— and maddening—Pen tool.

Ted Alspach, group product manager for Illustrator.

with traditional artists. Plus, she notes, Venus's flowing locks were an ideal showcase for PostScript's fluid lines.

Because Illustrator was unlike any program before it, Adobe knew it had to educate its customers. "There was definitely a learning curve," Brown says. Taking a cue from Apple, which shipped an explanatory audiocassette with the Macintosh, Adobe produced a videotape tutorial in which Warnock himself showed how to use the software. In the video, Warnock sits in front of a black-and-white Macintosh SE and goes through the steps of drawing a flower. Legend has it that Warnock was the only one who had used Illustrator enough to demonstrate the product's features, which were awkward. "Using the Pen tool was something only John could do," Geschke says wryly. Among Adobe aficionados, the tape is a collector's item.

To promote Illustrator, Adobe began a grassroots effort that established the company not only as a developer but also as a practitioner of products for design professionals. Traditional artists remained skeptical that drawing on the computer could produce results as fine as they created by hand. Art director Brown and his staff were charged with making promotional materials with Illustrator—T-shirts, posters, mugs, bottle labels, you name it—as a way of showing what Adobe applications could do. Along the way they became experts in the program themselves, uncovering new tips and techniques that unleashed the power of PostScript drawing. They went to trade shows to demonstrate the product, they taught classes, they conducted seminars—anything to preach the gospel.

They plowed their knowledge back into the company and into Illustrator. Engineers became accustomed to requests for improvements from the in-house art staff. They listened, and Warnock and Geschke listened. Ultimately this exchange between engineer and designer led to a product synergy that guides development even now.

Continuing Growth

Onscreen color and a host of new tools such as blending and freehand drawing were key features of Illustrator's second version. While a technical success, Illustrator 88 will forever be perceived as a marketing gaffe. Named for the year in which it was introduced, Illustrator 88 barely shipped before 1989 and then was not updated until 1990, a full two years later. Good-natured finger-pointing continues to this day as to who really approved that name.

As Adobe's first software application and one that directly leverages the power of PostScript, Illustrator has been released for six operating systems. With the LaserWriter and the first two releases of Illustrator, Adobe's fate had been intertwined with the Apple Macintosh. But in 1989,

the company recognized the potential of Microsoft's Windows operating system by releasing a Windows version of Illustrator. In 1990, versions for UNIX and the NeXT operating systems came out, followed by releases for Silicon Graphics and Sun SPARC workstations.

Illustrator's success was not uncontested, however, as competitive products like CorelDraw and, most notably, FreeHand came onto the market. Developed by Texas-based Altsys, FreeHand was licensed by Aldus in 1988 and later became the focus of a legal dispute. When Adobe acquired Aldus in 1994, Altsys alleged unfair business competition and succeeded in getting FreeHand returned before selling it to Adobe rival Macromedia.

Illustrator's popularity brought with it a new set of challenges for the company, such as the need to set up sales and distribution channels and develop marketing programs. Around the time Illustrator 88 was introduced, Adobe launched a division dedicated to application sales and development.

Illustrator was the flagship product of Adobe's new software initiative, which would soon expand to include the mega-bestselling Adobe Photoshop. It also included a little program called Adobe Type Manager (ATM), which figured prominently in what became known as the Font Wars of 1989.

Fine artist Bert Monroy latched on to Illustrator as soon as it came out. This 1987 drawing is among his first. Hidden in it is a tiny Macintosh that can be magnified many times over without losing detail—a testament to PostScript technology.

MacWEEK

WORKSTATION NEWS

26 September 1989 Vol. 3 No. 34

Investigative report: Macs bust sanctions in South Africa. See Page 89.

Thumbs up for Portable, IIci at show biz send-off

Apple sent off the two newest members of the Macintosh family into the marketplace last week in a razzle-dazzle rollout featuring heavy helpings of Apple philosophy and media spin control.

Countering pundits' pre-release criticism of the Portable's weight and price and of the model overlap between the IIci with its sister IIcx, Apple's top executives told customers not to compare the machines with competitors on the basis of power and features.

"It is an issue of integration and user experience," according to CEO John Sculley. "People who touch it will want it," said Apple Products President Jean-Louis Gassée. "You don't buy coal, you buy energy," concluded Apple USA President Allan Loren.

Now it's time for buyers to decide ...

Enthusiasm high for Portable

By Jim Forbes

Universal City, Calif. — The bottom line on the Mac Portable is that its allure outweighs its price, at least for many business users attending last week's introduction here.

Customers polled by MacWEEK are clamoring to get their hands on the unit despite its steep price, hefty weight (15.7 pounds) and ungainly shape.

"We're extremely interested in the Portable," said Gerald Thomas,

a systems specialist at the ARCO controller's office in Los Angeles. "It's good technology, offering what we need in the way of features.

See Portable, Page 8

Apple executives Jean-Louis Gassée (left) and John Sculley had reason to smile at the unveiling of Apple's Portable machine and new high-performance member of the Mac II line.

Apple, Microsoft font alliance goads Adobe into about-face

By Cliff Lehman

San Francisco — The rift between Adobe Systems Inc. and Apple over control of the outline font technology widened last week as Adobe struggled to defend its ... was formed

nology (see MacWEEK Sept 19).

The agreement calls for Microsoft to license Apple's outline font technology, code-named Royal, for use in OS/2 Presentation Manager. In return, Apple gets Microsoft's PostScript-clone technology for use ... Apple printers. The upshot

IIci lures number crunchers

By John Battelle

Universal City, Calif. — The newest member of the Macintosh modular line is out of the starting gate, and if buyers and analysts present at the introduction here last week can pick their horses, the IIci is a winner.

Apple CEO John Sculley let the IIci introduce itself by playing a photo-realistic color 3-D animation of a running horse. To demonstrate the IIci's heightened performance, Sculley showed the identical, but markedly slower, animation on a IIcx. With its 25-MHz 68030 chip, speedy memory access, built-in video and optimized motherboard design, the IIci represents a 45 percent performance increase over its predecessor, according to Apple.

According to many analysts and buyers, the IIci may be the first Mac to bring the Mac look and feel together with the performance standards of workstation computing.

See IIci, Page 8

Smiles from the new font allies...

"The world went from zero open formats to two."
Bill Gates

"We intend to be more in control than we were in other arrangements."
John Sculley

Seybold: Clash of the Titans

By Carolyn Said

San Francisco — In a rare public display of emotion and intrigue, industry Titans Bill Gates, John Warnock and Steve Jobs exchanged potshots and played out a power struggle on stage at the opening session of the Seybold Computer Publishing Conference here.

His voice shaking at times, Adobe CEO Warnock made the most dramatic impact. Calling the Apple-Microsoft font plan "the

See Seybold, Page 9

...a grimace from the odd man out

"...the biggest bunch of garbage and mumbo jumbo I've ever heard..."

John Warnock

LATE NEWS

Adobe plans $15 million stock buyback

Mountain View, Calif. — With its shares taking a pounding on Wall Street, Adobe announced late last week that it will repurchase up to $15 million worth of common stock in the open market over the next few weeks. The shares represent about 3.8 percent of its common stock at recent prices, the company said (see related story, Page 10).

Electric Image to turn on Spotlight

El Monte, Calif. — Electric Image last week announced Spotlight, professional-level 32-bit color, 3-D rendering and animation software for Mac II machines. The $7,495 program, under development for four years and scheduled to ship in January 1990, generated animations that were used by Apple CEO John Sculley to introduce the Macintosh IIci.

The Industry Backlash

Illustrator proved that Adobe could develop a second revenue stream to enhance the flow from PostScript licenses. The business was diversified and the money rolled in: revenues for 1989 doubled to $121 million from the prior year. Approximately 65 percent of that came from PostScript, 25 percent from applications, and 10 percent from fonts.

Adobe's PostScript and typefaces were the de facto standards for printing on both desktop laser printers and professional imagesetters—a fact noticed by other companies eager to grab a piece of the ever growing multimillion-dollar desktop publishing market. "Adobe was the 800-pound gorilla of type by that time," says Allan Haley, then with ITC and now director of words and letters at Agfa Monotype. "Other companies wanted to make money from this, too."

The way Adobe conducted its PostScript font licensing enabled it to retain its hold on the type business. PostScript fonts came in two flavors: Type 1 and Type 3. Type 1 fonts were developed by, or were under license to, Adobe and therefore contained critical information about how the font data was converted to PostScript, how device independence was applied, and how outlines were encrypted to work with PostScript interpreters. Fonts created by parties not under an official arrangement with Adobe lacked those details and were called Type 3 fonts. By keeping the nuances of Type 1 fonts secret, Adobe retained its competitive edge and high licensing fees and thwarted manufacturers of clone technologies who were unable to replicate PostScript controllers. The Type 1 format was considered the jewel in PostScript's crown.

"The problem for Adobe was: Do you publish all the specifications for PostScript, so anyone can copy it and anyone can make PostScript fonts? If so, how do you make money?" says Jonathan Seybold. "It was a dilemma from the very beginning. Adobe decided to keep control of PostScript by keeping the Type 1 font specifications secret."

Becoming a Target

Adobe was also working to extend its reach. It had been pushing its onscreen imaging model Display PostScript, which provided similar benefits to onscreen display as PostScript did for printers. Instead of displaying pixelated images, Display PostScript rasterized them to the screen so that graphics appeared smooth and crisp. Adopting Display PostScript also made Adobe's Type 1 fonts standard in the operating system.

"Adobe was the 800-pound gorilla of type by that time. Other companies wanted to make money from this, too."

— Allan Haley

With an entrenched place in a lucrative market and plans for expansion, the once small startup was on the radar as a threat to more established companies. In 1989 two such companies started gunning for Adobe: Microsoft, not yet the most powerful software company on the planet, and Apple Computer, the once dominant computer manufacturer, an old ally but, increasingly, an adversary.

In the years since Adobe helped save Apple with the LaserWriter, relations between the two companies had cooled. Steve Jobs was gone and his nemesis John Sculley ran the business. Sculley had questioned the wisdom of investing in Adobe back in 1983 and now, even as Apple's $2.5 million investment in the company had risen at least 3,000 percent, Apple management bristled at the royalties Apple was paying Adobe for its PostScript license. In 1988 Apple's royalty payments were 33 percent of Adobe's $83 million revenue, a substantial sum.

"Warnock sat with his back to Gates, which was not easy to do when both were facing the audience."

— Frank Romano

Moreover, Adobe's pursuit of printer OEMs cut into Apple's bottom line. With more vendors to choose from, customers could buy true PostScript printers from other manufacturers for many hundreds of dollars less than the price of the LaserWriter. This piqued Apple considerably.

And money wasn't the only issue. Apple increasingly saw its reliance on outside technologies—specifically Adobe's—as its Achilles' heel. To have control over its destiny Apple would need to develop its own font and printing technologies. So when Adobe approached Apple with Display PostScript, it declined. Apple had its own onscreen imaging model, QuickDraw, and wasn't inclined to enter into another licensing agreement with Adobe. Instead, the company had been working quietly since 1987 on a font format, code-named Royal, and had started development on new system-level typefaces that would cut Adobe out of the loop.

In anticipation of announcing its font strategy, in July Apple sold its share in Adobe Systems for more than $87 million, netting a profit of at least $85 million. When it caught wind of Apple's plans, Adobe announced that it had in development a product that could rasterize Adobe PostScript fonts onscreen—without Display PostScript, without a PostScript printer. The product, which would become Adobe Type Manager, was not yet in development, but its announcement was a preemptive strike in the escalating battle for font supremacy.

Microsoft and Apple Join Forces

Microsoft, too, had been looking for technologies to distinguish its new Windows operating system and to bolster the OS/2 Presentation Manager, which it had codeveloped with IBM until that alliance fell apart. It planned its own display system, thus ruling out Display PostScript, but it needed font and printing technologies. Microsoft's Nathan Myhrvold

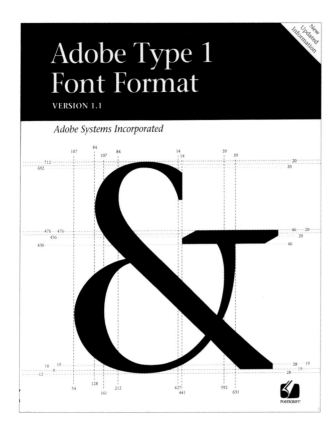

Adobe Type 1
Font Format
VERSION 1.1

New Updated Information

Adobe Systems Incorporated

POSTSCRIPT

Adobe's 1990 release of the Type 1 font format specification meant that now any designer could create a PostScript Type 1 font.

looked at every prospect on the market, including Adobe's. The stakes were high, as whatever imaging platform Microsoft chose would likely become the next standard. According to Geschke, Adobe was willing to let Microsoft use Adobe Type 1 fonts in its operating system for almost nothing, but Myhrvold flatly said no.

But another company did want Display PostScript: NeXT Computing, founded by Steve Jobs. NeXT agreed to license Display PostScript for its onyx-colored cube-shaped computer, and Adobe had begun development on Illustrator for Display PostScript that would run on NeXT.

NeXT was not yet a force in computing—and never would be—but its relationship with IBM played a role in this drama. If NeXT persuaded IBM to standardize on PostScript, Microsoft would be in a more vulnerable position. And there was was bad blood between Microsoft CEO Bill Gates and Jobs over Microsoft Windows, which Jobs saw as a misappropriation of the Mac's look and feel. If Adobe could be used as a pawn in this game, that was all to the good.

"A lot of animosity had been building toward Adobe within the industry," says Seybold. "Pressure had been applied for some time. And in 1989, the backlash finally happened."

After rejecting both Adobe and Hewlett-Packard, among others, Microsoft turned to Apple and its nascent Royal font technology. Apple and

BizStats: 1988

No. of employees: 291

Revenue: $83 million

Stock price range: $6 to $12 (2-for-1 split)

Product releases:
Font Folio
Illustrator 88

Other:
>> 33% of Adobe sales are from Apple

75% of Adobe revenues are from PostScript

Adobe's Font Folio is a $9,600 hard disk containing its entire font library

Patents #4,837,613 issued to William Paxton, Michael Schuster, John Warnock: a method for selecting the intensity level of each primary color for displaying or printing a predetermined desired color

RON CHAN

Ron Chan was invited to Adobe in early 1987 to test a new drawing application, code-named Picasso, based on the company's PostScript technology. As one of the first artists outside Adobe to use what we now know as Illustrator, Chan became an early advocate of digital drawing tools, and his commercial work helped promote Illustrator and its new graphic style. Shown here are a 1989 cover for the *San Francisco Chronicle*'s TV Week; a May 1989 cover for *Macworld* magazine's first issue to be produced by all digital means; a 1990 retail package for multimedia application Macromedia Director; and a 2002 illustration for the *New York Times* Circuits section. Now a freelance illustrator, Chan's work and inimitable style can be seen in major publications worldwide. (www.ronchan.com)

"With Illustrator, I can worry about how things look, instead of how to get there."

Microsoft—once bitter enemies—joined forces to usurp Adobe's font and printing dominance. Apple would develop an alternative font technology that Microsoft would use, while Microsoft would develop a competitive printing technology that Apple would use. This alliance was the next salvo in what has since become known as the Font Wars.

Lobbing Bombshells

In September 1989, the feud took center stage at the Seybold Seminars trade show and conference in San Francisco, a venue for many announcements affecting the industry. Apple's intentions to develop its own font format had been disclosed in its annual report, but the deal between Apple and Microsoft was known to only a few people, among them Seybold, who was bound by confidentiality agreements not to disclose what he knew. Yet as the event moderator, Seybold orchestrated a keynote session at which the speakers were Microsoft's Bill Gates, Adobe's John Warnock, NeXT's Steve Jobs, and IBM's Nick Donofrio.

Gates used the opportunity to extol the virtues of the new technologies. In time they would become known as the TrueType font format and TrueImage printer interpreter, although when Gates asked the audience what the new tools should be called, industry pundit Frank Romano yelled, "Why not call it off?"

Over the course of Gates's speech, Warnock grew more and more animated, his expression revealing irritation. That Gates and Microsoft, newcomers to publishing and printing, should claim technical superiority over Adobe and PostScript visibly irked him.

When Warnock took the podium, he not only reiterated the benefits and stability of PostScript and its related technologies, he also questioned the merits of developing new formats when a standard that worked very well was already in place. Then he dropped a bombshell: He stated Adobe's intention to publish the specifications for the Type 1 font format, PostScript's crown jewel. By releasing the hitherto unpublished technical documents, Adobe hoped to blunt the opposition's main barb, that in contrast to the PostScript Type 1 format, TrueType was a publicly available format open to anyone, without requiring a licensing fee.

"This was a tremendous blow to Adobe," says Seybold. "They had to open up the standard, which they clearly resisted doing and yet should have done earlier. Their resistance had put them in a box."

Jobs spoke next, downplaying both Microsoft's and Adobe's announcements and proclaiming IBM as the only player that mattered. However, he did discuss the importance of Display PostScript to the NextStep operating system. As the last speaker, Donofrio said that IBM would

---

BizStats: **1989**

No. of employees: 383

Revenue: $121 million

Stock price range: $8 to $15

Product releases:
  Adobe Type Manager 1.0
  Illustrator 88 for DOS

Other:
>> Apple sells off its 20 percent equity in Adobe and begins developing its own PostScript clone (Apple's $2 million investment nets it $87 million)

  Apple and Microsoft announce they will join forces to develop a competing open-font standard to PostScript for the OS/2 Presentation Manager and Macintosh System 7 (but the technology is never delivered)

  Adobe makes PostScript font technology an open standard

  Camp Adobe, design invitational for pre-release Adobe Photoshop, is held

  Adobe licenses PostScript to Agfa, Compugraphic, Monotype, and Varityper to develop Type 1 fonts

support both PostScript and TrueType/TrueImage for the time being until it figured out which way to go.

Sturm und Drang

Sparks flew during the question-and-answer period that followed, which became a defining moment for Warnock and Adobe. Warnock, by then quite upset, pointedly ignored Gates. "Warnock sat with his back to Gates, which was not easy to do when both were facing the audience," Romano says.

In response to a question, Gates again claimed that TrueType's quadratic splines were far superior to PostScript's Bézier curves and that a single font for both screen and printer would set a new standard for desktop publishing for years to come.

When asked to comment, an emotional Warnock called Gates's explanation "the biggest bunch of garbage and mumbo jumbo" he'd ever heard. It was raw and uncensored, but Warnock's heartfelt statement resonated with many. "It was the most dramatic moment in Adobe's history," says Romano. "Everything Warnock built could have fallen apart that day."

"I was proud when John said, 'That's a bunch of mumbo jumbo,'" says Steve MacDonald. "I said, 'Good, John. Your voice is cracking, but good for you.'"

It was an emotional moment for all of Adobe, not just Warnock. The company was under attack, and one of its attackers was a former ally. Warnock, who believed in loyalties more than royalties, felt betrayed by Apple. The event also generated a long-running feud with Microsoft. The announcement sent Adobe's stock into a tailspin: it immediately lost four points in one day. Investors questioned whether Adobe could stand up to the dual assault.

"The Apple-Microsoft deal opened up the font format when fonts were 10 percent of our business," says MacDonald. "Microsoft would get into the printer business and Apple got out from the licensing fee. And Microsoft was already approaching our PostScript clients to convince them to sign up for their technology."

"Their ambition was to drive the price of type to zero," says Geschke. "We were protective of the type technology, but when we saw what they were trying to do, we had to react."

Warnock's response was to do what Adobe did best. "We just said, We are going to out-invent the bastards," he says today. "They can do all this marketing crap, and we'll just out-invent them."

"That's the biggest bunch of garbage and mumbo jumbo I've ever heard."

—John Warnock to Bill Gates,
onstage at Seybold, 1989

The Triumph of ATM

Adobe counterpunched in two ways. Adobe kept its word and published the specifications for Type 1 in March 1990. As a postscript to his appearance six months earlier, a triumphant Warnock took the stage at Seybold Seminars in Boston and held aloft the slim white book written by Doug Brotz. "I said we'd publish the Type 1 format, and here it is," he said.

Issuing the Type 1 specifications signaled the end of Adobe's PostScript-font juggernaut. Now any type designer—or Apple or Microsoft, for that matter—could create a Type 1 font and thus siphon off dollars from Adobe's premium-priced type library. In fact, even before the format's publication, a few foundries had already figured out how to do just that.

If opening up the Type 1 format was rife with symbolism, releasing Adobe Type Manager (ATM) in December 1989 had far more actual impact. ATM successfully undercut Apple and Microsoft's strategy to ruin the market for PostScript.

Prior to ATM, PostScript fonts appeared onscreen as coarsely pixelated bitmaps with jagged edges. The transformation to smooth output occurred when the PostScript interpreter residing in the printer called up the equivalent outline font. As a result, PostScript type users did not see the typographic subtlety onscreen that they did with printed output. TrueType promised to eliminate that with a single font file that looked the same when viewed onscreen and when printed on paper. Advocates of the TrueType technology said the same couldn't be done with PostScript.

Adobe accepted the engineering challenge, but the threat was real. Not only was Adobe's type business at risk, but so too was its printer franchise. If users could get the same results onscreen and in print with an inexpensive non-PostScript printer, demand would surely dry up. "The perception internally was that, If we don't do this, we're really in trouble," acknowledges Advanced Technology Group (ATG) scientist Jim King.

A core team of engineers (including Mike Schuster, Bill Paxton, and Warnock) swung into action. In addition to the problem of rasterizing PostScript fonts onscreen, a second difficulty arose. Because TrueType would be built into the Macintosh operating system, Adobe also had to figure out a way to make PostScript fonts available to Macintosh users from within the OS and its applications. ATG scientist Ed Taft describes ATM's accomplishment this way: "There were two major breakthroughs: rendering good-quality text from outlines at display resolution, and figuring out a way for ATM to intercept text-drawing commands in the operating system."

From first learning about Apple's Royal font technology to shipping ATM was a six-month flat-out effort. Engineers toiled day and night, realizing

"*We are going to out-invent the bastards. They can do all this marketing crap and we'll just out-invent them.*"

— John Warnock

Adobe engineer Mike Schuster led the development of ATM 1.0.

that beating Apple and Microsoft to market was critical. David Lemon recalls the "manic" pace of development as he worked with Paxton and Schuster. "They'd look at me and say, 'Don't worry, David. It's not life or death if we get this out. It's only the future of the company.'"

Working at a breakneck pace, Adobe brought ATM to market at least a year before any TrueType fonts from Apple or Microsoft appeared. Lemon explains: "We had to get ATM established. If it had come out at the same time it wouldn't have worked because a TrueType juggernaut would be in place. If we hadn't gotten ATM out then, we would be living in an all-TrueType world now."

"ATM kept Microsoft from blanking us out of the font business. ATM signaled to the world that we were going to be there," King agrees. Adds David Pratt, who joined Adobe in 1988 to lead the new applications division: "It was a remarkable effort and talked about for years as Adobe at its best."

ATM opened up the PostScript font library for millions of users and in so doing helped preserve Adobe's market share. While TrueType is the default font format on the Macintosh and Windows operating systems, professional designers and printers prefer PostScript fonts because they work flawlessly with the PostScript output devices that designers rely on.

"The publishing industry rallied around Adobe," Seybold says. "Adobe had been there from the beginning. Adobe understood aesthetics. Apple without Steve Jobs did not really understand. Microsoft didn't understand at all. Adobe you trust. Microsoft and Apple you do not trust."

Microsoft's much vaunted attack on PostScript printing failed to materialize. Only a few TrueImage printers ever saw the light of day, and Microsoft quickly ceased its development. Thanks to ATM, though, buyers of low-cost inkjet printers and other non-PostScript output devices can get the same typographic fidelity that users of PostScript printers can.

In 1991, Apple and Adobe resolved their differences when Apple agreed to include Adobe's type rasterizer and fonts in Macintosh System 7. Then in 1996, Adobe and Microsoft reached rapprochement. The companies agreed to join forces over OpenType, a new cross-platform format they would codevelop. In effect, OpenType put PostScript fonts in a TrueType wrapper, simplifying font management while providing richer linguistic support and finer typographic control.

The Font Wars were over, and ATM had proved that Adobe was willing to do what it took to protect PostScript. But the company had felt the hot breath of competition on its neck. The need to diversify into other markets was all too clear. And in 1990, that's what Adobe did.

Adobe Type Manager improved the appearance of PostScript fonts onscreen, deflecting the threat posed by Apple and Microsoft's competitive TrueType format.

Although Apple and Adobe mended fences in the aftermath of the font wars, Microsoft remained an adversary for years to come. The prickly relationship was a favorite topic of Warnock's at subsequent industry events.

Seybold

SEYBOLD

Report on Desktop Publishing

Apple and IBM Gang Up on Microsoft 3

BELATEDLY RECOGNIZING that market share in the '90s depends on setting the software standards for the desktop, Apple and IBM have joined forces to develop a portable, open operating system. It will run on a range of central processors, including IBM's RS/6000 RISC processor as well as Intel's and Motorola's CISC lines. It will, we think, be available for licensing to all comers. It will be object-oriented and will support multimedia, peer-based interfaces and cross-platform communications.

As has been true of many front-rank hardware makers lately, profits and market shares at Apple and IBM have been declining. Both companies have recognized that they must act quickly, redefining themselves as systems software

*"John always said that if
we build great products
we'll have a good business."*

— Fred Mitchell

Charting New Directions

The new decade ushered in a new era for Adobe and for publishing. PostScript had democratized the publishing and type industries, but for Adobe, PostScript's popularity meant increased competition and declining prices. To ensure its livelihood, the company had to adapt. The world outside was changing, too, as computers became more powerful, color monitors more ubiquitous, and scanners more affordable. Yet the photographic, color-retouching, and video-production industries remained in the hands of proprietary systems operators. Adobe saw an opportunity to transform those businesses with desktop tools much as it had liberated the printing industry just a few years before. The company charted a new course to develop software for the creative professionals who drive the publishing process.

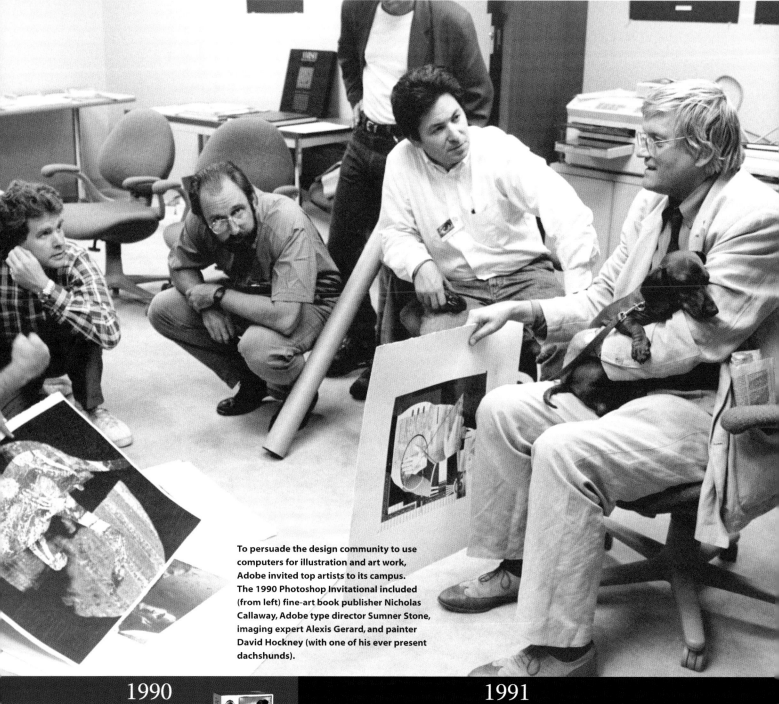

To persuade the design community to use computers for illustration and art work, Adobe invited top artists to its campus. The 1990 Photoshop Invitational included (from left) fine-art book publisher Nicholas Callaway, Adobe type director Sumner Stone, imaging expert Alexis Gerard, and painter David Hockney (with one of his ever present dachshunds).

1990

Adobe publishes Type 1 Reference Manual

Photoshop 1.0 launched

HTML developed; birth of the Web

PostScript Level 2 released

1991

Apple releases Macintosh Quadra 700 and 900, with 25-MHz 040 Motorola processors

America Online born from Steven Case's work at Apple

Apple introduces QuickTime

Fractal Software becomes Fractal Design and develops Painter, a natural-media art tool

Aldus acquires Ulead's PhotoStyler image-editing application

Premiere 1.0 released

Display PostScript introduced

BUILDING A BUSINESS

The Font Wars of 1989 had made crystal clear what executives at Adobe already knew: The company could no longer afford to bank its entire future on PostScript. Nor did it want to. OEM licenses continued to be the main revenue stream, but Illustrator's overnight success pointed to the possibilities inherent in graphics application software.

Warnock and Geschke understood that the market pressures leading to the introduction of ATM and to the increased competition in the clone and type markets would continue to chip away at PostScript. Adobe knew too that it could no longer depend on the Macintosh market for the bulk of its sales. ATM may have staved off the TrueType assault for the time being, but the company's faith in its former ally Apple had been shaken. While Microsoft was no friend, at least the Windows customer base was expanding and offered Adobe new market opportunities.

Stating the Case

In the spring of 1988, David Pratt joined Adobe as its director of support-products business, a division created for software applications. Pratt had experience in creating sales channels at peripheral maker Logitech and knew the PC market from seven years at Intel. According to Pratt, the consensus at Adobe was that he was a hatchet man hired to kill application development.

It was a reasonable assumption. PostScript fonts, Illustrator, and the Collector's Editions of patterns, symbols, and so on, brought in revenues

> *"The applications business lost money, but we kept plugging away at it because we knew PostScript could run out of gas."*
>
> — Bruce Nakao

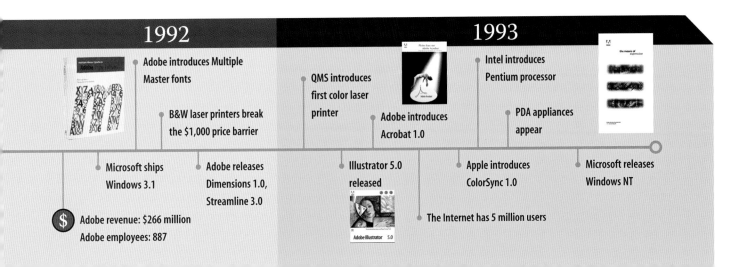

1992

Adobe introduces Multiple Master fonts

B&W laser printers break the $1,000 price barrier

Microsoft ships Windows 3.1

Adobe releases Dimensions 1.0, Streamline 3.0

$ Adobe revenue: $266 million
Adobe employees: 887

1993

QMS introduces first color laser printer

Adobe introduces Acrobat 1.0

Illustrator 5.0 released

Adobe Illustrator 5.0

Intel introduces Pentium processor

PDA appliances appear

Apple introduces ColorSync 1.0

The Internet has 5 million users

Microsoft releases Windows NT

of $19 million in 1988, rising to $35 million in 1989—nearly break-even, but a fraction of the $82 million PostScript system business. Adobe licensed a new product called Photoshop in the fall of 1988, but it was positioned to be an add-on to, or subset of, Illustrator, and the company had minimal revenue expectations for it. On top of everything else, the few applications in development couldn't even pay their own way; sales of PostScript systems subsidized the group.

But rather than rid Adobe of applications, Pratt's mission was entirely the opposite. Warnock believed that graphics applications would figure prominently in Adobe's future, and Pratt was there to justify his faith. "People inside the company said, 'Why are you spending this money on applications? Systems has 40 percent pretax margins. Get rid of applications and focus on systems,'" Warnock recalls. "But I knew that if we ended up a one-product company down the line we'd be short-sighted and eventually be in trouble."

"Applications development was Warnock's baby," says Linda Clarke, who was hired in 1990 to spearhead marketing for the division. "He was always playing in that playground."

Adobe hired David Pratt in 1988 to launch its applications business.

To kick-start the organization Fred Mitchell, then director of business development and strategic planning, organized an offsite meeting in 1989 in which Pratt, Warnock, product manager John Kunze, and Tom Malloy, then head of engineering, mapped out an applications strategy. "We needed to get people to understand that we could have a successful business," says Pratt. "I don't think anyone realized how successful we could be."

Mitchell and Pratt pulled together data to demonstrate the potential size of the graphics software market and to project a point where the division would make an acceptable profit margin. "The question was: Could we reach a stage where it could be profitable? That meant $40–$50 million," recalls Mitchell. "We put a forecast in place to prove that we could get to $200–$300 million in revenue. People laughed."

According to Mitchell, Warnock didn't blink when confronted with those numbers. He believed the potential was there. "He always said that if we build great products we'll have a good business, and if we build products that people need we'll have a good business," Mitchell says.

Fred Mitchell, then director of business development, helped map out the strategy for Adobe's desktop applications.

The group then charted out what types of applications Adobe needed to flesh out its product line. Among those identified were typefaces, graphics creation, image editing, page layout and video editing. "How to expand the product line and expand into new markets was part of that initial planning meeting," Pratt says, "and as a result we began to listen to people pitching their products." Two such pitches brought image-editing application Photoshop and video-editing software Premiere to Adobe.

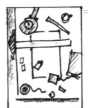

1. PLEASY LIGHTHEARTED LIKE VERY GRAPHIC SHOT OF ART STUDIO

2. PICTURE FRAME, COLLAGE

3. SURREAL LANDSCAPE W/ DRAWING TABLE

4. CASSANDRE-LIKE FACE W/ 4 DRAWINGS

5. STRAIGHT COLLAGE

6. HAND W/ ART TOOLS

7. MORE STRAIGHT FORWARD ARTIST STUDIO

8. TOP VIEW OF DRAWING TABLE

9. SPARE, MOUSE WRAPS AROUND TOOLS

10. PANES OF GLASS W/ DIFFERENT DRAWINGS

11. GRAPHIC, ABSTRACT COLLAGE

12. ARTIST STUDIO AGAIN W/ ARTIST

13. ART EMANATING FROM ARTIST, NAME ON TOP.

14. MANNIX / WILD, WILD WEST COLLAGE

15. DRAWINGS ON STUDIO FLOOR

16. FLOATING TOOLS AROUND COMPUTER SCREEN?

Adobe's creative department learned early that to persuade traditional designers to embrace technology, it had to produce packaging and collateral of the highest standard. Among those at this packaging review for the Adobe Collector's Edition (above) are Russell Brown, Don Craig, Elise Dorsey, and Laurie Szujewska. The storyboard at left shows options for an Illustrator campaign.

The establishment of the applications division meant a new internal structure for Adobe, with Pratt leading applications and Steve MacDonald heading systems, home of PostScript. Warnock and Geschke split their responsibilities, too. "Chuck was mostly on the systems side while John was heart and soul of the applications group," Pratt says.

The division brought some tensions to the surface. The systems group, justifiably proud of its accomplishments and secure in its role in the company, resented funding the upstart software group. Conventional wisdom held that a systems company should not develop, sell, and market shrink-wrapped software. "Adobe spent lavishly to sit at the table of applications," Dan Putman, Adobe's original hardware engineer and former senior vice president of the North American systems division, notes dryly. The applications group, on the other hand, had a mandate to succeed and chafed at their colleagues' lack of support. "We felt underappreciated and got tired of being second-class citizens," says Pratt.

The opposing camps often lobbied Warnock or Geschke to support their projects over the others'. "The PostScript people viewed me as their friend, while the applications people saw John as theirs," Geschke says. "But John and I both understood that we needed both, so we could play good cop and bad cop." Warnock adds, "It's always hard to get a well-run organization to change."

At the executive level cooler heads prevailed. It was a necessary time of transition, and PostScript enabled Adobe to expand. "We had to think about building more products," says former CFO Bruce Nakao. "The applications business lost money, but we kept plugging away at it because we knew PostScript could run out of gas."

Bootstrap Marketing

Even though the applications division had support from the top, the group had to earn its keep. "It was actually a rather poorly funded start-up," Clarke says of the division's early days. Adds Pratt: "Chuck and John didn't tell us what to do. They gave us the rope to either succeed or fail."

As at many other startups, grassroots promotional efforts often took the place of lavish marketing campaigns. "We learned to be creative," says Clarke. "It was guerrilla warfare."

In the early days, Adobe was not only marketing its products but also selling the very idea of using computers for design and illustration. The desktop publishing revolution had shown that it was possible to use a Macintosh—plus PageMaker, PostScript, and, increasingly, Illustrator—for limited forms of publishing; but professional designers still expressed doubt, scoffing that the results would never be good enough. "Computer graphics didn't have a good name. The design community was skeptical,"

These whimsical drawings were made by illustrator Chris Krueger for a PostScript product brochure.

acknowledges Luanne Seymour Cohen, an Adobe art director for 12 years and now an author and teacher. "They would only listen to us if the art-work looked beautiful."

Adobe let the products speak for themselves. The tactics employed by Adobe's creative team during the launch of Illustrator were now applied with greater intensity. Product packaging and collateral had to show-case not only excellent design and execution but also Adobe products. Potential customers had to believe that the purchase of a program and its related products would enable them to achieve the quality shown. "We set a high standard for packaging design," Clarke says. "It was a cheap form of advertising."

Along the way, an Adobe aesthetic was born. "We appreciated the aes-thetics of good design overall," says Russell Brown. In addition, "we had good typography from the beginning of time because the type guys sat right next to you. If you used type incorrectly they told you."

At the 1990 Design Invitational, members of Adobe's creative team (back row from left) Luanne Seymour Cohen, Min Wang, and Russell Brown, keep a watchful eye on the participants, along with an unidentified artist.

The creative team worked the booth at trade shows to dazzle prospective customers. Here Russell Brown chats with early adopter and fellow Art Directors Invitational instructor Diane Burns.

It was not uncommon for Warnock to stick his head in to comment on advertising and packaging, either. "John is an artist, a painter, and a photographer," Clarke says. "He had a view into the types of customers that Adobe served." Warnock's respect for good design and typography permeated the products, from feature implementation in engineering to display type in packaging.

That design legacy persists to this day. "John's love of books and typography shows through everything they do, from the programs themselves and the way they're marketed, from the collateral to the packaging," says Gene Gable, a longtime industry observer and the current president of Seybold Seminars and Publications. "Adobe gets the sophistication of its market and that makes a difference in its products."

Making Converts

Printed materials were not the only arena in which Adobe conducted guerrilla marketing. The company was no longer small enough that every employee worked the booth at trade shows, but the creative team reached out to designers through road shows and workshops. "We became evangelists for the products," says Cohen, who traveled worldwide speaking at seminars and teaching classes.

In 1987, both Brown and Cohen started teaching at the Stanford Art Directors Invitational Master Class (SADIM), where staff from some of the biggest companies in publishing went to learn about new tools and technologies. "All these art directors from magazines came out to SADIM, because the New York community hadn't adopted digital tools yet," Cohen says.

Recognizing an opportunity, Adobe hatched a plan to start its own version of SADIM. But instead of making people pay to attend, Adobe invited influential designers, artists, and photographers to come and learn how to use its software. The payback was twofold: First, the attendees would return home and talk about what they had done, perhaps inspiring others to try the tools and even influencing their companies to purchase the software. And second, during the event artists would produce graphics that Adobe could then use in its promotional materials, hence affirming to the rest of the design community that their big-name peers did indeed use digital tools.

The result was "real marketing, not fluff marketing," says Pratt, who knew firsthand what impact those events could have. Before joining Adobe, Pratt had attended a 1987 SADIM Illustrator class taught by Brown—and ended up buying Illustrator (serial number 73) the very next day.

The applications marketing group went through design magazines to research likely candidates for the first gathering. In the summer of 1989 a select group of artists, illustrators, and designers arrived at Adobe's Mountain View offices for the first Design Invitational, later dubbed Camp Adobe. The event featured Illustrator 88, so up-and-coming illustration artists like Ron Chan and J. Otto Seibold were invited along with *Time* magazine art director Nigel Holmes. Adobe was also looking for feedback on an unreleased product called Photoshop.

Because Adobe's goal was to convert traditional artists to digital tools, many of the attendees were computer neophytes. "Most of the designers didn't even use computers, so we had to teach them how to use a Mac," Brown says. Some of the younger illustrators caught on immediately. "Ron Chan's style lent itself to the computer, so he was going back and forth between the computer and scissors," Brown recalls. "J. Otto Seibold was cutting paper and then *bingo!* he was using Illustrator. We pushed him over the edge, and then he pushed others over the edge." New York photographer Sam Merrell, who attended the 1990 Photoshop invitational, recalls that some attendees were "profoundly mystified" by the

"*Computer graphics didn't have a good name. The design community was skeptical. They would only listen to us if the artwork looked beautiful.*"

— Luanne Seymour Cohen

ART DIRECTORS INVITATIONAL

Adobe's first Art Director's Invitational took place in 1989. Later dubbed Camp Adobe, the event brought in top designers from around the country to learn about digital tools and Adobe software, including Illustrator 88 and a prerelease version of Photoshop. The 1990 invitational focused on the just-shipped Photoshop.

This page, top: Artist Paul Davis ponders the screen; middle, Adobe's Russell Brown lends a helping hand; bottom, illustrator Lance Hidy, graphic artist Michael David Brown, Photoshop product manager Steve Guttman, and an unidentified artist review a print. Opposite page, Russell Brown explains Photoshop to Nicholas Callaway and David Hockney.

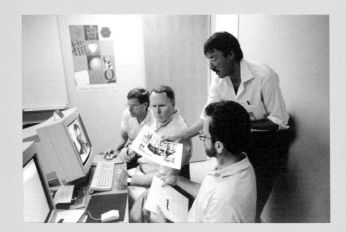

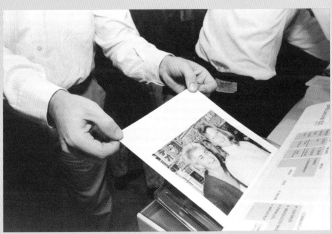

V V

"We always referred to Russell Brown as our secret weapon. No competitor had anyone like him."

— David Pratt

new tools and were ready to hop the first flight back East. "But by the third day, everyone in the group was working away, starting and finishing projects that would've consumed their first two days," says Merrell, an early convert to digital techniques.

The invitationals, fueled by Brown's gregarious personality and teaching antics, had the desired effect as attendees spread the word about the cool new computers and software they used. "We always referred to Russell as our secret weapon," says Pratt. "No competitor had anyone like him." Brown, who jokingly calls himself "Adobe's sanctioned ego trip," says, "I'm taking credit for pushing *Time* magazine into using the Mac. After the invitational, Nigel Holmes went back to New York and bought Macs for *Time*." Later Adobe used a similar strategy on journalists. For the so-called Press Invitationals, key media representatives were invited to spend the day at Adobe playing with new products.

SADIM is no longer held, but Adobe continues the tradition with both the Design Invitational and its own Art Directors Invitational Master Class (ADIM), with Brown as the main instigator and master of ceremonies and mayhem. Few art directors today need any persuasion to use digital tools, and ADIM today is "more of a celebration of Adobe's tools," says Brown. "We give them information that they can use and can disseminate back at the office. It's energizing and creative."

Turning the Corner

The early '90s was a period when Adobe, led by the upstart applications group, broke new ground both in the products it developed and in the way it reached customers. Adobe Type Manager epitomized Adobe's approach when it shipped in late 1989. Although the technical and political underpinnings of ATM were complex, its marketing pitch was simple: ATM got rid of the jaggies. Clarke remembers seeing raised eyebrows at the use of the word *jaggies* (the rough, ragged edges of bitmapped fonts onscreen). "But everybody knew what you meant. 'ATM ends the jaggies and makes type look better,'" she says.

Adobe had previously approached mail order catalogs with caution. "At the time we viewed them as shady characters and fly-by-night operators," Clarke says. But to push ATM into the market quickly, Adobe persuaded MacWarehouse and MacConnection to each purchase 10,000 copies (with no return guarantees) and then watched the software fly out the door. The company had been focused on the product as a strategic necessity and a technical achievement rather than a moneymaker. ATM was proof that selling inexpensive software could also prove lucrative for Adobe. "We sold it for as little as we could get away with so we could flood the market. It was never looked at as a way to make money, which it did end up doing," says Pratt.

BizStats: 1990

No. of employees: 508

Revenue: $169 million

Stock price range: $9 to $26

Product releases:
Photoshop 1.0
PostScript Level 2

Other:
>> Patent #5,185,818 issued to John Warnock: covers font substitution using multimaster fonts, emphasizing the quality resulting from matching the original character weight, x-height, etc.

In June, Adobe's stock drops 30% and stockholders file a lawsuit claiming that Adobe gave out misleading sales projections and artificially inflated the value of the company's stock (dismissed in 1992)

Type 1 Reference Manual published

Luanne Seymour Cohen chats with painter David Hockney while her son Charlie ogles Hockney's dachshunds.

Despite that early success, making applications a profitable enterprise was a long, hard road. "For the first two years the perception was that applications were a waste of money," Pratt says. By the third quarter of 1993, however, the applications division reached the goal it had set at the offsite years earlier: an annual run-rate of $200 million in revenue. At 53.4 percent of the annual total, application revenue had overtaken systems. "It took us four years, but we did it," says Pratt, adding that one product in particular helped push the division over the top.

That product was a software application called Photoshop.

GORDON STUDER

Gordon Studer is one of a group of Bay Area–based illustrators who cut their teeth in newspaper art departments. Hired by the *San Francisco Examiner* as a traditional artist, Studer began working with bitmapped graphics programs before glomming on to Illustrator in 1988. Studer's style quickly evolved from trying to imitate traditional techniques with the new tools to exploiting a computer-generated aesthetic of geometric shapes and two-dimensional planes. He credits the Macintosh and Illustrator with helping him to cultivate the abstract style that forms the basis of his more recent Photoshop collages, in which scraps of photos are distilled to their purest shapes. (www.gordonstuder.com)

∨
∨

"For me it's all about

'How simple can I get?'"

© BERT MONROY
1990

Digital artist Bert Monroy, an
early Illustrator advocate, enthu-
siastically embraced Photoshop
when it shipped in 1990. He coauthored (with David Biedny) the
first book on the product.

Unleashing Photoshop

When the first group of artists and designers went to Camp Adobe in 1989 at the invitation of Russell Brown, they didn't realize they were about to see a product that would ultimately revolutionize not only their immediate work but the entire graphic arts and publishing industries. Nor could anyone in the room be aware of the impact Photoshop would have on Adobe itself.

Photoshop represented a radically new direction for Adobe and its applications division. Unlike Illustrator, Photoshop was based not on PostScript curves but on raster pixels. Illustrator enabled artists to draw line art from scratch; Photoshop enabled photographers to work on images from other sources, such as those acquired from a scanner. And unlike Illustrator, which was emphatically homegrown, an outside party had developed Photoshop. No wonder Brown, Luanne Cohen, and other members of the creative team watched the Adobe "campers" carefully as they grappled with this new product.

Adobe needn't have worried. In time Photoshop would eclipse Illustrator in terms of popularity and overshadow even PostScript as Adobe's flagship product.

The Ph.D. Project

Photoshop began in 1987 as a private project of Thomas Knoll, a doctoral candidate in computer science at the University of Michigan. As a distraction from writing his thesis, he wrote a programming routine to display grayscale images on a black-and-white monitor. He showed the program, which he called Display, to his brother, John, who worked at filmmaker George Lucas's Industrial Light+Magic, the source of computer-generated special effects for movies such as *Star Wars* and *The Abyss*. Intrigued by Display, John asked Thomas to help him write a program for processing digital image files.

Thomas had gotten hold of a color Macintosh (intercepting one meant for his brother), so Display was now color capable. The brothers then expanded the program to include features that formed the foundation of today's Photoshop, such as soft-edge masks, tone and color adjustments, paintbrushes, plug-in filter support, and multiple file formats. It occurred to John that the software had commercial potential and, after convincing his initially reluctant brother, began to look for an outside investor to take the product into the public arena.

"I ran, not walked, to Mr. Warnock's office and said, 'We should buy this.'"

— Russell Brown

It was 1988, and a number of pixel-based painting and image-editing applications were on the market, among them SuperMac's PixelPaint and Letraset's ImageStudio, which later became ColorStudio. David Biedny, who consulted on all three of those products before making the leap to Photoshop, says that what made Photoshop different was how it approached images as mathematical constructs. "It's not about moving pixels around, which is what painting programs do, but it's about actually combining them together," says Biedny, who first saw Photoshop in 1988 and went on to coauthor the first book about it. "It's like a digital simulation of what you could do in a darkroom." Adds Clement Mok, who designed graphics for the Macintosh at Apple Computer and also consulted with Letraset, "When I first saw it I thought, Photoshop will kill ColorStudio. Photoshop's interface was much more intuitive, closer to the notion of MacPaint."

Knoll called a number of companies, among them Quark and Aldus, both of which had or were preparing competitive products. Adobe was interested but noncommittal, as it was looking at all the options on the market. Finally a small scanner manufacturer named Barneyscan agreed to ship the software as a tool for its scanner. The license for Barneyscan XP, as version 0.87 of Photoshop was known, had a limited duration, so John Knoll continued to look for long-term partners.

"Very early on we decided we'd like to have it," says Fred Mitchell, then director of business development and strategic planning, "but the Knolls said they were negotiating with other companies." Mitchell ran into John Knoll at the Macworld Expo in August 1988 and, impressed by what he saw, invited Knoll back to Adobe the following month.

Handshake Deal

In September 1988 Mitchell ushered John Knoll into a room where they were joined by David Pratt and Russell Brown, among others. Brown, for one, was excited. "I'd always wanted an image editor since playing with a Quantel Paintbox," says Brown of the first time he saw Photoshop. "Then John Knoll demo'd the Magic Wand. The fact that you could create a soft-edged mask! It blew me away." Brown had recently signed a nondisclosure agreement with Letraset over ColorStudio, but quickly recognized that Photoshop was the better product.

Warnock, deeply involved with applications and engineering, attended the demonstration but could stay for only 15 minutes. As Warnock was leaving, Pratt caught up with him at the door and asked him what he thought. "I think we should get it," Warnock said simply.

Brown's reaction was characteristically less reserved. "I ran, not walked, to Mr. Warnock's office and said, 'We should buy this,' and he said, 'We are.'"

Adobe acquired Photoshop from John Knoll (top) and Thomas Knoll (bottom), who developed it while writing his Ph.D. thesis.

According to Mitchell, the reaction from other parts of the company was less definite. "There wasn't as much enthusiasm around the company, but Warnock was really interested in it. He saw its potential. We had seen other image editors, and we saw real talent in the Knolls. Tom Knoll was a genius who wrote very precise code." The deal was sealed with a handshake in the fall of 1988 and a contract was finalized the following spring. "We were very lucky it didn't fall into someone else's hands," Mitchell says today.

But Adobe did not buy the software. It licensed it from the brothers, who would receive royalties on units shipped with a guarantee of no less than $250,000 over the first two years. "That was a huge amount of money then," Mitchell says. In hindsight such a deal seems ludicrously low considering Photoshop's phenomenal success, yet Adobe's initial plans for Photoshop were less ambitious.

Adobe saw Photoshop as an add-on to, or a subset of, Illustrator and therefore another way of selling more PostScript. "Everyone thought it was great program to promote PostScript and printing," says Brown. "We didn't know the influence it would have."

"At the time we acquired Photoshop the Mac had one megabyte of RAM and a 20-megabyte hard disk. You could keep maybe six images on your machine," remembers Warnock. "I had seen the big Scitex and Hell machines used to do color imaging, and then they bring in this little toy program. I thought we'd sell 250 per month, max."

Digital imaging was a relatively new business, but what Geschke and Warnock soon realized was that more people take photographs than draw line illustrations. Moreover, in the favorable climate of a desktop publishing revolution, Photoshop cut across a growing category of hardware devices as well. The market for scanning devices was starting to develop, with optical sensors improving in quality while declining in price. Color monitors and printers were becoming ubiquitous, too. Following Moore's law, personal computers were becoming faster, more powerful, and less expensive with each successive release. Photoshop was poised at the nexus of desktop publishing, computer imaging, and traditional photography.

Adobe Photoshop's first toolbar.

"Photoshop surprised everybody," says Pratt of the program's immediate success. "It was going to be a subset of Illustrator, but it addressed a market that brought in other markets." For example, he notes that in the late '80s no one at Adobe anticipated that the *New York Times* (and every other newspaper) would routinely use Photoshop to touch up its black-and-white (and, later, color) images, or that several years down the line Photoshop would be used to make graphics for a little-known experiment called the World Wide Web.

ADOBE AND THE DIGITAL IMAGING REVOLUTION

No one expected Adobe Photoshop to take off the way it did—not people within Adobe, not the photography community, not the prepress industry, not even the digital artists who recognized immediately that the new software was a notch above any other pixel-based product they'd seen. Today, no aspect of publishing has been untouched by Photoshop, and the juggernaut rolls on with its consumer version, Photoshop Elements.

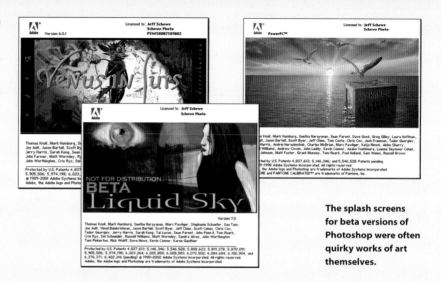

The splash screens for beta versions of Photoshop were often quirky works of art themselves.

FIRST LOOKS

Adobe first caught my attention at a New York Macintosh users group. Someone showed me a print from an Apple LaserWriter. Later I called Geschke to ask him about it. He really knew what he was talking about. I told the Knolls they should take Photoshop to these two guys [Warnock and Geschke] because they would get it.

David Biedny, digital artist

Throughout the '80s, photo retouchers used Scitex and Paintbox workstations that cost $300,000. High-end computer imaging cost $1,200 per hour, so to retouch an image cost $20,000 to $30,000 for a project. I went out and bought an entire Mac system for $24,000. I paid for it with one job.

Jeff Schewe, photographer

When Photoshop came out, imaging studios got rid of all the Quantels in the basement.

Bert Monroy, digital artist

PHOTOSHOP EVOLVES

When adjustment layers came out I almost fell to my knees in thanks. Layers gave us the ability to try out a color or tonal correction without changing the original file.

Katrin Eismann, digital artist

I stayed with Photoshop 2.5 for a long time even after version 3, with layers, came out. I liked the idea that I had to make a decision and stick with it. That's when men were men and boys were boys, because once you made up your mind, that was it. It was macho to have to commit to an image state.

Glenn Mitsui, designer and artist

I was stunned by the alpha channel. It gave me a nondestructive way to work with images. You could always get back to where you were.

Lynda Weinman, author and designer

When I opened my first image using the new Duotone feature, I instinctively reached for the phone and dialed Ansel Adams. He'd passed away eight years earlier, but I know he would have gotten in his Cadillac and driven up here to see it.

Stephen Johnson, landscape photographer

FAVORITE FEATURES

I had been an airbrush artist, so seeing the use of the airbrush in Photoshop was big for me. I could get smooth, soft tones and gradients much closer to what I was used to getting with traditional tools.

Bert Monroy

Before type could be anti-aliased in Photoshop, I remember fixing type edges by hand with the Eyedropper and Pencil tools. It was nuts.

Lynda Weinman

As I worked with higher-resolution images I kept pushing for Photoshop to accept larger image files. Finally Mark Hamburg said, "It's only you and the CIA that want a 30,000-pixel limit."

Stephen Johnson

IMPACT ON PHOTOGRAPHY

For a number of years, the photographic community was very hostile. I was lecturing in Santa Fe about Photoshop. This guys calls out: "Do you call yourself a real photographer?" And I said yes. He was really upset about the sea change he saw around him.

John Lund, photographer

If Ansel Adams were using Photoshop—and he would be using Photoshop, without any doubt—he'd only be using 25 percent of it.

John Paul Caponigro, author and photographer

I've always thought of my digital photography not as photography but as an accessory of my computer. The image is immediately a computer graphic. No matter what it is, I can always make it what I want it to be. That's very freeing.

April Greiman, artist and photographer

SLICING AND DICING

Photoshop is the Cuisinart of imaging. No matter where it's coming from, Photoshop can deal with it.

David Biedny

I've even seen a tattoo artist use Photoshop to show customers what a tattoo will look like on their bodies.

Jeff Schewe

THE CREATIVE PROCESS

I end up with things I couldn't do in traditional media. I'm not simulating anything. I'm integrating everything, traditional and nontraditional media. The dramatic thing is that it pushes you in directions you could never go with paint.

Sharon Steuer, illustrator and author

I like the unpredictable factor of working in Photoshop: the possibility of not having anything particular in mind, just setting out on a digital journey—what mistakes, what accidents, what can happen when you aren't attached to a product or a result. You can have a creative dialogue in this environment.

April Greiman

When I'm working with Photoshop I am carried into the process by listening to the image. Each image has its own voice, and if you listen to the image, the image will tell you what to do.

Katrin Eismann

The computer and Photoshop eliminate the barrier between imagination and execution. It's possible to make any vision into photographic reality.

John Lund

PERSONAL EPIPHANIES

Without Photoshop I don't know where I'd be. It allowed me to have a niche very early. We had a comfort level with it in Seattle that gave us a leg up on the rest of the country really quick.

Glenn Mitsui

When the IRS attached my account in 1991, I took my portfolio of the Photoshop work I'd done and showed it to the IRS auditor. He said he'd never seen anything like it and gave me another year.

John Lund

Which day did I realize that Photoshop had changed everything for me? The day I realized

"Every published picture we see today has had something done to it in Photoshop."

— John Lund

I would never shoot another roll of black-and-white film because I had so much more control by converting it after the point of capture. The day I realized all the colors were up for grabs, that I had a painter's palette in a photographic rendition. The day I realized that the color theory I had been trained with was based on qualitative terminology, like complementary colors, and that I could assign numerical or quantitative values and advance it even further. The day I realized I could change proportions. The day I realized that composition was completely up for grabs, the day that taking elements out of pictures became more important than putting them in, the day that I could make seemingly natural effects like fog or rainbows or stars, and on and on. What I look forward to is that next breakthrough.

John Paul Caponigro

IMPACT ON THE INDUSTRY

Photoshop was the source of revolution in several industries: prepress, motion pictures, fine arts, image making. It was the basis on which the battle of the pixel was waged.

Jeff Schewe

Photoshop revolutionized not only graphic design but the whole design field as well.

April Greiman

The impact of Photoshop is like a tsunami running through pop culture. It's made an elite technology democratic. There isn't an aspect of visual culture that hasn't been or won't be impacted.

John Paul Caponigro

Photoshop was the best deal Adobe ever got.

Frank Romano, Rochester Institute of Technology

The original Photoshop application fit on one 800 KByte floppy disk, accompanied by Installer and Extras disks.

Mark Hamburg has assumed the mantle of Adobe's chief Photoshop architect.

The First Version

Adobe considered changing the product's name—ImagePro and PhotoLab were possibilities, as were Impressionist and Artist, according to Thomas Knoll—but eventually kept "Photoshop." The Knolls wrote the first version to be released under the Adobe label. Thomas provided the core code. John worked on supplemental features similar to what was available to him with ILM's high-end workstations. According to Jeff Schewe, a photographer who has written a history of Photoshop, John was able to sneak favorite special effects into the program as the supplemental features we now know as plug-in filters.

This plug-in architecture, which made Photoshop extensible, spawned an entire subindustry of software companies that developed special-effects filters and productivity tools to add functionality to Photoshop.

Adobe Photoshop 1.0 shipped in February 1990 as a Macintosh-only product. It was immediately perceived as a technological breakthrough, but it was slow to take off. According to Pratt, only a few hundred copies of Photoshop sold each month in its first release cycle. Adobe had set low expectations for the product anyway, but it also realized that to grow the product, it needed more engineers than just Thomas Knoll. Among the new members of the Photoshop team was Mark Hamburg, who is now the senior-ranking Photoshop engineer and its chief architect.

The free exchange of ideas between engineer and designer—a hallmark of Illustrator's development—continued with Photoshop. Russell Brown, especially, was an active participant, suggesting features to Thomas back in Michigan and then to the new in-house engineers. "I'd say to Thomas Knoll, 'It would be really great if I could preview this printed page,' and then he'd send me the feature back and say, 'Try this,'" Brown recalls.

Brown's road shows and tutorials now included Photoshop demonstrations, so he constantly looked for ways to dazzle his audience and thus spread the word about this exciting new product. He found willing co-conspirators in the engineering department. "It was wonderful," says Brown. "I'd ask for special features, like a key combination shortcut, and they'd do it for me. Things weren't as controlled then as they are now, so if the programmer liked it and I liked it, we put it in the program. Later, I'd show it off to people and say, 'Did you know it did this?' They'd say, 'Hey! That's not documented!'"

Brown developed a reputation for slipping in features that he alone could use to wow the audience, but the explanation is much simpler: manuals and documentation are written and printed long before software code is final, so last-minute features slipped through the cracks. But the creative collaboration was so successful that up through version 3.0, Brown's name

BERT MONROY

As a traditional painter, Bert Monroy often found himself limited by the tools of his trade when changing a brush meant interrupting his creative flow. Monroy was already an Illustrator convert when he came across Photoshop in 1989 prior to its release. In Photoshop Monroy found the ability to paint unfettered. His street scenes are often sketched onsite with Photoshop on a Macintosh PowerBook: no scanners or tracing allowed. A member of Photoshop's alpha feedback team, Monroy tests new features—and occasionally contributes them—to the program. The maple leaves and fabric textures in "Late Afternoon" (2002) were created using Photoshop 7.0's custom brush and symbol features, for which Monroy made some patterns. (www.bertmonroy.com)

appeared on the Photoshop splash screen as a contributor to the program along with the Knolls and the engineering team.

Each release of Photoshop brought significant new features to the program, such as CMYK support in version 2.0, released in June 1991. That addition ignited a controversy similar to that of the early PostScript era, when traditional typesetters rebelled against digital fonts. Printers and color separators balked at the idea of untrained desktop publishers making their own color separations. But unlike the earlier typesetting manufacturers who were slow to adapt, everyone in the printing industry had seen enough to take the new threat seriously. Today nearly every printer in the industrialized world uses Photoshop for its color-separation and prepress tasks.

In Adobe's third fiscal quarter of 1991, Photoshop overtook Illustrator in terms of revenue—and it never looked back. Photoshop sales were boosted even more when Adobe worked deals with scanner manufacturers to include a copy of Photoshop with each scanner sold. Today similar deals are in effect with digital camera manufacturers for Adobe's consumer-friendly version, Photoshop Elements.

Embracing the PC

In 1993 Adobe took Photoshop to the Windows platform. Because of fundamental differences in the operating systems, developing Photoshop 2.5 required engineering two separate products. Bryan Lamkin, now Adobe's senior vice president of the graphics business unit, was hired from PC developer Harvard Graphics to lead the Windows team.

Although Illustrator for Windows had shipped in 1989, Adobe was still regarded as a developer of Macintosh software. "We were not a confident Windows company," Lamkin admits. Nevertheless, Photoshop 2.5 for Windows was an overnight success, earning $16 million its first year. "The numbers blew the doors wide open," says Lamkin. "We knew the imaging market was going to be huge, and this confirmed it."

Photoshop's ability to instantly create and mutate versions of an image lets artists work in entirely new ways. Shown here: Katrin Eismann's creative process.

Yet despite Photoshop's obvious success, the Photoshop team was careful not to get complacent. Competitors such as ColorStudio gradually fell by the wayside, but new challengers appeared, such as Aldus's PhotoStyler and MetaCreations' Live Picture. The latter was especially troubling because it allowed users to store image components on separate layers, which could then be worked on individually and stacked and reordered for different effects. Lamkin describes the Photoshop team's temperament at the time of having both "confidence and paranoia"—they were cocky in their abilities but nervous about losing market position.

Adobe responded with Photoshop 3.0, universally recognized as the product's most pivotal version. Released in late 1994, Photoshop 3.0 had its own implementation of layers, which then set the standard for the industry. The team had raised the bar so high that Lamkin recalls an exchange he had with Photoshop's lead engineer: "I told Mark Hamburg after Photoshop 3.0, 'We're done.'" Of course, in many respects they had just begun.

Photoshop also set standards within Adobe. Version 4.0, released in late 1996, was the first to sport a new user interface that later migrated to all Adobe graphics applications. The redesign—which changed the sequence of frequently used commands and the location of popular tools, among other things—created a maelstrom of protest within the tightly knit Photoshop community. Illustrator users added fuel to the fire when they discovered a few months later that much of Photoshop's interface had been grafted onto Illustrator 7.0, forcing them to relearn that program. With the passing of time, the common user interface initiated in Photoshop and now spanning Adobe's product line became a popular feature and a selling point for all Adobe software.

Although Photoshop now dominates the Windows platform, it's on the Macintosh operating system that Photoshop has its most fervent followers. So loyal are these users that many of them would not switch to Apple's new groundbreaking Mac OS X until Adobe released Photoshop for that operating system. Steve Jobs, who returned to helm Apple in 1997, publicly needled Adobe about its slow adoption of Mac OS X for Photoshop. When Photoshop 7 for Mac OS X shipped in April 2002, Adobe reported strong sales for the product. Of his jabs at Adobe, Jobs now says, "Success has a way of washing away those things."

The Cult of Photoshop

Once Photoshop took off, it never slowed down. As computers became more powerful—especially with Motorola's PowerPC chip for Macintosh computers and Intel's Pentium series for Windows PCs—Photoshop gained the horsepower to perform at levels equivalent to those of high-performance workstations. The improved machine performance also allowed Adobe to add processor-taxing features targeted for specialized industries such as print, film, photography, and online services. "Imaging is like oxygen when it comes to communications," notes Lamkin. No one, it seemed, didn't have Photoshop.

Today, millions of copies have been shipped. "We thought we'd be lucky if we sold a few thousand a year," Geschke says now.

Above, photographer Sam Merrell (left) talks Photoshop with product manager Steve Guttman.

BizStats: **1991**

No. of employees: 701

Revenue: $230 million

Stock price range: $14 to $35

Acquisitions: Emerald City Software

Product releases:
   Adobe Type Manager 2.0
   Photoshop 2.0
   Premiere 1.0 (Mac)
   Streamline 2.0

Other:
>> Display PostScript introduced. Licensees include NEC, Next, Apple, DEC, and IBM

   More than 1,400 fonts in Adobe Type Library

   Warnock writes memo about a project called "Camelot," aka Acrobat

Sharon Steuer uses Photoshop's blend modes to capture the feeling of paint strokes on canvas in her illustrations.

V
V

"We used to have a mantra: 'Thank God for Photoshop.' Every quarter it kept going and going."

— Tom Malloy

"We used to have a mantra: 'Thank God for Photoshop.' Every quarter it would keep going and going," says vice president and Advanced Technology Group director Tom Malloy. In 1995, Adobe ended its licensing agreement with the Knoll brothers and bought the product outright for $34.5 million. When Adobe moved into its impressive new corporate headquarters in San Jose, California, a joke about the source of financing for the twin 18-story towers made the rounds at the company. "Photoshop for the Mac built the first building, and Photoshop for the PC paid for the second," says Brown.

Photoshop now has a life of its own and a cultlike following. The Knoll brothers are as revered as the galactic heroes from *Star Wars*. More than 400 books on Photoshop are in print. Entire trade shows and conferences are devoted to it. Online forums serve thousands of dedicated users. And it gave rise to a new professional trade: the Photoshop guru.

Some Photoshop gurus got their start with the Photoshop forum on America Online, one of the earliest and most influential. On Tuesday nights one could log in and see freewheeling discussions and technique exchanges by such now legendary users as David Biedny, Kai Krause, Jeff Schewe, and others. Those informal think tanks not only fed ideas back to Adobe—Photoshop lead engineer Mark Hamburg was a regular—but also created an aura of glamour about Photoshop and its users. It's common practice among Photoshop devotees to boast about which version they used first. Saying you started with Barneyscan XP puts you in elite company, and claiming anything earlier means you breathe rarefied air.

Photoshop has entered the vernacular in ways no one could have imagined. Users frequently say they "photoshopped" an image. "When your product becomes a verb, you know you've defined your category," says Lamkin.

"Photoshop is an entity on its own," says Schewe, who consults on prerelease versions of Photoshop. "All other products from Adobe are known as Adobe products, but Photoshop nearly eclipses Adobe as a brand." Indeed, it's not uncommon for people to refer to Adobe as "the company that makes Photoshop."

"Photoshop launched us truly into the software business," says Brown. But Adobe wasn't content to stop there. Its next acquisition gave Adobe a key role on the multimedia stage. With Premiere, Adobe went to the movies.

KATRIN EISMANN

Katrin Eismann studied philosophy, politics, and photography before talking her way into a digital imaging class taught by Douglas Ford Rea at the Rochester Institute of Technology in 1991. She immersed herself in Photoshop while working at the Center for Creative Imaging in Maine, where she started as an intern and soon began teaching classes. Eismann's work resonates with a respect for nature with an awareness of politics, especially gender roles and class issues. She credits her digital camera and Photoshop with making her a better artist and photographer—the former gives her instant feedback on composition and the latter allows her to explore endless variations on a theme. (www.photoshopdiva.com)

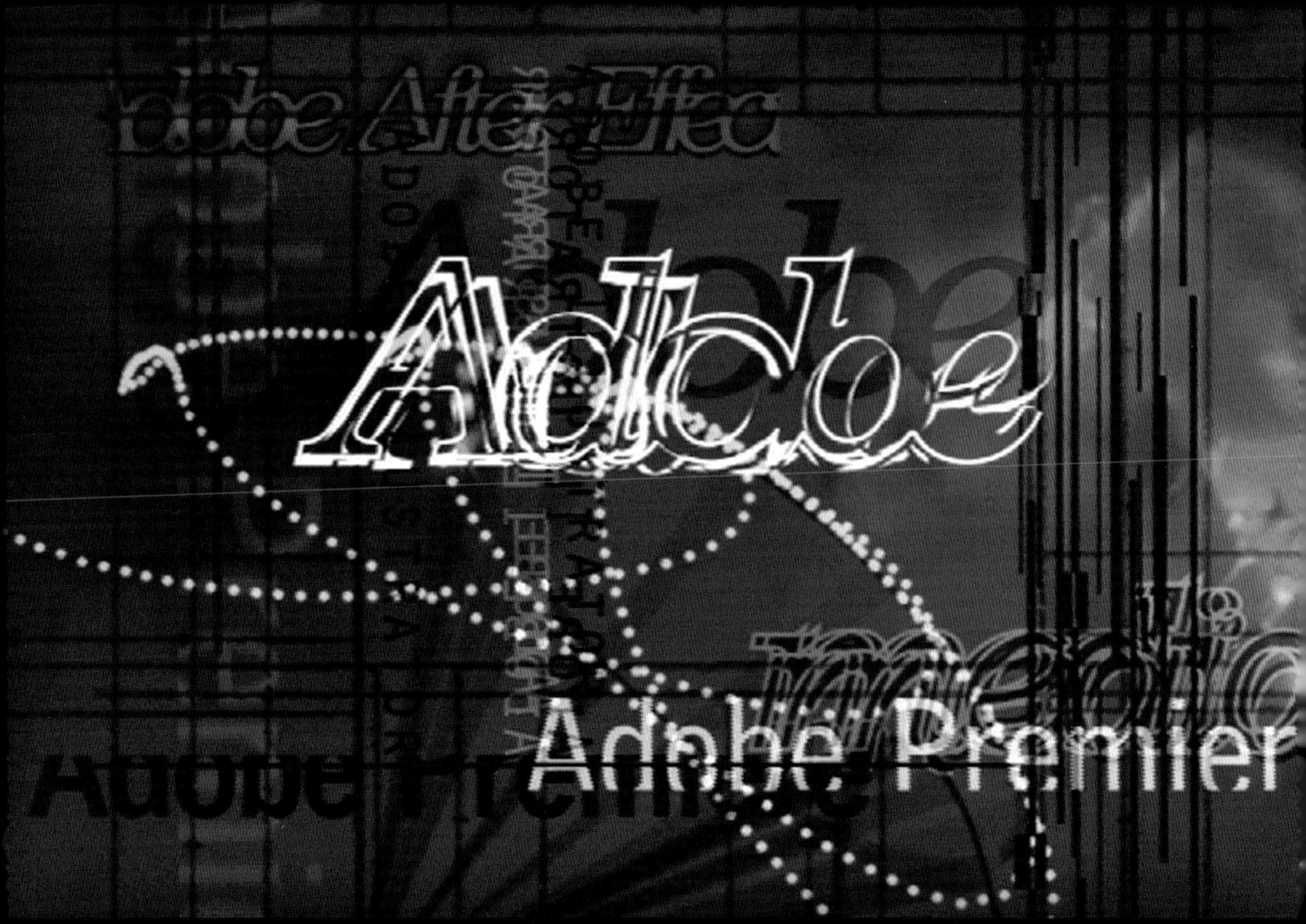
Adobe
Adobe Premier

Images in Motion

The applications group members who attended the strategic-planning offsite in 1989 identified several emerging markets for Adobe. By 1991, the image-editing market was well in hand as Photoshop turned heads, changed minds, and opened wallets. Page layout was a two-product race between Aldus PageMaker and QuarkXPress. Digital video, however, was new, especially for a company with its roots in print publishing.

History was repeating itself, however. The market conditions that Adobe faced with digital video were similar to what the company had confronted a decade earlier. Like typesetting businesses, the video-editing suites of the day were closed, proprietary systems. But like desktop publishing before it, a digital video revolution could put the power of professional systems into the hands of many. Adobe had conquered the printed page and the still image. Why not take on the moving image, too?

Digital video confirmed what Photoshop had already hinted at: Adobe was capable of moving outside the PostScript box. The company also had the acumen and talent to acquire a good product from another company and make it even better.

Setting the Stage

An early stand-alone video-editing program for desktop computers, Premiere helped kick-start the desktop video revolution. Interest in using personal computers for film editing was growing, and the computer-generated special effects seen in commercial films, such as those done at Industrial Light+Magic, inspired budding filmmakers. Anyone who played with filters in Photoshop saw that images could be manipulated in interesting ways—it was natural to want to experiment with moving images too. Indeed, Fred Mitchell recalls visiting Photoshop coauthor John Knoll at ILM and seeing a prerelease version of Photoshop in use at Lucasfilm's special-effects studio.

At that time, digital video editing was the domain of high-end workstations and proprietary software from companies like Avid Technology. The finished product was output to videotape. The hardware and software, sold as a complete system, cost anywhere from $20,000 to as much as $200,000, well beyond the reach of almost anyone but well-funded filmmaking studios.

In June 1991 Apple unveiled its QuickTime technology, which integrated multimedia capabilities into the operating system and let customers

"The day John Warnock signed the agreement for Premiere he said, 'I'm going to sign this, but this business is still some years away.'"

— Fred Mitchell

play video on their Macs. In response, hardware and software companies developed companion products for the creation and playback of QuickTime movies. Editing clips and playing movies heavily taxed computer performance, so personal computers needed to gain speed and power. Computer and peripheral makers tackled the problem with faster processors, video accelerator cards, and speedier storage devices. To bridge the gap between analog video sources and digital video editing, developers created video-capture cards, which allowed customers to import video from a VCR or High-8 camera into a personal computer, convert it to digital data, and play it back at high speed.

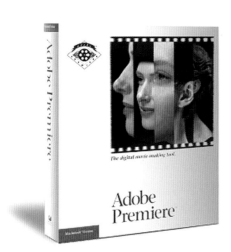

One of those companies developing products for this emerging market was SuperMac Technology, which sold several add-on processor boards that accelerated functions critical to digital video and that captured video frames from external sources. SuperMac also made software products—Photoshop competitor PixelPaint Professional among them—and had in development a nonlinear video-editing application as an adjunct to its film-capture cards. Called ReelTime, the software had been demonstrated publicly to great acclaim.

Like many other companies stretched too thin, SuperMac soon decided to disband its software division to focus on high-margin hardware sales. For most of 1991 SuperMac looked for a prospective buyer for ReelTime, talking to Adobe, Aldus, and Microsoft. In late summer Adobe not only purchased the software but also persuaded Randy Ubillos, its engineer and creator, to continue developing the software by coming to work at Adobe.

Fred Mitchell negotiated the deal. "The day John [Warnock] signed the agreement for Premiere he said, 'I'm going to sign this, but this business is some years away.' And he was right," Mitchell says now.

Desktop Video Revolution

Adobe rushed ReelTime, now called Adobe Premiere, onto the market. As the product had been almost ready to ship under the SuperMac label, few substantive changes were made to the program prior to its release.

Like Aldus PageMaker in the print arena, Premiere was lauded for putting an easy-to-use interface on what can be a complex process. With PageMaker, publishers placed text and graphics into a spatially organized page layout; in Premiere filmmakers combined images and sound into a time-based movie. That Premiere ran on desktop equipment available to anyone helped create a new generation of video artists for whom the cost of conventional systems was prohibitive. All that was needed was a Mac, Premiere, QuickTime, a video camera, and a video-capture card.

For users new to video editing, Premiere made the process accessible. Using a timeline as a metaphor, the editor assembled video clips in the desired sequence, marking start and end points, attaching a soundtrack, and applying dissolves, wipes, and other transition effects. Films could be previewed instantly with onscreen playback. Making a change was as simple as dragging it to a new location on the timeline.

What distinguished Premiere from other video-editing applications coming onto the market, however, was its ability to use Photoshop special-effects plug-in filters, like the ones John Knoll sneaked into the program during its early development at ILM and which Mitchell saw during his visit there. With the ability to add special effects to images, Premiere became more than just a video-editing program. Adding a graphical component made it as much a creative application as a production tool. The cross-fertilization between the two products also signaled Adobe's commitment to an extensible software architecture that invited plug-in development by third parties. Like Photoshop before it, Premiere soon had an active community of plug-in developers.

In marketing Premiere, Adobe faced a conundrum. Its previous work with Illustrator and Photoshop had made Adobe and its products acceptable in graphic design circles. But its customer base was not composed of video artists. The company hoped that its market of designers and graphic artists, already open to moving from typography to photography products, would be adventurous enough to try digital video—if it came from Adobe.

Back in Sync

But if Premiere was a revelation to amateur editors, professionals had a different reaction. The product impressed them, but the software had a few technical glitches that betrayed its origins in the desktop world. Professional filmmakers may edit on a computer, but the final product is still output to tape. The product seemed to have been designed more for computer playback than tape output, they believed. "Premiere always demo'd really well," says Fred Mitchell, "but it was years before it was used in production."

"Premiere 1.0 was an engineer's program more than a video editor's program," says David Pratt. "The engineers thought the video playback rate was 30 fps [frames per second]. Turns out it was 29.97 fps, so after a few minutes the sound and video got out of sync. We learned a lot about video doing Premiere." It took a few versions before the audio sync problem was finally resolved, but each version of Premiere showed steady improvement in performance and capabilities. By version 4.2, Premiere had come into its own as a complete video-editing tool.

The traditional video-editing companies took notice. Avid, which saw that desktop applications were making headway against its proprietary systems, launched its own software to run on off-the-shelf desktop hardware. Many

Produced by DV artist Glen Janssens, this promotional video emphasized Premiere's ability to create special effects using Photoshop filters.

APRIL GREIMAN

In the brief history of digital design few people are already legends—April Greiman is one of them. She developed an instant affinity with the Macintosh in 1984 and was one of the first professional graphic designers to use PageMaker. She has been using digital tools exclusively ever since. Her early work exploited the chunky pixelated look of early bitmap programs, but she quickly latched on to Photoshop shortly after its release. Ever changing and evolving, Greiman now uses Adobe After Effects in her multimedia pieces such as "light is always looking for a body," shown at the 2001 Aspen Design Conference. She often uses Photoshop and Illustrator to design environmental works such as these murals for the Amgen Corporation's café in Thousand Oaks, California. On a smaller scale, she recently designed the book *Something from Nothing* (text by Aris Janigian and published by Rotovision) with Photoshop, Illustrator, and PageMaker.

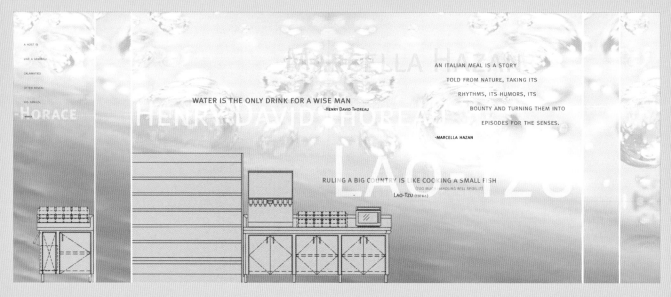

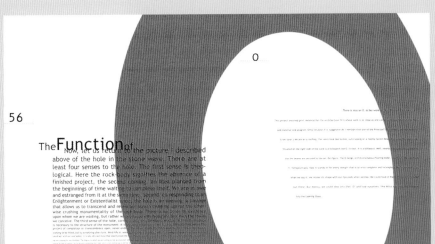

56

The**Function** of

Now, let us return to the picture I described above of the hole in the stone wave. There are at least four senses to the hole. The first sense is theo-logical. Here the rock-body signifies the absence of a finished project, the second coming, an idea planted from the beginnings of time waiting to complete itself. We are in awe and estranged from it at the same time. Second, corresponding to an Enlightenment or Existentialist sense, the hole is an opening, a passage that allows us to transcend and retain our human limits by against the other-wise crushing monumentality of the rock-base. There is no Order. It is we upon whom we are waiting, but rather who propose only, to fill the hole with the money we conceive. The third sense of the hole, corresponding to the Relativist mode, is necessary to the structure of the monument. It is itself a place. It projects of completion as transcendence open, never ended...

V V

*"I like the unpredictable
factor of Photoshop:
the possibility of
just setting out on
a digital journey."*

professional video editors who wanted to use desktop tools but wanted a familiar experience opted for Avid's software rather than Premiere.

Other competition came from Adobe's own backyard: Premiere's original engineer, Randy Ubillos, left Adobe for rival software maker Macromedia, where he was to develop a product to compete with Premiere. Ultimately Apple acquired the rights to Ubillos's in-development video product, and he went to Apple to finish what is now known as Final Cut Pro. On the Macintosh platform, Final Cut Pro currently outsells Premiere.

In 1993 Adobe released Premiere for the Windows operating system. Premiere 6.0 for Windows is now the market leader on that platform. Premiere has also been very successful in school settings where its price point and accessible interface make it an obvious choice for students.

Adobe added another tool to its digital video belt when it gained After Effects through its acquisition of Aldus in 1994. A postproduction video effects application developed by the Company of Science and Art (CoSA), After Effects is like Photoshop for the video world, and like Photoshop it democratized an industry dominated by high-end equipment and an elite cadre of practitioners.

With After Effects, video artists can layer moving images to make video collages and add special typographic effects that make title sequences come alive. As the software grew in sophistication, it migrated from adding spice to desktop projects to holding its own in commercial films. Many of the opening titles and closing credits used in Hollywood movies today are created in After Effects. Like Photoshop, too, After Effects includes filters for applying advanced visual effects so that objects can shatter or melt over time. After Effects has proven useful for media other than film. It's also used extensively in Web production as a means of animating graphics. An immediate hit when it was released, After Effects rules the roost for desktop video effects.

Warnock's insight when signing the Premiere contract proved to be right, however. Desktop video did not replicate the phenomenal growth of desktop publishing. For all the technical breakthroughs and educational efforts, digital video seemed too complicated to most users. The costs associated with it were still high, too. It required costly specialized hardware, expensive video cameras, additional software components, and so on. It wasn't convenient to share or distribute homemade videos, either. The files were too big to email, the CD-ROM playback quality was appalling, and videotapes were cumbersome to mail. Many of the companies that had staked their future on digital video were absorbed into other companies or went out of business. "Premiere predated the Internet, so there were a limited number of output options for it," says Mitchell. "But with the Internet, there are lot more options for how video is used

---

BizStats: **1992**

No. of employees: 887

Revenue: $266 million

Stock price range: $13 to $35

Acquisitions: OCR Systems, Nonlinear Technologies

Product releases:
 Dimensions 1.0
 Illustrator 4.0
 Premiere 2.0 (Mac)
 Streamline 3.0

Other:
>> Geschke held for five days by kidnappers

LYNDA WEINMAN

Lynda Weinman's career continues to evolve, from learning the ropes in traditional film to establishing herself as pioneer in Web graphics to creating a mini-empire in educational materials and instructional courses about Photoshop, After Effects, and other creative tools. As the author of the groundbreaking book *Designing Web Graphics*, Weinman was an early advocate of using Photoshop in conjunction with the World Wide Web. These images from her personal portfolio were created in After Effects. (www.lynda.com)

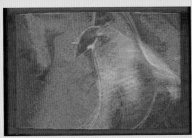  

and distributed." Today, too, all personal computers are video savvy, and many are equipped with drives to play and record video in the DVD format. Video playback can be onscreen, over the Internet, or on television. Digital video cameras and high-speed connections such as FireWire make it easy to bring home movies into the computer.

"Today, our video applications are our fastest-growing graphics product line," says Bryan Lamkin, senior vice president of Adobe's graphics business unit.

Premiere was an example of Adobe's being ahead of its time. It was not the last time Adobe had to wait for the market to catch up to its vision. But nothing tried the company's patience as much as a suite of tools and technologies it called Acrobat.

Adobe

Words → Take the Digital Road with Adobe

communication type proposals newsletter information numbers information

Acrobat: The Early Days

In 1993 Adobe released a product that signaled even more changes ahead for the company. Adobe's early era revolved around PostScript and the systems division. Its current growth stemmed from applications such as Photoshop and Premiere. But its future lay with Acrobat and PDF.

Acrobat is a suite of applications for creating and viewing documents in an Adobe-developed file format called PDF (Portable Document Format). It would take five years to gain momentum, but Acrobat, like PostScript and Photoshop, became a significant product and technology platform for Adobe and for the publishing industry. Given its less-than-auspicious start, no one at the time could have believed that Acrobat would play such an important role in Adobe's future—no one, that is, except John Warnock.

Imagining Camelot

In 1991, Warnock wrote a memo that outlined a technology enabling the exchange and delivery of documents, anytime, anywhere, and on any device. The project, then called Camelot, set out to eliminate the difficulties hampering "our ability to communicate visual material between different computer applications and systems."

Unlike common text files, which can be passed around via word-processing applications, the documents Warnock envisioned were visually rich, composed pages. Like PostScript, Camelot allowed complex layouts containing both text and graphics to be presented in a device-independent manner. But with Camelot the focus was not on printing to an output device but on displaying pages on any screen and on any platform. The similarity to PostScript was not accidental, of course. This new document format was, in fact, derived from the way PostScript renders text and graphics onscreen.

Warnock called this technology Interchange PostScript (IPS). "IPS will primarily contain the graphics and imaging operators of PostScript," he wrote. "The language will be defined so that any IPS file is a valid PostScript file. The file will have the appropriate baggage so that it is a valid EPS file. IPS files will print on PostScript printers and will be able to be used by applications that accept EPS files." He went on to say that IPS files would not need a full PostScript interpreter, only pieces of it. "The right way to think about IPS is as it relates to English. No person in the world knows every English word, but a small subset of the English words, and certain usage patterns enable people to consistently communicate."

"Today's paper-based information is hampered by the physical media. Acrobat technology liberates information and the flow of ideas."

— John Warnock

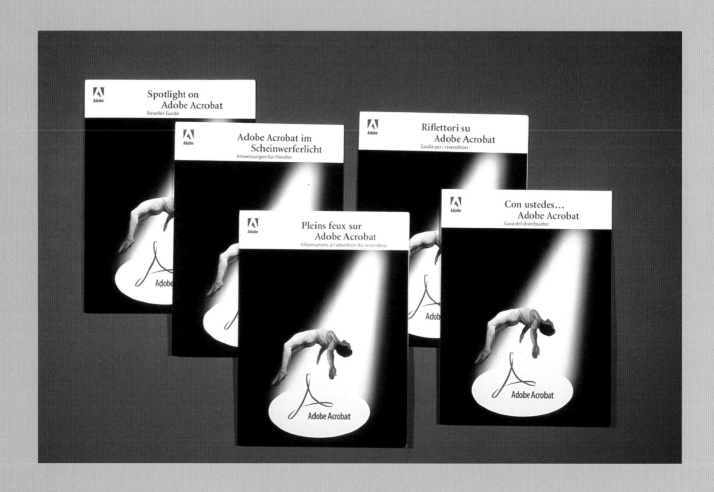

Calling the new technology a variation on PostScript was technically true—they shared the same imaging model—but it was also misleading. PostScript is a programming language that describes the attributes of a page and relies on an interpreter to place page elements in the proper position when the page is printed. PDF is not a language but a file format that contains a stylized PostScript font and graphics descriptions that can be referenced from any part of the file. The programming elements are eliminated, but the graphical elements remain, so that an original document can be perfectly replicated. A PDF file can be sent across networks and platforms with its visual integrity intact, regardless of the recipient's operating system or even whether the right fonts are installed on the viewing machine.

Another key technical distinction is that PostScript is designed for the linear process of printing. Even if you only want to print page 79 out of 80, the PostScript interpreter has to walk through the file page by page in sequence until it reaches the page in question. Acrobat, on the other hand, produces PDF files optimized for random access. If you want to read or print page 79, Acrobat takes you right to it. Compared with PostScript files, which can be large and unwieldy, PDF files are compact and readily available. Such a file structure lends itself to storage in databases and to efficient transmission via telecommunications.

"My frame of mind was that we had tons of PostScript files out there, but they required too big of a machine for widespread distribution," Warnock says. "I thought it would be great if we could print these files reliably anywhere even without the fonts. With PostScript if you didn't have the fonts, you'd have to ship them with the file, making it even bigger. We developed automatic font substitution and that worked like a champ."

The Camelot-IPS concept had its public debut under the code name Carousel in the fall of 1991 at Seybold Seminars in San Jose. Less than a year later, Adobe unveiled PDF. In 1993, the tools for creating and viewing PDF files were released, now bearing the name Acrobat.

The Paperless Office

For a company that up until then had staked its fortune on printing marks on paper, Adobe's positioning of PDF as a means to the "paperless office" seemed odd to some followers. The book-loving Warnock knew that Acrobat could never entirely replace paper in people's lives, but for document-centric organizations such as large corporations, accounting firms, and government agencies, Acrobat was an efficient and cost-effective means of communicating information.

One comparison Adobe made to tout the merits of the Acrobat solution was to faxed documents. Fax machines were dedicated devices that used

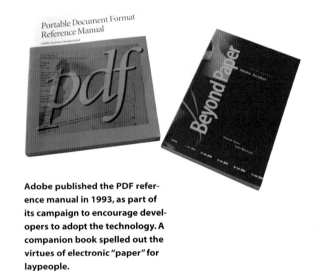

Adobe published the PDF reference manual in 1993, as part of its campaign to encourage developers to adopt the technology. A companion book spelled out the virtues of electronic "paper" for laypeople.

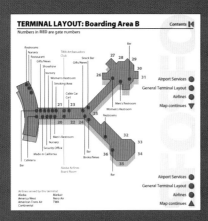

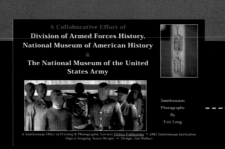

Acrobatic PDF Files

These examples show the breadth of the market Adobe was trying to reach with Acrobat, and the versatility of the PDF format.

a slow communications protocol in the phone line. The form of a faxed document remained true to the original, but the quality was poor and the appearance degraded over time. By contrast, electronic Acrobat files were high-quality, visually rich documents transportable via email or other network options. As Warnock said in a 1993 press release for Acrobat's formal unveiling, "Today's paper-based information is hampered by the physical media. Acrobat technology liberates information and the flow of ideas and allows it to enter the electronic age."

By having an electronic file that could be passed from user to user, from platform to platform, and across mixed networks, corporations could eliminate the paper memos piled in in-boxes and on desks. Of course, many Windows users believed they had such a solution in Microsoft Word, whose sheer ubiquity in the office environment ensured that anyone with a PC could open a .doc file. But using word processors as a file-exchange mechanism was like operating within a proprietary system: the recipient had to have the entire application installed, hope that it was the right version, and have the correct fonts available or else resort to standbys like Times or Arial.

Like PostScript, which liberated publications from the closed printing and typesetting industries, Acrobat freed documents from the constraints of vendor-specific applications and file formats. "We designed Acrobat

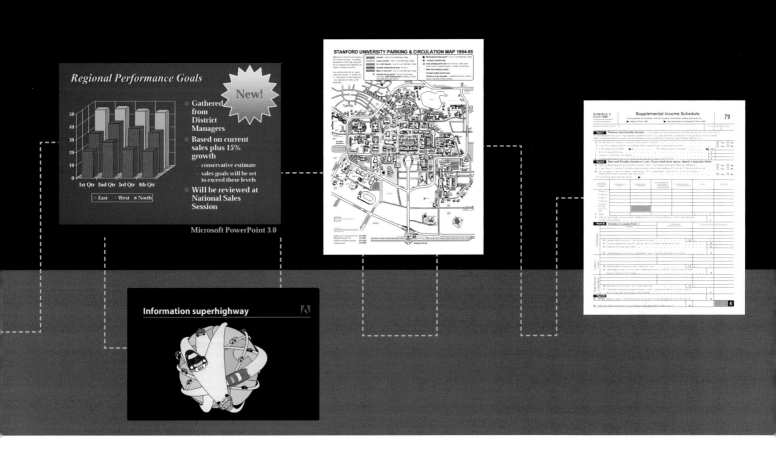

so that it grabbed the PostScript print stream, which meant that any application that could write PostScript—PageMaker, Microsoft Word, PowerPoint—could be captured as PDF," explains Warnock. With Acrobat, anyone could send bandwidth-efficient files via email to anyone else. For a printed copy, all the viewer had to do was press the Print key in the PDF reader application. "This way, you transfer the cost of paper printing to you and me," says Chuck Geschke. The financial upside for companies could be huge. By using PDF files for external communication, the sender communicated a visually rich message while cutting out the costs associated with printing and mailing. Using Acrobat for internal communications had an even greater upside. Adobe mandated early on that its own internal documents be produced as PDF files. After its first year of using Acrobat exclusively, Adobe said it had saved more than $1 million in printing costs.

PDF files had another compelling advantage: because PDFs are essentially images of the original document, PDFs were uneditable. They could be annotated but not materially changed, making them suitable for security-conscious institutions. A prime candidate for PDF would be something like a tax form. In fact, Warnock has said that he got the idea for PDF when hand-programming a federal tax-return form in PostScript back in 1984. By using a PostScript technique called "graph bind" Warnock was able to reduce the print time of the file from more than two minutes to just 22 seconds. Many years later, the IRS would become Adobe's biggest client by converting its paper forms into PDF files.

Market Contortions

Inside Adobe, Acrobat was a great idea and an exciting new direction for the company. Outside Adobe, it was another story. Adobe's freewheeling graphic arts customers were somewhat baffled by the company's embrace of corporate document management. There was nothing creative or sexy or imaginative about making an accounting form, no matter how good the graphics or font fidelity. "Acrobat just didn't fit the graphics mode," says Fred Mitchell.

Adobe hoped that adoption by corporate customers would lead to acceptance by its traditional customer base, but Adobe's product line and pricing structure initially deterred individuals from purchasing Acrobat. The suite of applications comprised three components, each priced separately: Acrobat Exchange, used for creating and viewing PDF files, cost $195 for a single-user license; Acrobat Reader, for viewing PDF files, cost $50 for a single-user license; and Acrobat Distiller, for converting PostScript files to PDF, cost $695 for a single-user license. Volume licenses were more cost-effective, of course. But even those individual users who could afford Acrobat wondered why they should bother. As there was negligible content available in PDF format, there was little need to purchase an application to read it.

But if Acrobat didn't fit the graphics mode, Adobe didn't fit the business mold. "Adobe didn't have an organization that called on the business market," says Steve MacDonald. Up until then, the Adobe sales force either sold PostScript licenses to OEMs or plied the retail and mail-order sales channel with graphics arts software. Adobe did make some sales to large corporations, but they were to the information technology (IT) department in charge of buying printers. Enterprise publishing sales were another matter entirely.

"The people we were used to calling on weren't the people we needed to be calling on," says Clinton Nagy, who left the PostScript sales division to head up Acrobat sales to the enterprise market. "It wasn't the IT department we should have been talking to but the publishing department." But when Adobe found its way to the right people, it often hit another wall. "The enterprise thought we were a graphic applications company. We spent a lot of time educating them," Nagy adds.

To say it was slow going would be an understatement. "We failed to meet revenue expectations every quarter," Nagy says of Acrobat's first three years. Internal debate raged about whether the product should be killed,

"I thought everybody would get Acrobat immediately. I didn't think it would take 10 years."

—**John Warnock**

yet the sales team doggedly pursued customers. "No one ever said, 'You guys aren't doing your job.' We had the funding and the internal support, so we had the confidence to go forward."

Acrobat's biggest supporter, of course, was Warnock himself. "I thought everybody would get Acrobat immediately," he says. "I didn't think it would take 10 years." His insistence that Acrobat continue was the main reason the product survived.

Equal Citizens

However slowly, progress was being made. Adobe's model for Acrobat within the corporation revolved around in-house communications—the central storage and widespread distribution of critical files via Acrobat. Many companies saw the benefit of such a strategy but didn't yet see the demand for it. Then with Acrobat Capture, which enables paper documents to be scanned and converted into PDFs, Adobe hit on another approach. "We'd tell them we could preserve the character of their documents—not only those created today but the ones created yesterday. We'd tell them to scan their old files: Go back to the paper files stashed away in cardboard boxes. Make your legacy paper docs equal citizens of your electronic files," says Nagy. That concept struck a chord.

As customers gradually signed on, the Adobe team tried to use those early adopters to leverage new prospects. But some customers balked, refusing to advertise their use of Acrobat and PDF because they considered it proprietary information or a secret weapon in corporate one-upmanship. Eventually word got out.

To those inside Adobe, Acrobat's slow adoption was perplexing. New products were rarely overnight hits—but to a company that had had a string of successes, Acrobat had the whiff of failure. Warnock persevered, insisting that Acrobat was a sound idea. The company continued to pour more money into its development, raising more than one eyebrow. "All these antibodies wanted to kill it internally," says Geschke.

Warnock and Geschke presented a united front to protect Acrobat. "By now we had an historical precedent," says Warnock. "Applications didn't pay for themselves; they had to be supported by systems. Now we wanted applications to support Acrobat. We were making an obscene amount of money on Photoshop, so why were we spending 200 man-hours on Acrobat? Because it's like the applications business. It'll take longer than we thought."

In 1994 Adobe released Acrobat 2.0, which included interactive features like the ability to embed multimedia elements and to link to external files. Adobe also made changes to the product lineup, and confusingly added two more packages: Acrobat Pro, which contained Exchange 2.0

BizStats: **1993**

No. of employees: 999

Revenue: $313 million

Stock price range: $15 to $37

Acquisitions: After Hours Software, CoSA (Company of Science & Art)

Product releases:
Acrobat 1.0
Illustrator 5.0 (Mac)
Photoshop 2.5
Premiere 3.0 (Mac) and 1.0 (Windows)

Other:
>> Adobe licenses PostScript software to printer manufacturers

2-for-1 stock split on August 11, 1993

and Distiller; and Acrobat for Workgroups, which contained Exchange, Distiller, and a new Catalog product for network environments.

Most important, Adobe decided to distribute the Acrobat Reader free of charge. This was a significant policy shift. "Our attitude was that we don't give away elegant technology," says Nagy. "But the impetus inside the company and with financial analysts was that we needed to do that." External pressure was strong. Competitive products did not charge for reading mechanisms, thus putting Acrobat at a disadvantage because Adobe charged a fee to both create and read PDF files.

Adobe realized it was necessary to sacrifice revenue in order to establish Acrobat as a standard. "It was a chicken-and-egg situation. We needed to get the reader out there, but we needed to have great content to read. Charging for the reader only made it worse," Mitchell says. "Making the reader free meant it was downloaded in higher volumes but still there was limited content. We had to have a ubiquitous reader and valuable content." With the free reader available in several ways, such as bundled with other Adobe products or downloaded from online services, the impediment to content creation was removed, and Acrobat started to gain traction.

But there was still the issue of PDF distribution. "The concept of Acrobat was to transfer a document all over the place while retaining its formatting," says Steve MacDonald, "but how did you get it to anyone?"

The answer came in 1993. At the University of Illinois a college kid by the name of Marc Andreessen had the idea to create a graphical user interface for the Internet, the global information network used primarily by educators and the military. As the first browser for the World Wide Web, Mosaic gave form to the vast amounts of data. In mid-1994 Andreessen joined with Silicon Valley veteran Jim Clark to start Netscape, a company based on the Netscape Navigator Web browser, formerly known as Mosaic. Back at Adobe, Warnock began talking about the Internet, pondering its applicability to Adobe and specifically to Acrobat.

Nagy recalls sitting with Warnock at Seybold Seminars in 1994 as Sun Microsystems technologist John Gage talked about Mosaic and its impact on the way information was published. "Gage finished and Warnock said, 'It's the Internet and that's the future.' The lightbulb went off. The Net became the transportation mechanism for Acrobat."

Acrobat still needed a few more years to reach its potential, but Adobe had more immediate concerns. At that same Seybold Seminars in September 1994, Warnock and Geschke had just announced the biggest deal of the company's existence: Adobe agreed to merge with old friend and occasional foe Aldus Corporation.

> "Our attitude was that we don't give away elegant technology"
>
> —Clinton Nagy

ADOBE HOLDS ITS BREATH

Adobe's period of prosperity and calm was horribly interrupted on May 26,1992, when cofounder Chuck Geschke was kidnapped from the parking lot of the Charleston Road offices. Spurred by media reports of Adobe's corporate and Geschke's personal financial success, two men who claimed to have ties to terrorist organizations held Geschke bound and blindfolded for five days in exchange for $650,000.

During his incarceration, few people outside Geschke's family and local and federal authorities knew what had happened. John Warnock was the first person Geschke's wife Nan informed. She feared that Warnock would suffer a similar fate, but it was more than that: The two men and their families are extremely close, and the Warnocks formed a tight circle around the Geschkes for the duration of the ordeal.

After the FBI eliminated the possibility that the kidnappers had come from within Adobe, Warnock informed six members of the executive team, who were sworn to secrecy lest any leaks jeopardize the negotiations with the kidnappers. The company had to appear as if it were business as usual. Adobe general counsel Colleen Pouliot had to remind anyone who knew about the kidnapping that they could not trade stock in case it was perceived as insider information. "That part was very surreal," recalls Pouliot. "It was just a horrible time. You had to act as if everything was fine, but all the time worrying if he was OK."

"John was worried and preoccupied but he knew he couldn't show it, so he kept his calendar but stayed close to the phone," remembers Janice Coley, Geschke's assistant and one of the first to know that something was wrong when Geschke didn't appear at the office.

Nan and Chuck Geschke

> *"You can't let people take your life away."*
>
> — Chuck Geschke

The FBI rescued Geschke and arrested his kidnappers on Saturday, May 30, but the operation didn't go exactly as planned. "I thought we'd lost him," says Warnock, still critical of the FBI's handling of the recovery. Geschke returned home to find a welcoming committee composed of family, friends, and colleagues. "The first thing he did when he saw me was to apologize," says Coley. "It was typical Chuck. He was apologizing that I'd been inconvenienced by his kidnapping."

Taking care of his immediate family came first, but then only two days after his safe return Geschke appeared before the entire company. "He wanted to tell us what had happened so we wouldn't just read about it in the newspapers," says Dick Sweet, who has worked with Geschke at Xerox PARC and Adobe. "As far as he was concerned, Adobe employees were his family, too." Adds Coley: "He knew that people needed to see him." It was an emotional gathering. "It was fabulous seeing him," says Pouliot. "We were bawling with a mixture of relief and concern and shock."

"I had to tell people. It's part of the company's history," Geschke says now. After his appearance at Adobe's offices, Geschke retreated to his vacation home for a month to recuperate, although he participated in board meetings by phone. He soon resumed his normal schedule.

While still deeply affected by the events of 1992, Geschke has willed his life to return to normal. He characteristically downplays the events of a decade ago. Friends say he is quieter and more aware of his surroundings than before the kidnapping, but Geschke has vowed to live his life on his terms. "You can't let people take your life away," he says.

Acrobat statues balance outside
Adobe's Mountain View offices.

"The Aldus acquisition was a huge turning point for the company. It changed the nature of Adobe."

— Linda Clarke

Expanding the Empire

The mid-1990s was a period of growth and change for both Adobe and the publishing industry. Adobe actively sought out and successfully completed acquisitions of several key companies, foremost among them its 1994 merger with Aldus Corporation, creator of the revolutionary page-layout program PageMaker. That deal alone catapulted Adobe into the upper tiers of personal software companies in terms of revenue. But increased revenue wasn't Adobe's only means of expansion. Publishing itself was undergoing a sea change, from paper-based production to online content distribution. Adobe tested new markets for its software, dipping a toe into the consumer arena and then wading into the tsunami that was the World Wide Web. As the company grew in both market share and influence, however, a raft of new challenges appeared.

1994

Adobe acquires Aldus

- Apple ships
  PowerPC Mac

- Aldus After Effects 1.0 released

- The Internet has
  25 million users;
  Netscape, Yahoo,
  launched

1995

- Industry consolidation: Fractal
  Design buys Ray Dream;
  Macromedia buys Altsys and Fauve

- WWW has 18 million pages

- Sun develops Java

- Acrobat integrated
  into Netscape browser

- Adobe
  acquires Frame
  Technology

- Adobe releases
  PageMaker 6.0,
  Photoshop 3.0,
  PageMill 1.0

1996

- Adobe moves into
  San Jose world
  headquarters

 Revenue: $787 million
  Adobe employees: 2,222

- Microsoft releases Windows 95,
  NT 4.0, and Internet Explorer

- Adobe releases
  Acrobat 3.0,
  PhotoDeluxe 1.0

- Steve Jobs returns
  to Apple, which
  then acquires NeXT

The Era of Acquisitions

The September 1994 Seybold Seminars in San Francisco was a celebration for Adobe. A few weeks before, the company had successfully completed its merger with Aldus Corporation, the creator of PageMaker and one-third of the alliance that had revolutionized publishing in 1985. The combined company—joined under the Adobe Systems name—was the fifth-largest personal software company in the world, occupying turf held by office applications companies like Microsoft and Novell.

The Aldus merger was a turning point for Adobe, but it was just one of several mergers and acquisitions Adobe undertook in the mid-1990s. As it gathered companies and expanded its products and services, Adobe grew in influence, stature, and revenue. At the close of the 20th century, Adobe Systems was one of the world's largest personal software companies, second only to Microsoft.

The Aldus merger, and the Frame Technology acquisition that followed, had a deeper significance for Adobe. The company—once an intimate family of a dozen people whose numbers Warnock swore would never exceed 50—nearly doubled in size from 1,000 to 2,000 people, altering Adobe's culture and forcing the second layoff in the company's history. As it acquired software, Adobe also wrestled with product integration and market development. Nowhere were those issues more pronounced than in Adobe's union with its former co-revolutionary, Aldus.

> *"It was a merger of equals. Aldus had as much to give in this deal as Adobe did. We had products that filled in gaps."*
>
> **— Paul Brainerd**

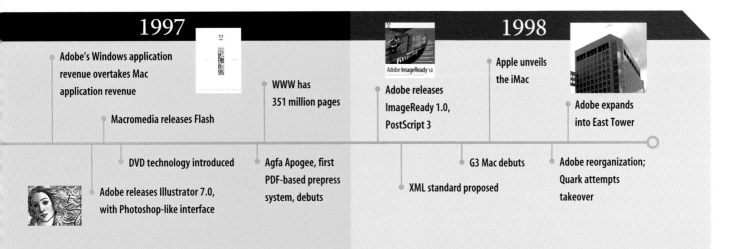

1997

- Adobe's Windows application revenue overtakes Mac application revenue
- Macromedia releases Flash
- WWW has 351 million pages
- DVD technology introduced
- Adobe releases Illustrator 7.0, with Photoshop-like interface
- Agfa Apogee, first PDF-based prepress system, debuts

1998

- Adobe releases ImageReady 1.0, PostScript 3
- Apple unveils the iMac
- Adobe expands into East Tower
- XML standard proposed
- G3 Mac debuts
- Adobe reorganization; Quark attempts takeover

Adobe ImageReady 1.0

Collision Course

Since 1985, the alliance that had created desktop publishing pulled apart, as Adobe, Aldus, and Apple each pursued individual agendas. Proving it could not be narrowly defined as a systems company, Adobe acquired and developed software in emerging markets. Aldus, similarly determined not to be a one-trick company, expanded its product line beyond PageMaker to other graphic arts software applications. Apple continued to reel from management changes—particularly the ouster of Jobs's replacement, John Sculley, and the uncertain leadership of Michael Spindler—and confusing product plans. The Adobe-Apple relationship, already frayed by the events of 1989, had been patched up under a new font-technology cross-licensing agreement, but the two former partners were no longer dependent on each other for their livelihood.

Adobe and Aldus, on the other hand, had been on a collision course for several years. Both companies had products that directly competed with the other's. In 1988 Aldus licensed a PostScript drawing program from Texas-based Altsys Corporation. Called FreeHand, the program was locked in a fierce battle for market share with Adobe's favorite son, Illustrator. While Adobe developed Photoshop for the Mac, in 1991 Aldus acquired PhotoStyler, a pixel-based image-editing program for Windows, and Adobe responded by releasing Photoshop for Windows in 1993. Also in 1993, Aldus acquired After Effects along with its developer CoSA (Company of Science and Art). After Effects, a postproduction special-effects package for moving images, was positioned as Aldus's entry into the video market—assuming a role similar to that played by Premiere for Adobe. Aldus had products that didn't compete with Adobe, too, such as the office presentation program Persuasion, a handful of consumer-oriented packages, and of course the granddaddy, PageMaker.

But whereas Adobe was prospering, Aldus was struggling. Its top two moneymakers—PageMaker and FreeHand—were second in their respective categories. QuarkXPress, developed by Denver-based Quark Inc., had overtaken PageMaker in the professional design market, and Illustrator was well ahead of FreeHand. Recent product and technology acquisitions like the purchase of After Hours Software, the developer of address book and calendar software, strained Aldus's resources. The company's profit margins were wafer-thin. For the 1992 fiscal year, Aldus reported revenues of $174 million but profits of just $6.8 million.

Paul Brainerd, who founded Aldus in 1984 with $100,000 of his own money, was tiring of the constant pressure. "I had been doing the annual update to our strategic plan as well as the three-year projections, and I could see that the industry was changing," says Aldus's former president and CEO. "The smaller niche players were struggling, the margins shrinking, the distribution channels consolidating. Plus, I was doing less

Aldus had recently acquired After Effects from CoSA, which bolstered Adobe's desktop video efforts.

"Aldus's culture was more like Apple's— freewheeling and loose. Adobe was much more conservative."

— Linda Clarke

Adobe and the Art of Acquisition

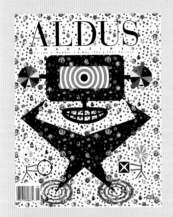

Adobe's vice president of venture development, Fred Mitchell, reckons he's seen thousands of companies since 1987, when he was first given the assignment of scouting new products and technologies. Some companies came to Adobe seeking an investment; others were ripe for acquisition. Mitchell decided which candidates made the cut to show John Warnock. "We'd been doing this a long time, John and I. He relied on my ability to do the early evaluation on these ideas, and he trusted me to not miss too many things," Mitchell says. "I've followed up on hundreds of opportunities and would show John two to five a month."

Warnock was a quick study. "He was adept at synthesizing the ideas and reducing the technology to its simplest terms," Mitchell says. "In each meeting he challenged himself to understand the product at a conceptual level." For entrepreneurs, making the pilgrimage to Adobe was akin to journeying to the gleaming city for an audience with the great and powerful Warnock. "It was hard to show him something really new," Mitchell says. Chances were, Warnock had already thought of it.

Here's a list of companies that Adobe acquired.

1991 Emerald City Software (TypeAlign font-manipulation software)

1992 OCR Systems (technology for Acrobat Capture)

1992 Nonlinear Technologies (handwriting-recognition software)

1993 After Hours Software (TouchBase and DateBook personal-information managers, acquired by Aldus)

1993 The Company of Science and Art (After Effects postproduction video software, acquired by Aldus)

1994 Aldus (PageMaker, Persuasion, FreeHand, PhotoStyler, TrapWise, PressWise, and more)

1994 LaserTools (font-scaling technology for non-PostScript printers; became PrintGear)

1994 Compumation (Color Central prepress software, acquired by Aldus)

1995 Frame Technology (FrameMaker)

1995 Ceneca Communications (PageMill and SiteMill Web site–creation software)

1995 Visualware

1995 Hyphen (printer software)

1996 Ares Software (font-scaling software)

1996 Swell Software (Web server software)

1997 DigiDox (personalized PDF-creation software)

> *"Just as we were starting to catch our breath, Frame happened."*
> — Linda Clarke

> *"I followed up on hundreds of opportunities."*
> — Fred Mitchell

1997 Sandcastle (two-way Internet communication technology)

1997 FinePoint (Web graphics software for ImageReady)

1999 GoLive (Web design software)

1999 Attitude Software (3D technologies)

1999 Photomerge (photostitching software for panoramic images)

2000 Glassbook (software for creating, reading, and deploying e-books)

2001 Fotiva (image-management and image-sharing software)

2002 Accelio (electronic forms solutions)

of the things I like to do—customer relations and product development—because I was spending too much time with stock analysts and attorneys."

As early as 1991, Brainerd told his board of directors that he wanted to relinquish the reins of the company when it reached its 10-year anniversary. Aldus retained an executive recruiter to find a successor for Brainerd, but replacing the founder of a company is always difficult and no viable candidate had appeared by 1993. The company's declining profits didn't help the search, and by the fall of 1993 Brainerd decided to look at selling or merging the company. "I went back to the board with a list of potentials. One of them was Adobe," Brainerd says. "I arranged to have breakfast with John Warnock."

Merging Traffic

On the surface the merger was a good fit. Aldus's products aimed at print publishing, interactive publishing, graphics, and production-service providers dovetailed with Adobe's. Aldus's prepress software meshed nicely with Adobe's PostScript systems division. Adobe wasn't terribly interested in Aldus's consumer products, but the low-end page-layout and graphics applications, such as Home Publisher, SuperPaint, and IntelliDraw, provided steady if unspectacular income.

There was significant overlap in the companies' graphics and interactive lineups, but the deal did secure for Adobe a foothold in the page-layout market. Adobe needed a page-layout program to sell its message of integrated communication products, and despite PageMaker's waning professional influence, it still had many loyal customers. Above all, a small group within Aldus was working on a next-generation page-layout program that Warnock and Geschke thought showed promise. Acquiring Aldus would be an investment in the future of page layout.

Warnock, Geschke, and Brainerd announced the merger at a press conference in March 1994. The deal was presented as a merger of equals but in reality was an acquisition. Aldus's revenues were approximately two-thirds that of Adobe's, but its profits were one-tenth. For the nine months prior to the merger, Aldus reported a net income of $5.1 million on revenues of $172.2 million while Adobe reported a net income of $49.3 million on revenues of $260.1 million. Aldus was a proud company, however. Although the basic terms of the deal were hammered out over the next four months, former CFO Bruce Nakao says the agreement underwent constant revisions. "An analyst described it to me as two fat pigs eating each other," says Nakao of the negotiations.

Regardless of what happened in the boardroom, each company was committed to making the transition as easy as possible for its employees. A team of representatives from Aldus and Adobe met regularly to work

breaking ground new

ALDUS

To explain the logic of the Adobe-Aldus merger, Geschke, Warnock, and Brainerd (pictured individually from left) made a videotape for employees, scenes of which are shown above.

through the details of the merger. "It was a textbook example of how to do it, marked by planning and communication and clarity," Brainerd says. "We were very focused. As we were two equal-size companies, we paid a lot of attention to the employees." Warnock, Geschke, and Brainerd held company meetings to answer questions and made videos to explain the merger to employees.

Gradually a picture of the new company emerged. The combined company, called Adobe Systems, would operate out of both Mountain View and Seattle. Each share of Aldus stock would be converted to a share of Adobe stock, for a final value of $440 million. Brainerd was given a seat on Adobe's board of directors, but he resigned from any day-to-day involvement in the company. As Brainerd owned 23 percent of Aldus, he stood to make a nice return on his $100,000 investment. (Brainerd used much of the proceeds to launch a number of nonprofit organizations, including the Brainerd Foundation, for funding environmental groups, and Social Venture Partners, for funding community activism.)

Aldus PageMaker helped start the desktop publishing revolution, but its market dominance had slipped prior to Adobe's acquisition of it.

Other details of the merger evolved over time. For example, not all of Aldus's 13 products were carried forward under the Adobe label. Except for PageMaker, which Adobe believed its branding would help revive, and After Effects, for which Adobe had no comparable product, Aldus's product lineup overlapped Adobe's. PhotoStyler was redundant with Photoshop. Hitchcock, freshly acquired from the defunct Digital F/X, competed with Premiere. Adobe tried to keep Persuasion afloat, but Microsoft's aggressive sales strategy for its PowerPoint buried it. The pre-press products stayed until 1996, when Adobe spun off its prepress division as Luminous.

Adobe's acquisition of Aldus prompted the construction of a new office complex in Seattle.

Aldus's second-highest revenue-producing product was another matter. FreeHand competed directly with Illustrator, and it also had a large and vocal customer base of users who had deliberately chosen FreeHand over Illustrator. Alienating those prospective Adobe customers would not help the merged companies' future. Adobe was noncommittal when asked about FreeHand's fate, vaguely promising that both would continue for the time being. But then FreeHand developer Altsys forced Aldus and Adobe's hand and nearly scuttled the merger.

Altsys's contract stipulated that Aldus could not market a program that directly competed with FreeHand, which Illustrator most certainly did. Fearing that Adobe would throw all its resources behind its own package and discontinue FreeHand, Altsys sued Aldus in May 1994. The Federal Trade Commission stepped in to investigate whether the merger violated antitrust laws by thwarting competition. "The FTC review got very messy and difficult," Brainerd says. "I think that John and Chuck had given up and thought that they couldn't pull it off. I worked night and day to resolve the issue in Texas."

In August, Adobe and Aldus came to terms with the FTC; they argued that the market for illustration software was large and diverse, as evidenced by the PC-only offerings from Corel and Micrografx as well as by other Mac applications. Aldus settled the lawsuit by agreeing to return

FreeHand to Altsys in January 1995. Adobe rival Macromedia purchased Altsys and FreeHand shortly thereafter.

Changing Lanes

When the merger was completed on August 31, 1994, the real work began of integrating not only the products and personnel of the two companies but also their cultures. Adding to the strain was Adobe's decision to lay off 500 people. Although the cuts affected both companies—Adobe employed about 1,000 people at the time and Aldus about 1,100—former Aldus employees felt singled out because many Aldus products had been cut as well. Remembers Linda Clarke, the former vice president of marketing for the applications division: "Adobe is such a nice company, but it had to show some teeth."

The split between two locations underscored the cultural division. A team of Adobe management embarked on a mission of shuttle diplomacy, flying to Seattle every week to meet with Aldus management. "Several of us would meet at the airport for the 6 a.m. flight," Clarke remembers. "We tried to be ambassadors of Adobe culture, but the distinctions remained. Aldus's culture was more like Apple's—freewheeling and loose. Adobe was much more conservative." A number of key Seattle employees were asked to relocate to the Bay Area. As the company grew to more than 2,000 people, Adobe initiated several construction projects—a larger facility in Seattle and a high-rise headquarters in San Jose, California. Still it would take years for the tension to dissipate between Adobe headquarters in San Jose and its Seattle outpost.

But despite the adjustments of personality and culture, strong positives emerged. Aldus gave Adobe several key products—PageMaker, After Effects, and the as yet unnamed next-generation page-layout program— to which Adobe applied engineering efficiencies and streamlined development processes. Aldus had had discrete teams (Warnock describes them as "silos" operating like separate companies) dedicated to each product. Adobe, on the other hand, shared critical components across product lines. It was clear to Adobe that a major restructuring of the Aldus business was in order. Warnock and Geschke agree that the product integration they envisioned when they bought Aldus was much harder to achieve than they had imagined.

On the other hand, Aldus had more robust marketing and distribution channels than relative applications newcomer Adobe. "It was a merger of equals," says Brainerd. "We had as much to give in this deal as they did. We had products that filled in gaps. Our distribution was better than theirs, especially internationally: at least 50 percent of our revenues came from international sales. Within 12 months of the merger, international sales increased 50 percent for Adobe."

Following the Aldus merger, Adobe expanded into international markets, setting up sales outposts in Canada, France, Japan, Scandinavia, and India, among other locations.

BizStats: 1994

No. of employees: 1,587

Revenue: $598 million

Stock price range: $30 to $39

Acquisitions: Aldus, LaserTools, Compumation

Product releases:
Illustrator 5.5 (Mac)
Adobe Type Manager 3.0
Premiere 4.0
Acrobat 2.0
Dimensions 2.0
After Effects 1.0

Other:
>> Aldus acquisition brings PageMaker to Adobe
Adobe Ventures founded
Construction begins on San Jose headquarters

Industry:
Macromedia acquires Altsys
HSC Software releases Live Picture
Netscape, Yahoo, and W3C launched

AN INTERNATIONAL MAGAZINE

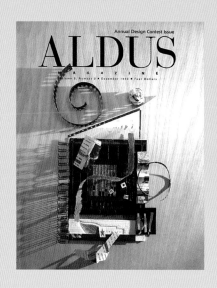

Launched in 1989, *Aldus* magazine was more than a marketing vehicle for Aldus products. It also earned a reputation for exemplary graphic design and sound technical advice.

Adobe continued the magazine's success, expanding international distribution and reaching 600,000 in circulation under its own imprint before suspending publication in 2000.

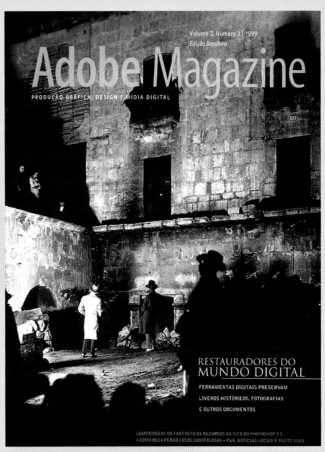

Adobe's marketing team began mining Aldus's customer base immediately. "We couldn't wait to start cross-marketing our stuff with Aldus," Clarke says. "Our sandbox had just gotten bigger." Because half of Aldus's sales were international, Adobe relocated its European headquarters to Aldus's base in Edinburgh, Scotland, under the direction of Aldus's Derek Gray. In fact, today approximately half Adobe's sales come from international markets. The seeds for Adobe's success overseas were sown in the European business started by Aldus and in the Japanese office created by Aldus in the late 1980s.

One of the marketing devices now available to Adobe was Aldus's highly respected self-titled magazine. Launched in 1989, *Aldus* featured tips and techniques for using Aldus products, written by the engineers and product managers themselves. Notable freelance authors and industry experts contributed stories on topics ranging from the best typefaces for a particular project to the specifications for paper in offset printing. Although primarily a marketing vehicle, the magazine competed favorably with established, independently published magazines and earned a reputation for offering useful information, showcasing great design, and exemplifying digital production values. Published six times a year and distributed free to registered users, the magazine peaked at a circulation of 600,000. Under the Adobe imprint, the magazine continued to thrive until it was discontinued in 2000 as part of a cost-cutting move.

Given the expanded customer base and increased marketing opportunities, Adobe put initiatives in place to achieve profitability by the end of the first quarter of 1995—six months after the merger was final. Mission accomplished: The fourth quarter of 1994 ended with a net loss of $48.1 million; the first quarter of 1995 ended with a net gain of $36.1 million. The turnaround was proof that Adobe's merger with Aldus, despite the rough spots, was a success. Adobe would not be so lucky with its next acquisition.

Building a Framework

Unlike the Aldus deal, which was positioned as a merger, Adobe's acquisition of Frame Technology was just that: an acquisition. Adobe had considered buying Frame, developer of the structured-document layout package FrameMaker, in August 1993, but the timing wasn't right. "John was enamored of the Frame technology," Nakao says. "He thought it superior to PageMaker." But when Geschke tallied up how many people would need to be laid off, he balked.

In 1995 Frame's management put the company up for sale. Warnock's interest hadn't waned. He perceived in FrameMaker an entrée into the technical- and long-document publishing market, one dominated by Unix workstations in government and corporate installations. Although

The Aldus and Frame acquisitions filled gaps in Adobe's page-layout lineup, with PageMaker and FrameMaker, respectively.

FrameMaker is technically a page-layout program, the market served by FrameMaker, which requires that the content of templated documents be updated frequently, is very different from that served by PageMaker, which emphasizes creative expression through graphic design. In FrameMaker, too, Warnock saw a kindred application to his other pet project, Acrobat. FrameMaker supported SGML (Standard Generalized Markup Language), a cross-platform, database-like method of presenting information, and it even had an Acrobat Viewer–like application in FrameViewer.

But few people in Adobe's top tier of management shared Warnock's passion. "Nobody wanted to do the Frame acquisition except John," says David Pratt, head of the applications division. "We couldn't justify the purchase, but John believed it would pay off in the long run." The lack of enthusiasm also stemmed from fatigue. The year of nonstop effort that had gone into integrating Aldus into Adobe had taken its toll on key staff members. "Just as we were starting to catch our breath, Frame happened," Clarke says. "As a result there was not the level of zeal and commitment that we had with Aldus."

But Warnock was undeterred, and in June 1995 Adobe announced its intention to acquire Frame in a deal valued at more than $500 million. In the following week, Adobe's stock took a beating, losing 18 percent of its value. There was more bad news. After the deal was finalized in October 1995, Adobe discovered that it had to absorb unanticipated restructuring expenses of $21.1 million from Frame's previous operations. As a result, Adobe reported a net loss of $11.7 million for the fourth fiscal quarter of 1995. Overnight its stock lost 30 percent of its value.

Greg Gilley, now vice president of engineering for the graphics business unit, helped bring Aldus's product line into the Adobe fold.

Warnock remains bullish on FrameMaker to this day, asserting that the program fits nicely with Adobe's new Network Publishing initiatives, especially now that FrameMaker has supplemented SGML with support for the industry-standard XML (eXtensible Markup Language) and Adobe's own XMP (eXtensible Metadata Platform), which enables the publishing of dynamic content on multiple platforms and in multiple media types. "FrameMaker is a wonderful product," Warnock says, adding that "XML will rule the world of structured documents." He explains that magazines, newsletters, brochures, or advertisements—the types of documents produced in programs like PageMaker—are almost never updated. "FrameMaker is targeted at user manuals, database publications, and long documents that are constantly updated," he says. "Because Web sites themselves are like long, complex documents that are also constantly updated, FrameMaker fits with where the Web is going."

Growing by Leaps and Bounds

Adobe's period of expansion didn't stop at large companies or deals worth a half-billion dollars. In October 1995, it also acquired Ceneca

Communications, developer of the Web applications PageMill and SiteMill, for $15 million. Prior to its merger, Aldus had been in the process of acquiring several companies subsequently absorbed by Adobe, including prepress systems developer Compumation in March 1994 and font and clip-art supplier Image Club Graphics in May 1994. Adobe ultimately spun off all prepress operations into a separate company called Luminous in January 1996. Image Club morphed into Adobe Studio, a source for visual design elements, before it returned to its original owners under the EyeWire label in 1998.

"The Aldus acquisition was a huge turning point for the company," Clarke says. "It changed the nature of Adobe." There was one other way in which the merger changed Adobe: it brought in a consumer-products division headed by a software veteran named Bruce Chizen.

Finding the Consumer Market

When Adobe acquired Aldus in 1994, it inherited a division dedicated to consumers who dabbled in layout and imaging for personal projects or for fun. This class of customer was a far cry from the creative professionals who formed the core of Adobe's clientele, those who made a livelihood from the design and production of publications and documents. The products targeting the home or small-business user by necessity had lower sticker prices, and by extension lower margins, than their professional-level cousins, which made it difficult to justify development expenses.

The consumer market did represent new opportunities. The cost of computers had been declining steadily, making it easier for average folks to purchase a system for home use. Low-cost scanners and printers were more readily available, too, which inspired computer-savvy parents and kids to incorporate photos into home-printed calendars, greeting cards, and school projects. A new product category for digital cameras was attracting the dollars of snapshot-happy hobbyists. In time, this market segment would become an area of phenomenal growth for graphics and imaging companies. Much as desktop publishing had wrenched control away from proprietary typesetting shops, so did the availability of inexpensive equipment and easy-to-use software make it possible for average folk to publish materials.

Adobe had little interest in entering that market at first. It was a distraction, and shedding the division would mean one less thing to worry about in the merger's aftermath. But one voice successfully urged the company to reconsider and in so doing helped Adobe build a new business.

Consumer Central

In fall 1993, Aldus CEO Paul Brainerd met with a candidate to lead Aldus's consumer group. Bruce Chizen had been general manager at the Claris Clear Choice division of Claris Corporation, an Apple subsidiary and maker of database software FileMaker. Because Aldus's board was still searching for a successor to Brainerd, Chizen realized he'd be taking a job where he didn't know who his boss would be. "I told Paul that I wasn't interested if there wasn't a president," Chizen says. The two men promised to stay in touch.

In January 1994, Brainerd recontacted Chizen and asked if he would meet with someone. He was told go to a hotel near the San Francisco airport, where he would be required to sign a nondisclosure agreement. After

"My first thought was, Why would Chuck Geschke want to leave Adobe to be president of Aldus?"

— Bruce Chizen

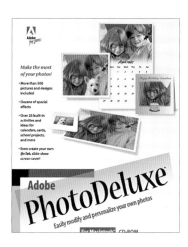

PhotoDeluxe, the first Adobe product targeted to consumers, quickly became the best-selling consumer photoediting product on the market in 1998.

Photoshop Elements, released in 2001, replaced PhotoDeluxe and advanced Adobe's consumer-oriented initiatives.

he signed, Chizen knocked on a hotel-room door and, as he entered, saw Geschke sitting with Brainerd. "My first thought was, Why would Chuck Geschke want to leave Adobe to be president of Aldus?" Chizen recalls. Brainerd informed Chizen of the impending merger and asked him again if he was interested in heading up the consumer division. According to Chizen, Geschke acknowledged that none of them really knew what the future held as a result of the merger. "I didn't know what was going to happen either, but I knew I liked this guy," Chizen says. Chizen joined Aldus in February 1994, just prior to the merger's announcement, and became the vice president and general manager of Adobe's Consumer Products Division when the merger was completed in August.

The consumer division, which operated under both Aldus and Adobe as a separate business unit, grew out of Aldus's acquisition in 1990 of San Diego's Silicon Beach Software. The product lineup—including graphics program SuperPaint, illustration software IntelliDraw, and Home Publisher, a repackaging of Personal Press—was based on software previously developed by Silicon Beach. The division had also strayed into personal productivity software like the personal-information manager TouchBase and the calendar application DateBook, both obtained from Aldus's purchase of After Hours Software in 1993.

"After my first visit to San Diego, Bruce and I agreed that if Adobe was going to pursue the consumer business, then it would not be done by engineering products from scratch, as was being done at Silicon Beach," Warnock says. "Instead, consumer products would be highly leveraged from Adobe's core technologies. The reason for this approach was that a consumer product could never pay for its development cost if it was not leveraged from some other effort." Warnock gave Chizen the charter to see what he could do.

Chizen rose to the challenge. He quickly realized that the company knew little about the consumer business. Only minimal research on the market opportunities had been done, nor was there a strategy in place for marketing. "The attitude was that customers would find their way to these products," he says. He had different ideas. Chizen believed there was an audience for consumer graphics products, especially in the realm of imaging. He had been impressed by the Casio QV-10 digital camera, one of the first reasonably priced consumer-oriented cameras from Japan that boasted such friendly features as an LCD screen that could be used for previewing and displaying images on the spot. Photoshop had tapped into the high end of the imaging and photography markets, so couldn't a similar but simpler product do the same for the low end? He argued his case. "It was a constant battle to get attention within the company," Chizen says.

"Adobe was not interested in the consumer division," says the former vice president of marketing for the applications division, Linda Clarke. "But Bruce pleaded with them to give him six months to turn it around."

Making the Case

Chizen brought in a few trusted players from his days at Claris, including marketing director Melissa Dyrdahl, who is now Adobe's senior vice president of corporate marketing, and Kyle Mashima, who joined the rechristened Home and Office Products Division in 1996. Chizen pared down the product line—selling TouchBase and DateBook to Now Software—then started making changes to the products that remained. One such change was to rework SuperPaint into Art Explorer, an easy-to-use painting program that nearly exploded with colorful graphics. But Art Explorer wasn't the product he had in mind when he spied that Casio digital camera. Adobe had been selling a "light" version of Photoshop through scanner OEMs, but Photoshop LE (Limited Edition) was just that—it had fewer features than the regular version, but it was still Photoshop and a complex product. What was needed was an application like Photoshop but much easier to use. Chizen persuaded David Pratt, by then senior vice president and general manager of the application products division, to allow him access to Photoshop's engineering talents.

The result was PhotoDeluxe, a version of Photoshop geared toward the home or small-business user. It addressed problems common to hobbyist photographers, such as the "red eye" caused by camera flashes and the need to repair damaged or creased photos. It offered many of Photoshop's special-effects capabilities but stripped them down to the essentials. PhotoDeluxe also included guided tutorials that walked customers through the steps of, for example, enhancing a photo, cropping it, and adding a border. It wasn't an entirely graceful solution: glimpses of its high-end sibling poked through occasionally, making the professional Photoshop features stick out in an otherwise consumer-friendly environment.

PhotoDeluxe shipped for Mac and Windows in 1996. It was a moderate success as a stand-alone product, but Adobe knew the software made a more powerful impression when viewed in the context of capturing images from scanners and digital cameras. As a result, Linda Clarke says, Adobe "bundled the dickens out of it," selling it in conjunction with imaging hardware. According to the research firm Dataquest, PhotoDeluxe was the number-one-selling consumer photoediting software in the world by 1998. "They didn't believe that there was going to be a market," Chizen says of the reaction from executive team. "But it turned into a nice $20- to $30-million business." The same Dataquest report showed that the entire category grew 237 percent in 1997 alone.

BizStats: 1995

No. of employees: 2,322

Revenue: $762 million

Stock price range: $28 to $70

Acquisitions: Frame Technology, Ceneca, Visualware, Hyphen

Product releases:
Adobe PageMaker 6.0
Illustrator 6.0 (Mac), 4.1 (Windows)
Photoshop 3.0
After Effects 3.0

Other:
>> Netscape integrates Acrobat into Navigator browser

More than 5,000 applications support PostScript output

Adobe Type Library exceeds 2,000 Type 1 typefaces

Industry:
Sun develops Java
Apple licenses its OS, giving rise to Mac clones
Fractal Design acquires Ray Dream
Macromedia acquires Altsys, Fauve Software
Iomega introduces Zip and Jaz drives

Adobe Dimensions 2.0

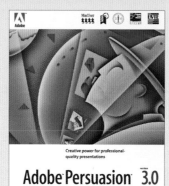

Adobe Persuasion 3.0

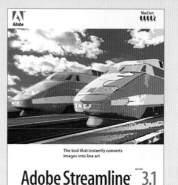

Adobe Streamline 3.1

Not every product acquired by Adobe makes the transition to its new owners. Some are gutted for pieces of code. Some are killed because they compete with existing products. And some are given a shot at continuing but don't make it in the long run. The following is a list of software acquired or developed by Adobe that either never made the grade or that did only for a while before being discontinued.

Adobe Circulate
Adobe File Utilities
Adobe Type Align
AfterImage
Ares Font Utilities
Art Explorer
Audition
ChartMaker
CheckList
Collector's Editions for Illustrator
Color Central
Configurable PostScript
Interpreter
Curo Document Manager
DateBook
Digital Darkroom
Dimensions
Display PostScript
DocuComp

Fetch
FontChameleon
FontFiddler
FontHopper
FontMinder
FontMonger
FreeHand
Gallery Effects
Hitchcock
HomePublisher
Image Library
InfoPublisher
IntelliDraw
PageMaker Database Edition
PageMill
Personal Press
Persuasion
PhotoDeluxe for Mac
PhotoDeluxe Business Edition
Photoshop LE
PhotoStyler
PixelBurst coprocessors
PostScript Fax
PrePrint
PrePrint Pro
PressReady
PressWise
Print Central
PrintGear

Publishing Packs
ScreenReady
Separator
SiteMill
SmartArt
Streamline
SuperATM
SuperCard
SuperPaint
Supra
TextureMaker
TitleMan
TitleSoft
TouchBase
TranScript (Unix)
TrapMaker
TrapWise
TrueForm
Type 1 coprocessor
Type Align
Type On Call
Type Reunion
Type Sets
Type Twister
Video F/X
Viewer 3.1
Viewer 95
Word For Word

PhotoDeluxe proved to be a fertile test bed for Adobe in many respects. Version 2 introduced Adobe Connectables: Internet hooks embedded in the program that provided a constantly updated source of tips, techniques, and tutorials for downloading from the Web. The combination of consumer digital imaging and the Web also led to the development of ActiveShare, a means of sharing family photo albums over the Internet. PhotoDeluxe also tested different market slices as it split into different versions for home and business users.

The success of PhotoDeluxe and the boom in the digital-camera market led Adobe to develop consumer-oriented Photoshop Elements in 2001. Unlike PhotoDeluxe, which distanced itself from Photoshop in name, appearance, and interface, Elements banked on its relationship to the professional product and its name recognition. Elements melded aspects of both PhotoDeluxe—guided tutorials and Web links, for instance—and Photoshop, especially its interface and tools. Like PhotoDeluxe, Elements was also bundled with scanners and digital cameras, but Adobe also aggressively marketed it as a stand-alone product.

Based on his track record with the consumer business unit, Chizen was tapped to lead Adobe's graphics division in December 1997, and the consumer group was merged into the main trunk of the company. The company had entered the mainstream and tapped into the rapidly growing audience for personal publishing and image sharing.

This represented a major shift for Adobe, one that was not viewed with equanimity by all. Contingents both within the company and among industry observers felt that the company was, at the least, diluting its brand's association with graphics professionals and, at the worst, moving away from that core market entirely. Industry pundits questioned whether Adobe was reaching too far, too fast.

Compounding the challenge was the rise of an entirely new communications medium, one that Adobe had yet to grapple with successfully. While Adobe was reaching out to consumers, graphics professionals were venturing into a new territory of their own: the World Wide Web.

"A consumer product could never pay for its development cost if it was not leveraged from some other effort."

— John Warnock

LOUIS FISHAUF

Designer Louis Fishauf was accustomed to hiring illustrators for his design work. Then he encountered Adobe Illustrator and quickly figured out that he had a knack for drawing himself. That was back in 1987. Now he's one of the most honored commercial artists of the last decade, whose work includes that epitome of 1990s graphic chic, an Absolut ad. Today Fishauf moves fluidly between vectors in Illustrator and pixels in Photoshop.

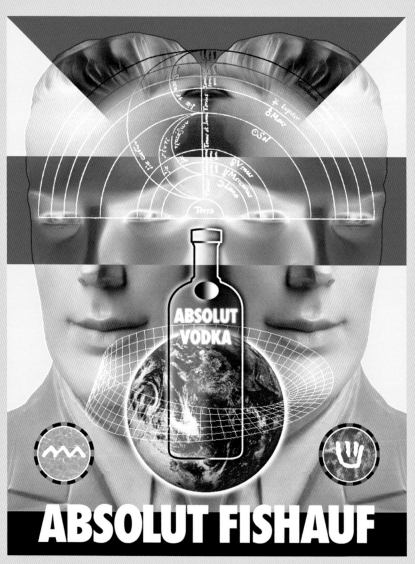

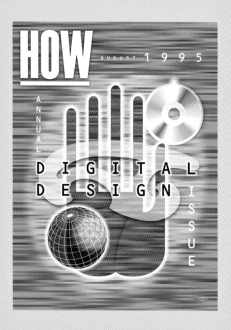

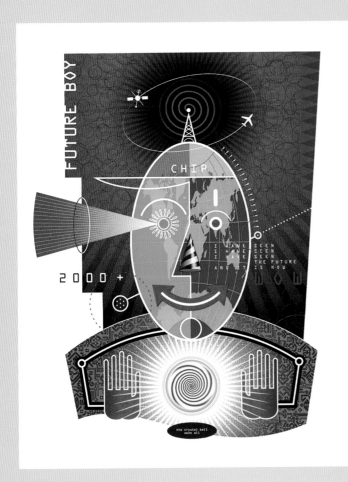

"Illustrator blew my mind when I saw my first output."

Adobe art director Luanne Seymour Cohen took a literal leap of faith—from an airplane—for a promotional video about the fear of Web design.

Working the Web

Few people could have predicted the impact that the World Wide Web would have when it came roaring into the 1990s. What had started as a means for government, military, and educational institutions to transmit information became, virtually overnight, a marketing and cultural phenomenon. Companies scrambled to keep up with the tsunami of changes bearing down on them, and Adobe was no exception.

Adobe was certainly aware of the rush to the Web, but in 1994 Adobe was dealing with issues closer to home. The Aldus and Frame acquisitions had sapped much of the company's vigor, and the company focused what energy it had left on integrating new software into its product line and especially on making Acrobat and PDF a cross-platform publishing standard. As a result, the leader in print communications struggled to keep pace with the rapidly evolving Web market.

The Web presented perplexing and potentially far-reaching problems for Adobe. The HyperText Markup Language (HTML) used by the Web to present data offered little control over the presentation of information, which flew in the face of Adobe's aesthetic. Adobe Acrobat had been developed for just that purpose: to transmit richly formatted documents over a network. If HTML and the World Wide Web became a standard, would that obviate the need for Acrobat? If individuals connected to a worldwide network could access information using only a Web browser, then what role did Acrobat play?

The answers to these questions were not obvious at first, but by fits and starts, Adobe worked through them and laid the groundwork for a future in which the Internet played as large a role in publishing as paper did.

A Leap of Faith

For a company that had started the desktop publishing revolution, it was natural to see the Web publishing revolution as a similar opportunity. Like print, with its brotherhood of typesetters and secret codes, the Internet had been the domain of scientists and engineers, and the main method of producing pages for the Web required typing commands and codes into a text editor that understood HTML, the WWW's de facto programming language proposed by Tim Berners-Lee in 1989. A viewing application converted the commands into formatted text and graphics, not unlike an interpreter for pages written in PostScript. And as in an earlier era, what brought the Web out of the back room and into the

"Acrobat was a way of taking Warnock's appearance-based model and making it acceptable for the Web."

— Jonathan Seybold

BizStats: 1996

No. of employees: 2,222

Revenue: $787 million

Stock price range: $29 to $74

Acquisitions: Ares Software, Swell Software

Product releases:
Adobe PageMaker 6.5
Adobe Type Manager 4.0
Photoshop 4.0
Acrobat 3.0
FrameMaker 5.0 (+SGML)
PhotoDeluxe 1.0

Other:
>> Adobe moves into San Jose world
headquarters

Adobe spins off its prepress application
products business as Luminous
Corporation

Industry:
Microsoft ships Windows 95,
Windows NT 4.0, Internet Explorer

Steve Jobs returns to Apple, which then
acquires NeXT

Microsoft releases Internet Explorer

mainstream was the development and popularization of a software application, in this case the Mosaic Web browser, closely followed by its commercial successor, Netscape Navigator.

With such parallels, it's not surprising that Adobe approached the Web the same way it had approached desktop publishing. The mechanism for publishing content on the Web existed, but a PageMaker-like program that facilitated the production of Web pages did not. Those who wanted to make Web pages had to learn HTML codes and use a text editor like Bare Bones Software's BBEdit. For designers used to working in the WYSIWYG (what you see is what you get) environment of print page-layout applications, the situation was less than ideal. Indeed, in many instances designers were being cut out of the Web design process, their role filled by code-savvy newcomers with engineering chops but little design background. Adobe knew that software had to make a similar leap if designers and publishers were to embrace the Web.

Near the end of 1994, a few months after the Aldus merger, Adobe found the answer in the cubicles of Ceneca Communications. The six-month-old company authored two products for the Web: PageMill for creating Web pages and SiteMill for managing Web sites. PageMill was one of the first of the so-called WYSIWYG editors for the Web that gave HTML a visual interface. Instead of typing in code, designers could drag and drop content into preprogrammed frames. Perhaps PageMill could do for Web page design and construction what PageMaker did for print design and production—the similarity in names was a happy coincidence but underscored the association.

It was a reasonable approach to take. Designers accustomed to producing pages printed with dots on paper were now confronted with creating pages displayed as dots onscreen, and it scared many of them. In addition to its daunting markup language, the new medium had an entirely new set of constraints, chief among them a minuscule file-size requirement (for fast-loading pages) that made graphics-intensive pages impractical, draconian limits on fonts and font sizes, a less-flexible (vertical) page format, and an inability to control the appearance of the final display (overridden by the browser and monitor settings). In typical Adobe fashion, the dynamic duo of Russell Brown and Luanne Seymour Cohen decided to address designers' fears head-on through a creative short film. During the SADIM (Stanford Art Directors Invitational Master) class, a film crew taped magazine designers as they browsed the Web and reflected about how their roles as designers might change as a result of it.

The footage was spliced into a short film that encouraged designers to face their fears and try something new. "Its purpose was to help designers understand that the Web might be a new and frightening frontier, but

The dynamic duo of Russell Preston Brown and Luanne Seymour Cohen made it their mission to champion Web design and encourage art directors to try it.

that they weren't alone in their fear," Cohen explains. To demonstrate that working outside the comfort zone could be both scary and exhilarating, the filmmakers came up with the metaphor of jumping out of an airplane and persuaded Cohen to do just that.

The rest of the movie showed Cohen confronting her fear of skydiving. The entire process from suiting up to jumping to landing was taped. Cohen made connections between her personal fear of jumping from airplanes—"I was so afraid that I couldn't actually make myself jump out of the plane; the guy had to push me"—with her fear as a designer of losing control with new technology. Shown at a 1995 AIGA conference in Seattle, the finished film marked a time in publishing's history when many designers were making a leap of faith—although few made as literal a leap as Cohen did.

Web-Page Maker

But producing pages for the Web is very different from preparing pages for a web press, as Adobe soon learned when it released PageMill for the Macintosh in late 1995. The program was a hit with HTML-impaired designers, thanks to its accessible interface, which was greeted with enthusiasm by its target audience, but its execution did not meet the standards demanded by Web professionals. PageMill was marred by a lack of table support and a propensity to replace tags and generate code

ADOBE AROUND THE GLOBE

Over the years Adobe has become a truly global company. Today more than 50 percent of its business is derived from international sales to such regions as Japan, Germany, the United Kingdom, France, and Scandinavia. Adobe's product development has also taken on an international flavor. The company has research and development facilities in India, Germany, Scotland, and most recently, Canada, with the purchase of Ottawa-based Accelio Corporation. The Adobe Acrobat team quips that the sun never sets on Acrobat development. This page, right: Edinburgh; below, Tokyo. Opposite page, top and lower left, Noida, India; lower right, Ottawa.

Adobe and the Growth of the Web

When the World Wide Web exploded as a cultural and technological phenomenon, Adobe was caught flat footed. Individuals like John Warnock recognized the Web's importance, but the company had no organized response to the maelstrom of changes whirling around it. Today the Web is an integral component of all Adobe's strategic initiatives, but early on it was a different story.

Missing the Boat

Adobe stuttered at the time of the Web.

Roger Black, chairman, Danilo Black USA

We were looking the other way when the Web happened. No one's eye was on the ball. The Internet train was running down the track and we jumped on the caboose.

Melissa Dyrdahl, senior vice president, corporate marketing and communications

Adobe didn't accept the reemergence of the content-driven side of things. They couldn't come to grips with content over appearance. John fought an ongoing rear-guard battle. Each time he was assaulted by the Web he'd move a little, then a little bit more, then a little bit more. It was a migration step by painful step.

Jonathan Seybold, Seybold Seminars

Nice Try

PageMill was exciting when it first came out, but Adobe approached the Web as a single HTML page, not realizing its complexity. That set them off on the wrong track.

Lynda Weinman, Web maven

Adobe acted fast with the acquisition of a Web authoring tool—the right thing to do—but as they didn't fully grasp the design needs of Web

"At the peak of the Internet bubble we were on the outside looking in."

— Bryan Lamkin

development, they made the wrong choice with PageMill. Because of that Adobe moved away from design dominance in terms of the Web.

Clement Mok, cofounder, NetObjects

We gave Macromedia the Web in the professional space.

Bryan Lamkin

Making Progress

ImageReady made it easier to be a Web publisher. Before that you had to slice images in Photoshop using the selection marquee.

Lynda Weinman

We were just starting to play around with hidden features of ImageReady, like designing rollovers and having it remember different slices. We had to do massive changes to a design that would have taken six hours to do. We hadn't even read the manual yet, but we discovered these cool features that let us deploy changes in a couple of minutes. It was sweet.

Melvin Rivera, cofounder, Mostasa.com

Vision or Hindsight

Early on Adobe wasn't leading in the Web space but following. Now Adobe is creating leadership-level products, but it took them a long time to get it right.

Lynda Weinman

Chuck and I always thought it had helped that we'd been around awhile before we started this thing. We had seen the mainframe and time-sharing eras. We knew this current phase couldn't last, especially the Net explosion.

John Warnock

John was a pillar of strength during the dot-com boom. He was skeptical that it would last.

Melissa Dyrdahl

that, while technically accurate, mangled the designer's intention. SiteMill was reviewed more favorably for its smooth automation of behind-the-scenes processes such as dead-link removal, a time-consuming task that most Web publishers are loath to do. Developing back-end processes for the World Wide Web was clearly out of Adobe's purview, however, and SiteMill was discontinued in January 1997.

Adobe's early success with PageMill was soon thwarted, as a host of WYSIWYG editors flooded the market in the months surrounding its release. Competitive products developed at a pace so fast and furious that it was difficult to keep up. Initially PageMill's competition included Home Page, released by Apple's software arm, Claris; HoTMetaL Pro, shipped in 1994 by SGML developer SoftQuad; and FrontPage, released in late 1995 by upstart company Vermeer Technologies, who sold it to Microsoft in January 1996, about the time Adobe released the Windows version of PageMill. For that release, Adobe repositioned PageMill as part of its home and small-business product line, but it ran smack-dab into FrontPage, which Microsoft had included as part of its Office suite of products, virtually guaranteeing FrontPage the lion's share of that market.

Although PageMill broke new ground for Adobe, it was quickly out-gunned. The company needed a more sophisticated product if it was going to compete for the hearts and minds of Web designers. NetObjects Fusion, released in late 1996 and developed in part by prominent designer Clement Mok, provided fledgling Web designers with familiar features such as style sheets and templates. By 1998, there were upwards of a dozen WYSIWYG Web authoring applications on the market, including two promising newcomers that targeted the professional design market: CyberStudio, developed by the German company GoLive and noted for the remarkable level of control it gave designers over the position and appearance of elements on a page, and Macromedia Dreamweaver, noted for its ease of use and clean code.

Within a year it became apparent that designers who embraced the Web were gravitating toward Macromedia Dreamweaver, particularly with the advent of Macromedia's Flash graphics and animation technology. "Macromedia had Flash, so we had to look at PageMill and ask, what piece of technology does it have as an enduring component?" Warnock says today. Adobe countered Macromedia in January 1999 by purchasing GoLive. PageMill's fate was sealed. Adobe ceased development of PageMill in March 2000 with an eye toward migrating users to its latest acquisition.

"We did PageMill—which was HTML done in a small way—and it failed," Warnock concedes. "But had we done PageMill in a big way, we would have failed in a big way."

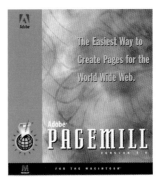

SiteMill and PageMill, both acquired through the purchase of Ceneca Communications, were Adobe's first Web products.

Although not planned as a Web tool, Photoshop quickly became the standard for Web image processing, making Adobe a player in the Web space.

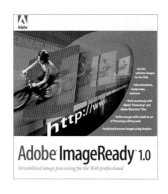

ImageReady, conceived as a companion to Photoshop, gave designers more control over Web graphics.

Photoshop to the Rescue

As the Web gained momentum, designers were forced to come to terms with it. Clients requested Web-site designs in addition to or instead of printed materials. Designers were faced with a daunting wave of Web design and authoring applications; deciding which product to use and then learning how to use it took precious time in the nonstop Web whirl. More often than not, designers and graphic artists new to the Web relied on familiar products to help them navigate this new landscape. And fortunately for Adobe, the vast majority of them reached for an old standby they knew they could trust: Photoshop.

Photoshop hadn't been developed with the Web in mind, but it had many features Web designers needed, such as the ability to slice images into pieces, to save images at reduced resolutions (which therefore had smaller file sizes), and to convert them to Web-friendly color spaces and file formats (GIF and JPEG). Photoshop also allowed Web artists to create graphics to exact pixel specifications. Web-savvy designers soon figured out how to work around Photoshop's print-centric point of view. In a remarkably short period of time, the world's leading image-editing application became the standard tool for creating graphics for the Web. Its dominance was further cemented as the scope of Web projects shifted toward large-scale service and e-commerce sites on which teams of specialists collaborated. For those given the task of creating Web graphics, there was no reason to use anything other than Photoshop.

Overnight, and somewhat by accident, Photoshop made Adobe a player on the Web.

Recognizing that it could apply its hard-earned graphics-application know-how to this new medium, Adobe set about creating specialized graphics tools for the Web. First out of the gate in the summer of 1998 was ImageReady. Conceived as a companion to Photoshop and intended for sophisticated users, ImageReady facilitated the production of Web graphics: color conversion, file conversion and export, image-mapping, and so on. It incorporated such tools as image slicing, for cutting images into tiled pieces that loaded more quickly into a Web browser; file optimization, for compressing images into smaller byte packages for faster onscreen display; and animation features, for making moving graphic elements out of static files.

Adobe followed ImageReady in December 1998 with ImageStyler, a Web graphics tool aimed at the business or home user. The program combined the graphics-creation capabilities of Photoshop with bits of ImageReady, such as the ability to prepare graphics for the Web, although it lacked ImageReady's animation features.

While both were solid products, neither ImageReady nor ImageStyler ever really found its niche. The crowded Web market confused potential customers, many of whom ended up buying Photoshop on name recognition alone or using a dedicated Web graphics program like Macromedia Fireworks. In 1999, only a year after its debut, ImageReady 2.0 was rolled into Photoshop 5.5. The decision ended ImageReady as a stand-alone application, but it solidified Photoshop's position as the premier graphics tool for the Web as well as print. ImageStyler never made it to a second version. Adobe replaced it in January 2000 with LiveMotion, a graphics creation and Web animation package geared for the professional market. Adobe's Photoshop Elements, a scaled-down version of Photoshop, now serves the business and home Web graphics market.

Working with a Net

Adobe's track record in producing new applications for the Web had been uneven thus far, but the company recognized it needed an overall strategy that incorporated the Web's infrastructure into both its applications and its systems.

In May 1995 Adobe unveiled the first phase of its Internet strategy, which appeared to be a mishmash of ideas. On the one hand Adobe touted PageMaker's and Persuasion's HTML-export features, which made page layouts or office presentations Web ready. Both efforts were poorly executed and made little impression. On the other hand Adobe introduced a system by which customers could manage individual printers worldwide using the Internet. Called PrintMill, it would allow corporate communications specialists working in, say, New York to locate a printer in the Los Angeles office and send a file to that printer for review by long-distance colleagues. The concept of Web-ready printing was incorporated into the third generation of PostScript.

But those steps toward the Internet didn't address the more fundamental problem nagging Adobe: in Adobe's worldview, HTML was simply too limiting a language. It could not produce the visually rich pages on which Adobe had staked its reputation. That's why Adobe was intent on pushing Acrobat as the standard means of transmitting composed pages across networks, and there was no bigger network than the World Wide Web. What Adobe needed was an Internet partner who recognized the value of PDF, the Portable Document Format.

Netscape Communications, formed in 1994, became that partner. The ambitious young company had the popular Netscape Navigator Web browser, and Adobe became an early investor (in fact, Warnock sat on Netscape's board). In March 1995 Adobe and Netscape announced a joint strategy by which Adobe would embed Web links in PDF files and Netscape would include a PDF plug-in for Navigator. This meant that when a URL link was double-clicked in a PDF document, a Netscape Navigator browser window opened, thereby providing instant access to the Internet. It also meant that a version of the Acrobat Viewer, code-named Amber, became part of the Netscape browser. When a person surfing the Internet came across a PDF file, Navigator launched the Acrobat plug-in so that the user could read the PDF file without leaving Navigator's HTML-native environment.

The agreement with Netscape was pivotal in terms of Adobe's Internet and Acrobat strategies. "Warnock resisted information separated from its appearance," says media consultant Jonathan Seybold. "Acrobat was a way of taking his appearance-based model and making it acceptable for the Web." However, Adobe's alliance with Netscape put Adobe once again in the crosshairs of Microsoft, which was developing its own Web browser software to compete with Navigator.

As Web hysteria reached a fever pitch in the late '90s, Adobe was perceived by many industry watchers to be sitting on the sidelines. Rival companies like Macromedia and Microsoft took the lead in Web design and deployment applications, while Adobe fumbled its Web applications and plugged away at promoting Acrobat. Had it not been for Photoshop and Acrobat, Adobe would have missed the '90s Web boom entirely. But given the dot-com bust of 2000, Adobe's hesitation seems prescient in

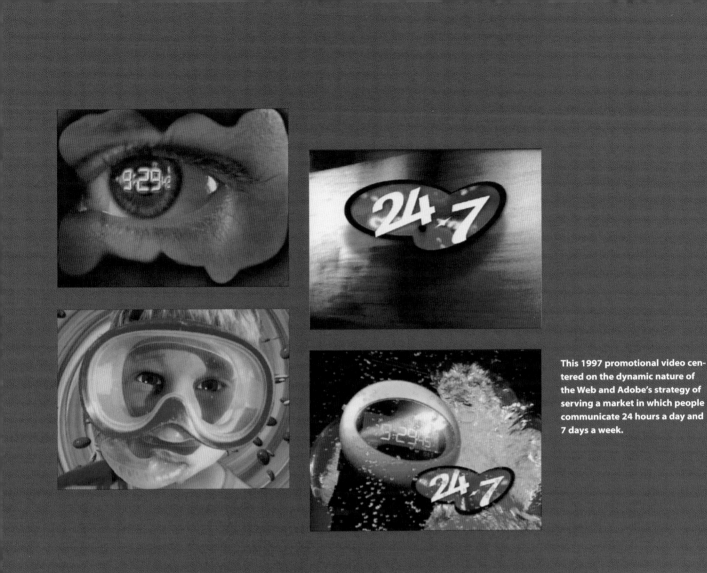

This 1997 promotional video centered on the dynamic nature of the Web and Adobe's strategy of serving a market in which people communicate 24 hours a day and 7 days a week.

hindsight, and indeed Warnock spins it that way today. "I didn't want to jump on the Internet and go along for the ride," he says. "If we were like everybody else, we wouldn't have a sustainable business."

The market changes wrought by the Web were only one business challenge Adobe confronted during the latter part of the 1990s. In 1998 it met perhaps its greatest test as a company, one that arose not out of external circumstances but from internal conditions.

HILLMAN CURTIS

Known for his minimalist Web designs and simple, effective animations, Hillman Curtis has created award-winning designs for clients such as Cartier, MTV, RollingStone.com, and Goodby, Silverstein & Partners. His signatures include clean navigation systems (seen here in the Greenwich Street Project and Adobe Studio sites) and powerful, compact animations such as these created for RollingStone.com and Adobe. Curtis's book, *MTIV: Process, Inspiration, and Practice for the New Media Designer,* outlines his straightforward and respectful approach to design. (www.hillmancurtis.com)

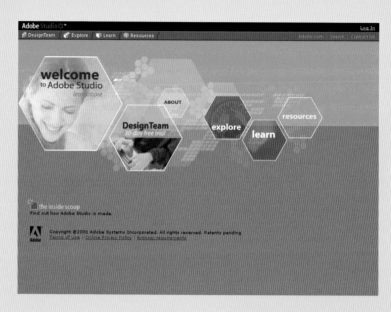

"Find the theme...then communicate it clearly."

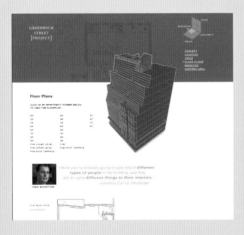

Regrouping

The Internet boom continued to escalate in 1998. It was a time of unprecedented prosperity for Silicon Valley and especially for the myriad of dot-com companies sprouting up in its fertile soil. The euphoria of limitless potential perfumed the air. But the mood in Adobe's executive boardroom was far different.

For Adobe, the summer of 1998 was marked by frustration and discontent. After years of steady growth and clear direction, the company was grappling with stalled sales and a loss of focus. Like a ship caught in a meteorological "perfect storm," where three weather fronts collide, Adobe was buffeted by slow product sales, a slumping Japanese economy, and political infighting. Already reeling from these factors, Adobe was dealt another blow when archrival Quark announced it wanted to buy the company.

The only way to get back on track was to make some hard decisions. Several years later, cofounder Chuck Geschke described the year as perhaps the most pivotal in Adobe's history.

The Endless Summer
The Adobe Systems of 1998 was a far cry from its origins, in which two men with a good idea built a company from scratch with the help of a couple dozen handpicked hires. By that summer, Adobe employed 41 vice presidents and supported four large business units that often competed with each other for customers and resources. The structure was becoming unwieldy; different divisions duplicated efforts that would have been better served by a coordinated, centralized system.

In anticipation of retirement, the cofounders had been pulling back and laying the foundation for the team that would take Adobe into the future. On the executive level Warnock and Geschke's longtime lieutenants—people such as Steve MacDonald, David Pratt, and Bruce Nakao—had left the company. Adobe had replaced the departed executives, but with mixed results. "The executives we had hired all came from search firms. All had great credentials; but these political fiefdoms were developing," says Warnock. Geschke concurs: "We could never get them to work as a team."

The lack of teamwork was taking its toll on product development, sales, and marketing. "Our stock was in the tank and we didn't have a coherent business plan on the horizon," Warnock says. "Our employees all had different ideas about the company's direction. If you asked them what our

"It was a drag to come into work every day."

— Chuck Geschke

mission was going forward, they'd tell you what they had been told by the last VP who'd talked to them. We'd lost control."

"We were starting to lose our customers too," says Geschke. Adding to Adobe's woes was the so-called Asian flu. The Japanese market, which contributed $60.3 million in revenues in the third quarter of 1997, was off 40 percent for the same period in 1998, and Adobe's stock was getting hammered.

The executive staff meetings had become "nightmares," in Warnock's words, and the infighting was having an effect on the two cofounders. "It was a drag to come into work every day," Geschke remembers. After a frustrating meeting in July 1998, Geschke called Warnock on vacation and said, "I'm at my wit's end," Warnock recalls. They played out some options, including early retirement. But they knew that Adobe as it stood then was not the legacy they wanted to leave. They had worked too hard to see it end that way. It was time for the cofounders to reassert themselves. "I finally said, 'We have to get rid of them all,'" Warnock says. But before they could put the wheels in motion, they needed to line up a team they could count on.

Like Warnock and Geschke, Bruce Chizen was frustrated by the state of affairs at the executive level. "We couldn't get anything done," Chizen says today. "I was getting ready to move on. I talked to Chuck about it and told him that I thought he had to make some changes." Chizen then left for a family vacation at the New Jersey shore. Coming in from the beach one day, he was told he had a message from John Warnock, who wanted Chizen to call him. "John never called me. So I thought, What does he want?" On the phone Warnock told Chizen that he and Geschke were eliminating the bulk of the executive staff the next Monday. Then Warnock asked Chizen a question with far-reaching implications: "What role do you want to have?"

Chizen, then vice president and general manager of the graphics products division, said he wanted to take on all product marketing and development, which would include engineering. Chizen's forte at that time was sales, so assuming engineering was a big transition. On top of that, Chizen would now report directly to Warnock, the engineer's engineer. But Warnock and Geschke reassured him. "They said, 'Everybody thinks highly of you. You don't have to be a technologist as long as you have the respect of the technologists,'" says Chizen, who would take on the title of executive vice president, products and marketing.

Back in San Jose, Warnock scheduled one-on-one meetings with the affected executives for Monday morning. The weekend before was filled with dread for the cofounders. On Monday, the executives met individually with Warnock, who accepted their resignations.

"Our stock was in the tank and we didn't have a coherent business plan on the horizon."

— John Warnock

After the 1998 management shake-up, a new executive team emerged: back row, from left, Geschke, Chizen, Warnock, CFO Hal Covert, executive VP of sales Fred Snow; front row, from left, VP Jim Stephens, general counsel Colleen Pouliot, VP Rebecca Guerra.

Warnock and Geschke, now supported by a single group of like-minded lieutenants, swung into action. Adobe had to develop a plan and execute it. Working with Chizen, they began restructuring the company. "We broke down the business divisions into functional organizations," Chizen says. They consolidated finance, operations, and marketing into a single infrastructure. They laid off 350 people. Chizen assembled his team, which included Shantanu Narayen, who would direct engineering; Bryan Lamkin, who took over graphics products; and Melissa Dyrdahl, who would lead a unified marketing effort.

Knowing the road ahead would be challenging, Chizen called a meeting of his senior staff to test their resolve. He went around the room and asked each person: "Are you in or are you out?" Everyone replied "in"—except Lamkin. "I said, 'Let me get back to you on that,'" he says somewhat sheepishly today. Internet fever was running high and Lamkin yearned for change and excitement. "Adobe at a Zen level had stayed the same," he says. Chizen gave him a night to think it over. The next morning Lamkin said he was staying. "What made me stay was what made me come here in the first place: the products and the people," he says.

The triage had been successful, but the company's earnings report for the third quarter reflected the summer of turmoil: a net income of just $152,000, or one cent per share, on revenues of $222.9 million; a layoff of 350 people with restructuring charges of $37.1 million, and a decline of $25.2 million in revenue in Japan alone.

With internal problems abating, Adobe turned its attention to external relations. After the restructuring announcements, the financial community held back, waiting to see what Adobe would do. But for Adobe, it was time to be proactive. Traditionally Warnock had been Adobe's public face while Geschke tended the corporate fires. Now a change was needed. "I told John that I had to go on the road to cement our outside relations and that John had to be Mr. Inside for a while," says Geschke. He and Jim Stephens, vice president of corporate development and former vice president of investor relations, took to the skies. "Jim Stephens and I visited every major account. We spent months on airplanes. We logged 250,000 miles and visited 30 countries."

But before Geschke and Stephens took off and before the turnaround had a chance to take effect, Adobe was dealt one more blow, this time from a rival software maker.

A Catalyst to Change

Ever since QuarkXPress had eclipsed PageMaker as the page-layout application of choice for professional publishers, there was no love lost between Quark and Adobe. The two companies had different philosophies about business, customer relations, and product development. For the most part, they agreed to disagree and stayed away from each other. But as Adobe suffered through the tumult of 1998, Quark saw an opportunity to change Adobe's fortunes or, at the very least, unnerve its founders.

On August 18, Quark CEO Fred Ebrahimi sent a fax to Warnock and Geschke expressing interest in merging the two companies. The two men were surprised—and incensed. Adobe saw the offer as yet another example of Quark's arrogance. On August 21, Warnock and Geschke wrote Ebrahimi indicating that they had no wish to discuss such a scenario. The reply prompted another, public exchange. On August 25, Quark issued a press release announcing its overture and then posted the two previous letters on its Web site. Now Adobe was forced to confirm Quark's proposal and to deny its own interest. Adobe's press release concluded that Quark's correspondence had "failed to state any material terms that would constitute a firm and bona fide offer." If Quark's faxed letter had proffered actual terms, Adobe as a publicly held company would not have been able to comment. Instead it was able to fight back on the stage of popular opinion.

The timing of Quark's letter was auspicious—it had come just before the opening of the influential publishing-industry trade show Seybold Seminars, held each September in San Francisco—which led some observers to view it as a publicity stunt. The drama being played out via fax and Web site was indeed the buzz of the show (one industry magazine gave out buttons that read, "I'm betting on Adobe!" and "I'm betting on Quark!"). But a telling moment came during a conference session whose topic was the possible takeover. After some onstage debate, the

BizStats: **1998**

No. of employees: 2,664

Revenue: $895 million

Stock price range: $24 to $52

Product releases:
Illustrator 8.0
Photoshop 5.0
Premiere 5.0
PhotoDeluxe Home Edition 3.0 (Windows)
PhotoDeluxe Business Edition (Windows)
ImageReady 1.0
ImageStyler 1.0
PageMill 3.0 for Mac
PostScript 3

Other:
>> Hostile takeover bid from Quark Inc.

Adobe expands into East Tower, San Jose headquarters

Patent #5,831,632 issued to John Warnock and Michael Schuster: for a technique that replicates, bends, and miters tiles to match the curvature and corners of a specified PostScript path

The Evolution of the Annual Report

Over the years Adobe's annual
reports have served as a reflection
of current trends in graphic design,
as a showcase of Adobe products
in action, as a digest of an industry
in transition, and as a record of the
company's financial success. In recent
years, its annual financial review is
also available in PDF format, which
can be downloaded from its Web site,
www.adobe.com.

1986

1989

1990

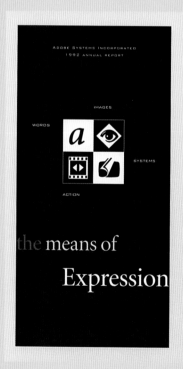

1992

1994

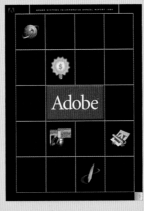

1996

1998

1999

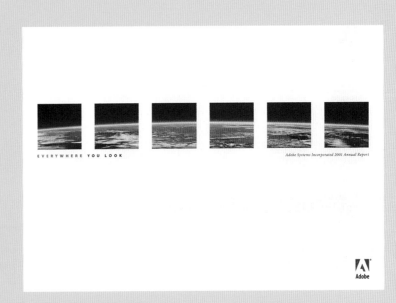

2001

moderator asked the audience for a show of hands in favor of Quark's bid. Not a single hand was raised.

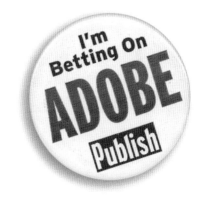

Never a company to shrink from a fight—witness its response to the Apple-Microsoft type alliance in 1989—Adobe used the conference as an opportunity to debut an as yet unseen product. The surprise demonstration came during a keynote speech by Steve Jobs, back at the helm of Apple, in which he invited Adobe and Quark onstage to show support for the Macintosh. With Quark founder and chief technology officer Tim Gill onstage, Adobe unveiled its brand-new page-layout application and QuarkXPress competitor, code-named K2. Clearly Adobe was not about to let Quark get the upper hand.

Adobe refused to talk to Quark. Recognizing the futility and expense of a hostile takeover, Quark withdrew its offer less than three weeks after the initial fax.

But Quark's gambit achieved its desired effect: It told the world that the once mighty Adobe was in trouble. And Adobe was. The company's stock price had dipped to $24.44 on August 24, about the half its value four months earlier. If Quark, a privately held business, could come up with the money to purchase a company four times its size, Adobe's future did not look promising.

But internally the bid had the opposite effect. "The Quark takeover attempt catalyzed the company," Warnock says today. "Our response was, We're going to be damned if we get taken over by these turkeys. We're going to annihilate them. We'll just out-engineer them." Six months later, in March 1999, Adobe released the page-layout program K2, now called InDesign.

"Our response was, We're going to be damned if we get taken over by these turkeys."

— John Warnock

By the end of 1998, Adobe's stock had climbed back to $46.75. With new senior managers Adobe was poised to tackle the challenges of the 21st century. More important, the company was developing a coherent product strategy, one that wove together threads from its systems heritage, applications success, and future technologies. At its center was Adobe Acrobat.

"Show me any publisher on earth who does not print out or publish using some piece of Adobe technology."

— Frank Romano

Planning the Next Wave

If the first battle of the publishing revolution was waged on paper, then the next would be fought on the World Wide Web. By the close of the 20th century, the Web was transforming communication in terms of content distribution and commercial transaction. Unwilling to abandon its hard-won position in the printing and graphic arts markets, Adobe embraced the model of cross-media publishing, in which content once created is distributed through multiple methods, whether print or online. The company expanded its product line to include more-robust Web authoring tools, reinvigorated its page-layout line, and refined the software that served as a fulcrum between the print and online worlds. With PDF, like PostScript before it, Adobe had developed another industry standard.

ACROBAT TAKES HOLD

If 1998 was a year of inner turmoil for Adobe, the company entered 1999 determined to reassert itself. Adobe's traditional graphic arts products continued to sell well, but Adobe executives knew that, as with PostScript before it, diminishing returns were inevitable. The more mature the product, the fewer features can be added with each update, leading to a sales plateau. If Adobe was to thrive into the 21st century, then it had to look to new markets. The challenge before Adobe wasn't just to come up with sexy new software, either. What was needed was a technology platform around which a cohesive product strategy could be built.

The company didn't have to look far for the way out. It was right under their noses in the form of Adobe Acrobat.

In the years immediately following its public debut under the name Carousel in 1991, Acrobat seemed to many observers like a solution in search of a problem. The product had long been cast in the shadow of its flashier graphics siblings. But surrounded by fundamental changes in communications and guided by Warnock's tenacity and unwavering faith, Acrobat had slowly transformed itself into an indispensable part of Adobe customers' daily work. As features were added to the technology and its suite of applications, Acrobat expanded its scope in Adobe's product lines: from printing, where it has virtually replaced what we knew as PostScript; to graphics, where it can serve as the Esperanto of file formats; to the Internet, where millions of Web pages are posted as PDF files; to corporate communications, where it provides secure document transmission.

"If Chuck and I agreed, then the board of directors would go along. Chuck and I agreed about Acrobat."

— John Warnock

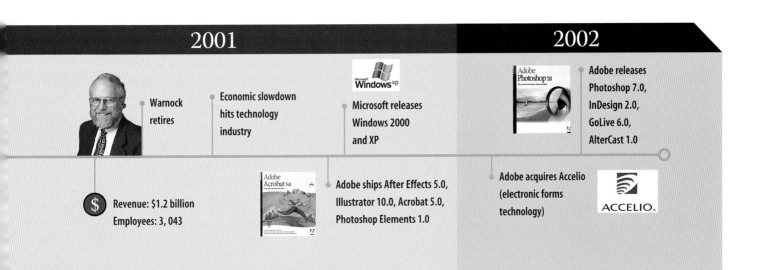

2001

Warnock retires

Economic slowdown hits technology industry

Microsoft releases Windows 2000 and XP

Revenue: $1.2 billion
Employees: 3, 043

Adobe ships After Effects 5.0, Illustrator 10.0, Acrobat 5.0, Photoshop Elements 1.0

2002

Adobe releases Photoshop 7.0, InDesign 2.0, GoLive 6.0, AlterCast 1.0

Adobe acquires Accelio (electronic forms technology)

ACCELIO

Adobe's advertising campaigns focused on Acrobat's ability to solve everyday office problems, such as the need to copy and distribute large volumes of paper files.

Sales of each successive version of Acrobat indicated that the buying public had finally glommed on to Acrobat, too. It was clear that the unglamorous, misunderstood Acrobat would not only be the foundation of Adobe's future initiatives but also become a cornerstone of modern publishing and communications.

To Web and Print

Acrobat's transformation happened gradually. The 1994 decision to distribute the Acrobat Reader free of charge did a great deal to perpetuate the technology. Acrobat then caught the wave of the World Wide Web in 1995, when Adobe formed an alliance with Netscape over the Amber technology, which enabled the Navigator browser to open PDF files on the Web. With Acrobat 3.0, released in November 1996, the PDF-Netscape integration was complete, making PDF a standard for posting richly formatted pages on the Web. Adobe later made PDF available for the rival Microsoft Explorer browser as well. "Getting into the browser made Acrobat an Internet product," says director of Acrobat engineering Bob Wulff, who started on Acrobat engineering when Warnock grabbed him in the hall in 1990, saying, "I just need you for two weeks." Twelve years later Wulff still works on Acrobat.

But the Web wasn't the only place in which customers were gravitating toward Acrobat and PDF. Print publishers, too, started using the format as a convenient means of distributing complex pages via email or on CD-ROM. A growing number of businesses recognized that they could send advertisements to publishing enterprises in a single PDF file with images, logos, and pricing information intact. PDF was an economical way to preserve the format and graphical intent of a publication or an advertisement.

Newspapers especially saw the value of allowing clients to submit files via PDF, which increased timeliness and reduced overhead. As more advertising agencies sent files in the PDF format to AP AdSEND—The Associated Press's online service that delivered advertisements to publishing entities worldwide—the demand grew for more robust print publishing capabilities in Acrobat and in PDF.

While color has always been supported in PDF, early versions lacked the color controls demanded by graphic artists. It was sufficient for newspaper publishing, but advertisers and publishers both clamored for more sophisticated color in PDF. Adobe responded in Acrobat 3.0 with print-savvy color-content support such as the ability to specify PDFs in CMYK for four-color printing and to output files in a prepress workflow. Magazine publishers and packaging designers asked for Pantone spot-color support, and they got it. Acrobat and PDF, originally an offshoot of the PostScript printing technology, was now becoming part of the print production process. "We realized we had an interesting replacement for PostScript," Wulff says. "Now people recognized that PDF was essentially portable PostScript."

The coupling of print capabilities with online delivery proved to be valuable for Adobe clients and publishers in general. Sarah Rosenbaum, who has worked on Acrobat since 1992 and who is now director of product management for the Acrobat desktop group, remembers receiving a phone call in early 1996 from the prepress manager for the Macy's West department store chain. Just before an ad was due to AP AdSEND, an error was found—an item was priced $40 less than it should have been—and as Macy's West had stores in most states west of the Mississippi River, the mistake could have been costly. Had the ad been produced as separated films, correcting the error would have been time consuming and expensive. Using a beta version of Acrobat 3.0, Rosenbaum talked the prepress operator through the correction. "We were able to change the price and get it into the system five minutes before deadline," she says.

But while Acrobat 3.0 was finding converts in Adobe's traditional graphic arts audience, it was also gaining fans outside Adobe's usual sphere of influence. Acrobat 3.0 was the first version to support Japanese, thereby spreading Acrobat across the Pacific. The Internal Revenue Service began using Acrobat 3.0's interactive capabilities, which meant that tax preparers could fill in data fields on PDF tax returns. Acrobat 3.0 also included a plug-in linking it to Acrobat Capture, thereby enabling corporations to more easily scan legacy paper documents and turn them into searchable PDF files. The latter proved especially useful during a lawsuit brought against a large tobacco company that sent the equivalent of semitrailer trucks of documents to the opposing attorneys. The plaintiff's counsel used Acrobat Capture to scan the files into PDF for easy categorization.

Sarah Rosenbaum, who has worked on the Acrobat team since 1992, is currently director of product management for its desktop group.

A 1998 promotional video shows a welder consulting specifications in a PDF document.

A keyword search of the PDF files uncovered critical evidence—"the smoking gun," quips Rosenbaum—that led to a conviction.

The Quest for Security

If Acrobat gained traction with version 3, the next one put it into high gear. Acrobat 4.0, released in 1999, offered a host of features that endeared it to the corporate user, such as the ability to annotate and review files in collaborative environments. PDF is, in effect, electronic paper, and the idea was to bestow on it as many properties of paper as possible. The digital equivalents of sticky notes, highlighters, and pencils were included for marking up pages, along with text styles like strike-through and underline for editing copy. Acrobat could compare two annotated files and indicate where changes had been made. Simple touch-up tools were also added for basic text and image editing.

Financial institutions responded favorably to Acrobat 4.0's new security features, such as password protection and digital signatures. Also compelling for enterprise environments was Acrobat's ability to embed other file types in a PDF. So, for example, if the PDF contained financial data from a spreadsheet, the recipient could launch the actual spreadsheet from within the PDF for closer inspection. Windows PC users could also use Microsoft Office macros within Acrobat.

The drive to integrate Acrobat with the Web continued as well. One of Acrobat 4.0's more ingenious features was the ability to capture Web pages as PDFs. In a kind of reverse twist to displaying PDFs in a Web browser, Acrobat could reach out to the Web and take snapshots of Web pages and instantly convert them to PDF files, with graphics and hyper-links intact and pages scaled to fit a target size. Users could even specify how many levels of a Web site they wanted captured at any one time. As was so often the case at Adobe, Web capture arose out of an investigation by an individual—this time, Advanced Technology Group principal scientist Dick Sweet—who showed it to Warnock. "He thought it was pretty cool," says Sweet, "so we did it." This feature has been incredibly useful for archiving Web sites, especially in the aftermath of the dot-com bust, during which so many sites disappeared.

Thanks to these and other enhancements in Acrobat 4.0, sales for the ePaper division, which houses the entire Acrobat product line, sky-rocketed in 1999. Revenues increased 123 percent from 1998, more than doubling from $58 million to $129 million.

Moving Ahead

Released in April 2001, Acrobat 5.0 became a star. Adobe expanded on earlier themes: For instance, PDF annotation was married to the Web, so that collaborators can mark up files from within a browser. Electronic

ADOBE AND THE ASCENT OF ACROBAT

The early days of Acrobat were full of both promise and discouragement. As championed by John Warnock, Acrobat and PDF were technologies that would take Adobe boldly into the next century. Convincing a hesitant marketplace was another matter. Eventually, two events helped propel Acrobat into the mainstream: Adobe's decision to give away the Acrobat Reader free of charge and the rise of the Internet as an information platform. But in the early days, the application had plenty of naysayers, both within and without the company, and Acrobat would not have survived at all without Warnock's dogged determination.

CONCEPT

No one thought anything about Acrobat at the time. Microsoft thought it already had the answer. It was called ".doc."
Roger Black, publication designer

This was the Holy Grail: How do you move documents across networks and platforms? For 30 years people have been trying to solve this problem. IBM tried, DEC tried. Then we did it with PostScript, by snatching the print stream away from the printer.
John Warnock

We understood what Acrobat could do from a technology point of view, but not from a marketing point of view.
Bryan Lamkin, senior vice president, graphics business division

VISION

Acrobat was a start-up within Adobe. It took us years to get our arms around it, but then it started to take off.
Fred Mitchell, vice president, venture development

"People called it the Roach Motel of documents. You get documents into it, but they never come out."

— John Warnock,
speaking at Seybold
Seminars, 1999

Acrobat was a vision of John's. He had the strength of conviction to see it through.
Dick Sweet, principal scientist, Advanced Technology Group

Acrobat was part applications and part system software. It took us a long time to figure out how to market it.
David Pratt, former co-COO and original head of the application products division

The bell went off for Adobe when printers started requesting PDF files.
Roger Black

I was working late one night in my office, which was next to Warnock's. We had to use Acrobat for everything and the beta software was hard to use and took me a long time to do this simple thing, so I started cursing aloud about this stupid software. John stuck his head in to see what was the matter and saw it was Acrobat. I told him that if I had old-fashioned paper files in my in-box, I'd be finished and at home by now. When he sat down

in the chair opposite me and leaned back, I knew that I was in trouble. He was going to wax poetic about Acrobat. It was going to be a long night.
Linda Clarke, former vice president of marketing, application products division

PROOF

Warnock was the lone voice in the wilderness saying we would make money on PDF and Acrobat when all anybody else saw was that we were giving it away for free.
Doug Brotz, principal scientist, ATG, and Adobe's longest-tenured employee

We started making headway when we were giving the Reader away for free. Through Adobe Ventures we went out of our way to fund companies to do PDF development. We needed to find companies to make PDF a standard. Warnock had the vision in his head but translating it into marketing took some time.
Linda Clarke

DETERMINATION

The board of directors always challenged our commitment to Acrobat. But if Chuck and I agreed, then they'd go along. We've been right often enough. Chuck and I agreed about Acrobat.
John Warnock

Had it not been for the individual support of John Warnock and the support of the executive team and the rest of the company, Acrobat wouldn't be here.
Clinton Nagy, former Acrobat sales director

All these antibodies wanted to kill Acrobat. Then they came back and said, Oh, shit. John's right again.
John Warnock

PAMELA HOBBS

Pamela Hobbs' illustrative style has been called "retro-modern" or "James Bond meets the Jetsons." With Illustrator she creates patterns, textures, and environments that, when used in combination with Photoshop, result in unique, "multiplexed" images. Her vibrant, contemporary style has garnered such clients as Swatch, Absolut, and Sony. Hobbs has lived and worked around the globe, teaching computer graphics at the School of Visual Arts, Parsons School of Design, and the California College of Arts and Crafts. Now based in London, the native Brit might best be described as the Emma Peel of illustrators: stylish, distinctive, and ahead of her time. (www.pamorama.com)

"It's not about creating effects in Photoshop and Illustrator but about allowing my individuality to come through."

BizStats: 1999

No. of employees: 2,800

Revenue: $1 billion

Stock price range: $9 to $40 (adjusted for 2-for-1 stock split, October)

Acquisitions: GoLive, Attitude Software, Photomerge

Product releases:
Acrobat 4.0
After Effects 4.0
Adobe Type Manager 4.5 Deluxe/Mac
PageMaker 6.5 Plus
Photoshop 5.5 and ImageReady 2.0
InDesign 1.0
PhotoDeluxe Home Edition 4.0 (Windows)

Industry:
LivePicture files for bankruptcy

forms can be published online and data filled in. Interoperability with the corporate standard Microsoft Office was extended: Users can instantly create PDFs from Word, Excel, or PowerPoint; and they can quickly extract text from a PDF file for reuse in Word or other applications. Yet at the same time, Adobe has beefed up security controls if the document author wishes to prevent the repurposing of content.

Acrobat continued to offer inducements to the graphic arts community. Version 4 had allowed graphic artists to export images in formats suitable for Illustrator and Photoshop and to apply graphics options such as compression and resolution on the fly. Added to version 5 were transparency effects and color-management features consistent with what's available in other Adobe applications. The extended font format OpenType is also supported.

Perhaps the feature that most propelled Acrobat forward was its support of XML (eXtensible Markup Language) and the subset XMP (eXtensible Metadata Platform). XML classifies content by the information it contains and the use of that information as defined by its author. In the case of Acrobat and other Adobe products, the syntax used to define information is XMP. Content defined with XML tags can be used on flexible database-like applications, making it suitable for e-commerce on the Web, for instance. By supporting XML, PDF becomes a medium for financial transactions, not just for static images. PDF provides the form's appearance while XML/XMP supplies the data. Other Adobe applications followed Acrobat's lead in supporting XML: Illustrator 10.0 in the fall of 2001 and InDesign 2.0 in early 2002. XML and XMP will soon be implemented across Adobe's entire product line.

Doing Cartwheels

After the release of Acrobat 5.0, the year 2001 marked a milestone for Acrobat Reader: more than 400 million copies of Acrobat Reader have been distributed worldwide. According to the Web research firm Jupiter Media Metrix, PDF is second only to HTML in terms of ubiquity on the Web. "In 1994 we would go to the Web and count the PDFs by hand [using spidering technology] as an indicator of how well Acrobat was doing. In the beginning there were tens of thousands of PDFs. But when it hit 100,000, we stopped counting. We knew that it was going to take off," Wulff says.

After years of operating at a loss, Acrobat now more than pays its own way. Sales for the Acrobat family of products continued its upward trajectory in 2001, rising 40 percent (67 percent in the second quarter alone) and accounting for 24 percent of Adobe's revenue. All other Adobe business units, including graphics and PostScript, posted declines for the year. Acrobat is now Adobe's lead revenue generator, surpassing former

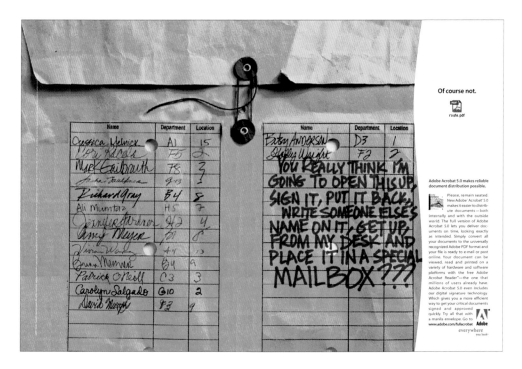

kingpin Photoshop. Acrobat rivals Photoshop in another area as well: As with Photoshop before it, an entire sub-industry of PDF developers has taken root, with several hundred companies currently making plug-ins for Acrobat and related products.

For those who toiled in obscurity on a project that, to paraphrase a comedian, got no respect, being top dog is somewhat unnerving. "When you have a big product with big revenues, you can have big problems," Wulff says. Rosenbaum says that a Photoshop engineer jokingly thanked her for taking the pressure off his team.

But the rise of Acrobat signals more change than who has bragging rights within Adobe's stable of products. Acrobat is wending its way into every aspect of the company's development and marketing strategies and working its way into every corner of the publishing and communications fields as well. Adobe pictures a future in which everyone—from studio-bound graphic artist to on-the-run corporate executive—relies on Adobe Acrobat and its related products.

But before Adobe could unveil that vision, a few more pieces of the puzzle had to be put in place. The company needed a robust page-layout program that bridged the gap between Adobe's traditional PageMaker customer and its emerging Acrobat client. InDesign was that program.

WASHINGTON'S INAUGURAL ADDRESS

FELLOW CITIZENS OF THE SENATE AND THE HOUSE OF REPRESENTATIVES. AMONG THE VICISSITUDES INCIDENT TO LIFE, NO EVENT COULD HAVE FILLED ME WITH GREATER ANXIETIES THAN THAT OF WHICH THE NOTIFICATION WAS TRANSMITTED BY YOUR ORDER, AND RECEIVED ON THE FOURTEENTH DAY OF THE PRESENT MONTH. ON THE ONE HAND, I WAS SUMMONED BY MY COUNTRY, WHOSE VOICE I CAN NEVER HEAR BUT WITH VENERATION AND LOVE, FROM A RETREAT WHICH I HAD CHOSEN WITH THE FONDEST PREDILECTION, AND, IN MY FLATTERING HOPES, WITH AN IMMUTABLE DECISION, AS THE ASYLUM OF MY DECLINING YEARS: A RETREAT WHICH WAS RENDERED EVERY DAY MORE NECESSARY AS WELL AS MORE DEAR TO ME, BY THE ADDITION OF HABIT TO INCLINATION, AND OF FREQUENT INTERRUPTIONS IN MY HEALTH TO THE GRADUAL WASTE COMMITTED ON IT BY TIME. ON THE OTHER HAND, THE MAGNITUDE AND DIFFICULTY OF THE TRUST TO WHICH THE VOICE OF MY COUNTRY CALLED ME, BEING SUFFICIENT TO AWAKEN IN THE WISEST AND MOST EXPERIENCED OF HER CITIZENS, A DISTRUSTFUL SCRUTINY INTO HIS QUALIFICATIONS, COULD NOT BUT OVERWHELM WITH DISPONDENCE, ONE, WHO, INHERITING INFERIOR ENDOWMENTS FROM NATURE AND UNPRACTISED IN THE DUTIES OF CIVIL ADMINISTRATION, OUGHT TO BE PECULIARLY CONSCIOUS OF HIS OWN DEFICIENCIES. IN THIS CONFLICT OF EMOTIONS, ALL I DARE AVER, IS, THAT IT HAS BEEN MY FAITHFUL STUDY TO COLLECT MY DUTY FROM A JUST APPRECIATION OF EVERY CIRCUMSTANCE, BY WHICH IT MIGHT BE AFFECTED. ALL I DARE HOPE, IS, THAT, IF IN EXECUTING THIS TASK I HAVE BEEN TOO MUCH SWAYED BY A GRATEFUL REMEMBRANCE OF FORMER INSTANCES, OR BY AN AFFECTIONATE SENSIBILITY TO THIS TRANSCENDENT PROOF, OF THE CONFIDENCE OF MY FELLOW-CITIZENS; AND HAVE THENCE TOO LITTLE CONSULTED MY INCAPACITY AS WELL AS DISINCLINATION FOR THE WEIGHTY AND UNTRIED CARES BEFORE ME; MY ERROR WILL BE PALLIATED BY THE MOTIVES WHICH MISLED ME, AND ITS CONSEQUENCES BE JUDGED BY MY COUNTRY, WITH SOME SHARE OF THE PARTIALITY IN WHICH THEY ORIGINATED. SUCH BEING THE IMPRESSIONS UNDER WHICH I HAVE, IN OBEDIENCE TO THE PUBLIC SUMMONS, REPAIRED TO THE PRESENT STATION; IT WOULD BE PECULIARLY IMPROPER TO OMIT IN THIS FIRST OFFICIAL ACT, MY FERVENT SUPPLICATIONS TO THAT ALMIGHTY BEING WHO RULES OVER THE UNIVERSE, WHO PRESIDES IN THE COUNCILS OF NATIONS, AND WHOSE PROVIDENTIAL AIDS CAN SUPPLY EVERY HUMAN DEFECT, THAT HIS BENEDICTION MAY CONSECRATE TO THE LIBERTIES AND HAPPINESS OF THE PEOPLE OF THE UNITED STATES, A GOVERNMENT INSTITUTED BY THEMSELVES FOR THESE ESSENTIAL PURPOSES: AND MAY ENABLE EVERY INSTRUMENT EMPLOYED ON ITS ADMINISTRATION TO EXECUTE WITH SUCCESS, THE FUNCTIONS ALLOTTED TO HIS CHARGE. IN TENDERING THIS HOMAGE TO THE GREAT AUTHOR OF EVERY PUBLIC AND PRIVATE GOOD I ASSURE MYSELF THAT IT EXPRESSES YOUR SENTIMENTS NOT LESS THAN MY OWN, NOR THOSE OF MY FELLOW-CITIZENS AT LARGE, LESS THAN EITHER. NO PEOPLE CAN BE BOUND TO ACKNOWLEDGE AND ADORE THE INVISIBLE HAND, WHICH CONDUCTS THE AFFAIRS OF MEN MORE THAN THE PEOPLE OF THE UNITED STATES. EVERY STEP, BY WHICH THEY HAVE ADVANCED TO THE CHARACTER OF AN INDEPENDENT NATION, SEEMS TO HAVE BEEN DISTINGUISHED BY SOME TOKEN OF PROVIDENTIAL AGENCY. AND IN THE IMPORTANT REVOLUTION JUST ACCOMPLISHED IN THE SYSTEM OF THEIR UNITED GOVERNMENT, THE TRANQUIL DELIBERATIONS AND VOLUNTARY CONSENT OF SO MANY DISTINCT COMMUNITIES, FROM WHICH THE EVENT HAS RESULTED, CANNOT BE COMPARED WITH THE MEANS BY WHICH MOST GOVERNMENTS HAVE BEEN ESTABLISHED, WITHOUT SOME RETURN OF PIOUS GRATITUDE ALONG WITH AN HUMBLE ANTICIPATION OF THE FUTURE BLESSINGS WHICH THE PAST SEEM TO PRESAGE. THESE REFLECTIONS, ARISING OUT OF THE PRESENT CRISIS, HAVE FORCED THEMSELVES TOO STRONGLY ON MY MIND TO BE SUPPRESSED. YOU WILL JOIN WITH ME I TRUST IN THINKING, THAT THERE ARE NONE UNDER THE INFLUENCE OF WHICH THE PROCEEDINGS OF A NEW AND FREE GOVERNMENT CAN MORE AUSPICIOUSLY COMMENCE. BY THE ARTICLE ESTABLISHING THE EXECUTIVE DEPARTMENT IT IS MADE THE DUTY OF THE PRESIDENT "TO RECOMMEND TO YOUR CONSIDERATION, SUCH MEASURES AS HE SHALL JUDGE NECESSARY AND EXPEDIENT." THE CIRCUMSTANCES UNDER WHICH I NOW MEET YOU, WILL ACQUIT ME FROM ENTERING INTO THAT SUBJECT, FARTHER THAN TO REFER TO THE GREAT CONSTITUTIONAL CHARTER UNDER WHICH YOU ARE ASSEMBLED; AND WHICH, IN DEFINING YOUR POWERS, DESIGNATES THE OBJECTS TO WHICH YOUR ATTENTION IS TO BE GIVEN. IT WILL BE MORE CONSISTENT WITH THOSE CIRCUMSTANCES, AND FAR MORE CONGENIAL WITH THE FEELINGS WHICH ACTUATE ME, TO SUBSTITUTE, IN PLACE OF A RECOMMENDATION OF PARTICULAR MEASURES, THE TRIBUTE THAT IS DUE TO THE TALENTS, THE RECTITUDE, AND THE PATRIOTISM WHICH ADORN THE CHARACTERS SELECTED TO DEVISE AND ADOPT THEM. IN THESE HONORABLE QUALIFICATIONS, I BEHOLD THE SUREST PLEDGES, THAT AS ON ONE SIDE, NO LOCAL PREJUDICES OR ATTACHMENTS; NO SEPERATE VIEWS, NOR PARTY ANIMOSITIES WILL MISDIRECT THE COMPREHENSIVE AND EQUAL EYE WHICH OUGHT TO WATCH OVER THIS GREAT ASSEMBLAGE OF COMMUNITIES AND INTERESTS: SO ON ANOTHER, THAT THE FOUNDATIONS OF OUR NATIONAL POLICY WILL BE LAID IN THE PURE AND IMMUTABLE PRINCIPLES OF PRIVATE MORALITY; AND THE PRE-EMINENCE OF A FREE GOVERNMENT BE EXEMPLIFIED BY ALL THE ATTRIBUTES WHICH CAN WIN THE AFFECTIONS OF ITS CITIZENS, AND COMMAND THE RESPECT OF THE WORLD. I DWELL ON THIS PROSPECT WITH EVERY SATISFACTION WHICH AN ARDENT LOVE FOR MY COUNTRY CAN INSPIRE: SINCE THERE IS NO TRUTH MORE THOROUGHLY ESTABLISHED THAN THAT THERE EXISTS IN THE OECONOMY AND COURSE OF NATURE, AN INDISSOLUBLE UNION BETWEEN VIRTUE AND HAPPINESS, BETWEEN DUTY AND ADVANTAGE, BETWEEN THE GENUINE MAXIMS OF AN HONEST AND MAGNANIMOUS POLICY AND THE SOLID REWARDS OF PUBLIC PROSPERITY AND FELICITY: SINCE WE OUGHT TO BE NO LESS PERSUADED THAT THE PROPITIOUS SMILES OF HEAVEN, CAN NEVER BE EXPECTED ON A NATION THAT DISREGARDS THE ETERNAL RULES OF ORDER AND RIGHT, WHICH HEAVEN ITSELF HAS ORDAINED: AND SINCE THE PRESERVATION OF THE SACRED FIRE OF LIBERTY, AND THE DESTINY OF THE REPUBLICAN MODEL OF GOVERNMENT, ARE JUSTLY CONSIDERED AS DEEPLY, PERHAPS AS FINALLY STAKED, ON THE EXPERIMENT ENTRUSTED TO THE HANDS OF THE AMERICAN PEOPLE. BESIDES THE ORDINARY OBJECTS SUBMITTED TO YOUR CARE, IT WILL REMAIN WITH YOUR JUDGMENT TO DECIDE, HOW FAR AN EXERCISE OF THE OCCASIONAL POWER DELEGATED BY THE FIFTH ARTICLE OF THE CONSTITUTION IS RENDERED EXPEDIENT AT THE PRESENT JUNCTURE BY THE NATURE OF OBJECTIONS WHICH HAVE BEEN URGED AGAINST THE SYSTEM, OR BY THE DEGREE OF INQUIETUDE WHICH HAS GIVEN BIRTH TO THEM. INSTEAD OF UNDERTAKING PARTICULAR RECOMMENDATIONS ON THIS SUBJECT, IN WHICH I COULD BE GUIDED BY NO LIGHTS DERIVED FROM OFFICIAL OPPORTUNITIES, I SHALL AGAIN GIVE WAY TO MY ENTIRE CONFIDENCE IN YOUR DISCERNMENT AND PURSUIT OF THE PUBLIC GOOD: FOR I ASSURE MYSELF THAT WHILST YOU CAREFULLY AVOID EVERY ALTERATION WHICH MIGHT ENDANGER THE BENEFITS OF AN UNITED AND EFFECTIVE GOVERNMENT, OR WHICH OUGHT TO AWAIT THE FUTURE LESSONS OF EXPERIENCE; A REVERENCE FOR THE CHARACTERISTIC RIGHTS OF FREEMEN, AND A REGARD FOR THE PUBLIC HARMONY, WILL SUFFICIENTLY INFLUENCE YOUR DELIBERATIONS ON THE QUESTION HOW FAR THE FORMER CAN BE MORE IMPREGNABLY FORTIFIED, OR THE LATTER BE SAFELY AND ADVANTAGEOUSLY PROMOTED. TO THE PRECEDING OBSERVATIONS I HAVE ONE TO ADD, WHICH WILL BE MOST PROPERLY ADDRESSED TO THE HOUSE OF REPRESENTATIVES. IT CONCERNS MYSELF, AND WILL THEREFORE BE AS BRIEF AS POSSIBLE. WHEN I WAS FIRST HONOURED WITH A CALL INTO THE SERVICE OF MY COUNTRY, THEN ON THE EVE OF AN ARDUOUS STRUGGLE FOR ITS LIBERTIES, THE LIGHT IN WHICH I CONTEMPLATED MY DUTY REQUIRED THAT I SHOULD RENOUNCE EVERY PECUNIARY COMPENSATION. FROM THIS RESOLUTION I HAVE IN NO INSTANCE DEPARTED. AND BEING STILL UNDER THE IMPRESSION WHICH PRODUCED IT, I MUST DECLINE AS INAPPLICABLE TO MYSELF, ANY SHARE IN THE PERSONAL EMOLUMENTS, WHICH MAY BE INDISPENSABLY INCLUDED IN A PERMANENT PROVISION FOR THE EXECUTIVE DEPARTMENT; AND MUST ACCORDINGLY PRAY THAT THE PECUNIARY ESTIMATES FOR THE STATION IN WHICH I AM PLACED, MAY, DURING MY CONTINUANCE IN IT, BE LIMITED TO SUCH ACTUAL EXPENDITURES AS THE PUBLIC GOOD MAY BE THOUGHT TO REQUIRE. HAVING THUS IMPARTED TO YOU MY SENTIMENTS, AS THEY HAVE BEEN AWAKENED BY THE OCCASION WHICH BRINGS US TOGETHER, I SHALL TAKE MY PRESENT LEAVE; BUT NOT WITHOUT RESORTING ONCE MORE TO THE BENIGN PARENT OF THE HUMAN RACE, IN HUMBLE SUPPLICATION THAT SINCE HE HAS BEEN PLEASED TO FAVOUR THE AMERICAN PEOPLE, WITH OPPORTUNITIES FOR DELIBERATING IN PERFECT TRANQUILITY, AND DISPOSITIONS FOR DECIDING WITH UNPARELLELED UNANIMITY ON A FORM OF GOVERNMENT, FOR THE SECURITY OF THEIR UNION, AND THE ADVANCEMENT OF THEIR HAPPINESS; SO HIS DIVINE BLESSING MAY BE EQUALLY CONSPICUOUS IN THE ENLARGED VIEWS, THE TEMPERATE CONSULTATIONS, AND THE WISE MEASURES ON WHICH THE SUCCESS OF THIS GOVERNMENT MUST DEPEND.

GEORGE WASHINGTON

APRIL 30, 1789

The Return to Page Layout

When Adobe acquired Aldus Corporation in 1994, one of its key motivations was to bring a page-layout program into its product line. The ability to produce complex pages containing both text and graphics, replete with fine typography, stylish composition, and detailed imagery, was a cornerstone of the publishing revolution. That Adobe prior to 1994 didn't have such a product was somewhat embarrassing to the maker of the world's leading publishing tools.

"We essentially acquired Aldus to get a page-layout application," admits David Pratt, former president of the applications division and COO. In addition to procuring a best-selling program in Aldus PageMaker, Adobe gained a much needed piece of the graphic arts and publishing workflow to work with its other applications, such as Illustrator, Photoshop, and, above all, Acrobat.

There was one problem: PageMaker was not the solution Adobe needed.

PageMaker was a sturdy program, but the world had passed it by. Professional designers and high-end production facilities had long since abandoned it for QuarkXPress. That program's developer, Quark, had won customers—including some of the biggest publishing houses in the world—with sophisticated typography, precision controls, and an extensible architecture that allowed users to custom-tailor the application to suit their needs. The very foundation of publishing and page layout was changing, too. With the rise of the Web, anyone who produced a page layout for print was usually asked to create a Web companion, which required separate tools and techniques and resulted in duplicated efforts. Professional content creators sought products that allowed them to leverage their graphic assets and translate them easily from one medium to another—a phenomenon dubbed "cross-media publishing." This was not the publishing world into which PageMaker had been born.

PageMaker still sold well, but its users were primarily small-business owners, nonprofit organizations, and office workers who produced in-house newsletters, bulletins, and the like, and who mostly used Windows-based PCs. While Adobe saw those customers as important, they did not make up the high-end market its publishing strategy required.

Unfortunately, there was very little that could be done to PageMaker to get that audience back. The technical foundation of PageMaker was old and creaky. The core application had barely been modified since 1990.

"The success of InDesign is inevitable. Buying QuarkXPress now would be like looking in the rearview mirror."

— Shantanu Narayen

THE ART OF PAGE DESIGN

With its suite of versatile tools, InDesign allows designers to create dynamic pages that are more than just static containers for graphics. Michael Mabry combines old and new techniques in his Declaration of Independence (opposite page, top). The type on the left page of the spread is hand-lettered with quill and ink, while text fills the sinuous shapes (created in InDesign) behind the tax collector. (www.michaelmabry.com)

Seattle-based Modern Dog designed this poster (opposite page, bottom) to show the graphic flexibility of InDesign 2.0. (www.moderndog.com)

Trek Bicycle (this page) uses InDesign to create eye-popping ads and product brochures for the cycling equipment used by Tour de France winner Lance Armstrong and others. (www.trekbikes.com)

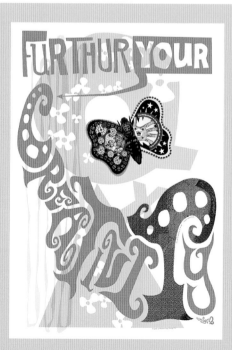

> V V

"Photoshop is a nearly perfect program. InDesign is approaching that."

— Mike Strassburger, Modern Dog

As vice president of cross-media publishing, Susan Prescott weaves together Adobe's integrated publishing strategy.

Because its structure did not allow the seamless integration of additional components, new features had been grafted onto the program. Over time, additions were often written with different programming methods, making the application a software Tower of Babel. Fixing one bug—let alone adding a feature—might break other parts of the program. In some software areas, no one knew how large parts of PageMaker worked. The engineers who had originally implemented the features had left Aldus long before the acquisition, and their knowledge was never captured.

As Warnock puts it, "The code base was in terrible shape, and modifying anything was tough." To get PageMaker in fighting trim to take on QuarkXPress and meet the demands of a changing marketplace would require a complete overhaul of the program, perhaps even a complete rebranding. It was easier to start from scratch.

InGestation: Plotting the Future

As early as 1990, a small team of Aldus engineers had been working in secret on the next incarnation of PageMaker. The seven-person group pondered the question, If we were starting all over again, what would we want PageMaker to look like? They developed the program's conceptual framework, which included an extensible architecture that went well beyond that offered by its rival. QuarkXPress allows specialized features to be plugged in to the program—called XTensions in Quark parlance—but the core program consists of a monolithic chunk of code that is less flexible to work with. The concept behind the next-generation PageMaker was to make the entire program out of modular components so that features could be swapped in and out or updated when needed.

The Aldus team never got a chance to test their concepts under the Aldus flag—PageMaker engineers were often redeployed to put out fires in other parts of the company—but a group of Adobe engineers, including Warnock, saw the work in progress during the discovery phase prior to the 1994 merger. What they saw impressed them. It became clear that Adobe was purchasing that unfinished application and the engineering talent to produce it. PageMaker would function as a placeholder marketed to business communicators until the new page-layout program was ready. That took longer than expected, however.

"At the time of the merger, I ultimately believed that we could integrate it with our products so that they would work well together," Warnock says today. "This turned out to be much tougher than any of us thought at the time." After the merger, Adobe bridged the gap between the way engineers from the two companies worked by supplementing the former Aldus team with engineers from San Jose. This expanded team turned to the task of writing code and constructing the software's skeleton.

The project became known under the code name "K2"—the world's second-tallest mountain but the most technically difficult to climb. Throughout the process, Adobe's engineering team was driven by one thought: to outdo the competition and set new standards. "We knew we could do it one better than Quark," says Al Gass, senior director of cross-media publishing products. "Where we could go a generation ahead, we did, with transparency, XML [eXtensible Markup Language], and OpenType. We could change the underlying paradigm of what a page-layout application could do."

InDesign 2.0, which shipped in 2002, made up for the product's earlier stumbles and was critically lauded.

Key to K2's assault on Quark was its modularity. The program is actually a collection of software plug-ins, 170 or so, coordinated by a plug-in manager. This structure means that conceivably every component of the program can be replaced without the entire application being rewritten. If a particular client needed specific hyphenation and justification controls for its typography, that piece of the program could be swapped for one from a third-party developer or for an improved version from Adobe. Such an architecture gives Adobe engineers and third-party developers the freedom to develop features at a quicker pace than under the traditional software archetype, which means a speedier time to market for developers and faster update cycles for customers. Broken down into pieces, the entire application is much easier to maintain and update.

After its surprise debut under the K2 name during the Quark-takeover episode in fall 1998, InDesign was launched in March 1999. It was the publishing community's most eagerly anticipated product in years, as the rumor mill declared it the only product capable of toppling QuarkXPress from its perch. The InDesign that shipped in September 1999—and version 1.5, which followed six months later—piqued customer interest with their advanced typographic controls (including support for the OpenType font standard), interface components that were shared with Photoshop and Illustrator, and built-in graphics tools. Sales of InDesign skyrocketed initially—curious customers of both QuarkXPress and PageMaker wanted to see what the fuss was about—but then dropped off quickly. InDesign wasn't quite yet the "Quark killer" the public had expected from Adobe.

InControl: The Strategic Hub

Adobe continued work on InDesign even as it updated PageMaker in late 2001. As product features evolved, so too did the philosophy behind it. InDesign was more than a page-layout application. It was the hub of a cross-media publishing strategy that spanned print, Web, and even wireless communications. InDesign needed to work seamlessly with Adobe's other graphics applications such as Photoshop and Illustrator as well as dynamic-media applications such as GoLive and LiveMotion. InDesign, too, would become the authoring application for PDF files that could be distributed across the Internet, or deployed on handheld devices, or read as electronic books.

InDesign therefore had to support anything Adobe's other applications could throw at it—not just PDF but also a host of evolving file formats and technologies like XML, XMP, SVG, and WebDAV, all of which make it possible to share and repurpose content across platforms and devices. "InDesign will be a machine—a machine for publishing highly automated documents," Warnock says.

InDesign also needed to work around the world. It supports OpenType—the extended font format that allows for greatly expanded character sets and rich typographic controls—and Unicode, the universal font-encoding scheme that standardizes languages across platforms, applications, servers, and other devices. Because InDesign supports both OpenType and Unicode, it is well suited for Japanese and other non-Latin-alphabet languages, in which a single font can contain thousands of characters. InDesign-J, designed specifically for the right-to-left and vertical text composition of some Asian languages, takes advantage of the program's modular construction. Instead of trying to modify an existing left-to-right-reading application for a Japanese audience—the method previous page-layout programs used—Adobe can swap out InDesign's Latin-alphabet composition engine for the appropriate Japanese one. As a result, desktop publishing is finally taking off in Japan, nearly 15 years after Adobe landed on those shores with PostScript fonts and printer interpreters.

When InDesign 2.0 shipped in January 2002, it garnered accolades almost immediately and certainly shook up the status quo. "The success of

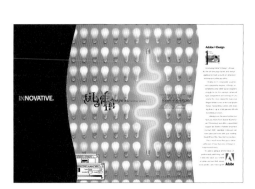

Adobe's first advertising campaigns for InDesign 1.0 played off words beginning with "in"—such as *Innovative* and *Inspiring*.

"We knew we could change the underlying paradigm of what a page-layout application could do."

— **Al Gass**

This poster by Michael Mabry showcases InDesign's ability to flow text into graphic shapes.

InDesign is inevitable," says Shantanu Narayen, Adobe's executive vice president. "Buying QuarkXPress now would be like looking in the rear-view mirror."

If InDesign 2.0 had shipped under the old paradigm of desktop publishing, it would be the most significant page-layout application released in a decade. But InDesign reaches far beyond the printed page to a publishing environment that takes many forms, including the World Wide Web.

Second Story Interactive was one of a new breed of Web design firms Adobe sought to cultivate with its Web product offerings.

Building a New Infrastructure

With InDesign, Adobe delivered a product that addressed its core constituency: creative professionals who produce pages for print. But with its hooks to PDF and XML, InDesign also showed that publishing in the 21st century had to reach beyond the printed page and embrace different media, including the Web. Adobe may have stumbled out of the gate in the early days of the Internet boom, but it had quickly regained its footing. It saw the Web not only as a publishing platform but also as the digital network for an evolving communications strategy.

No longer just the domain of scientists and Net nerds, the Web had worked its way into the mainstream. For publishers, the Web created new opportunities for customized content, dynamic delivery, and lower production costs. For information consumers, the Web offered distinct advantages over print media for getting up-to-the-minute news. Like cable television the Web was live 24 hours a day, seven days a week. But even accessing the Web from a desktop computer was too limiting under some circumstances. As a result, a new breed of portable devices emerged that enabled customers to take the Web with them.

Most companies at the time were operating under the theory that content needed to be freed from its form so that it could be deployed anywhere—on paper, on the Web, even on the new raft of mobile communications devices like cellular phones, personal digital assistants, and electronic books. Adobe recognized the trend, but struggled with the unaesthetic output that resulted from it. The notion of separating content from its formal appearance was a radical departure from the Adobe of old, which believed that presentation—through layout, typography, graphics, and PostScript printing—was as important as the message itself. But with PDF as the linchpin of the publishing workflow, the visual integrity of a document could remain intact even as the content changed dynamically through database tie-ins and the use of XML.

Before Adobe's vision could become a reality, however, it had to bolster its Web presence in applications, systems, and even communications.

Buying GoLive

To become a force in the Web publishing market, Adobe needed better Web tools than its earlier offerings. So in January 1999 it acquired GoLive Systems and its Macintosh-only Web authoring tool CyberStudio. Lauded as one of the best WYSIWYG editors for creating robust Web

The notion of separating content from its formal appearance was a radical departure for Adobe.

Adobe's marketing for its GoLive Web authoring application targeted a younger, hipper Web crowd.

sites, GoLive CyberStudio was already in use at commercial-caliber Web sites in the music industry and had recently garnered several influential awards. A few months later, in the spring of 1999, Adobe released its first version of the product, now renamed GoLive and available for both Mac and Windows.

With GoLive 4.0, Adobe aspired to give Macromedia's Dreamweaver a run for its money. The program included such features as a QuickTime-movie editor, which gave Web jockeys the ability to create streaming video without leaving the GoLive application. By the next version, released in the summer of 2000, Adobe made good on its promise of interoperability between Adobe applications. In addition to sporting the same user interface as its siblings, GoLive could open, edit, and save native Photoshop and Illustrator files.

Having a viable Web tool also gave Adobe the opportunity to remake its established, print-centric image to appeal to a younger, hipper, Web crowd. Ad campaigns during this period featured themes like "Smashstatusquo.com," "Shred the Web," and "Splatterpunk.com." Adobe spent hundreds of thousands of dollars as a sponsor of the extreme-sports X Games in 2000 and 2001. But while GoLive did establish a respectable foothold in the market, Dreamweaver continued to dominate the field. Adobe needed to go a step further and tie GoLive into the company's long-term publishing strategy.

The Web was evolving into a sophisticated communications medium, and Adobe wanted to provide the tools for dynamic-media publishing. GoLive 5.0 incorporated formats and protocols for Web authoring beyond standard HTML. It supported Acrobat PDF, Microsoft's Active Sever Pages, and, importantly, XML (eXtensible Markup Language), which classifies content not by how it's labeled with preset tags, as in HTML, but by what information it contains as defined by its author. Web pages written in XML function more like database records, thus enabling dynamically driven Web site pages to be updated automatically.

As Adobe's publishing strategy evolved, so did GoLive. Version 6.0, which shipped in early 2002, included the ability to produce pages in WML (Wireless Markup Language) and WAP (Wireless Application Protocol) for transmission to wireless devices such as cellular phones. GoLive 6.0 for Windows even included an emulator that let developers preview pages in an onscreen simulation of a Nokia mobile phone. This ability to package content in a variety of formats for a variety of devices would prove critical to Adobe's future direction.

As a companion to GoLive, Adobe unveiled LiveMotion in March 2000. LiveMotion gave designers the ability to animate graphics and add audio or video to Web pages, thus taking advantage of the dynamism

ADOBE AND THE ÜBER-APPLICATION

I n 1995, Adobe undertook an ambitious project to overhaul its entire line of applications with an eye toward making them look and act the same. The goal was a consistent software interface that gave customers a familiar user experience no matter which Adobe product they were in. The first product to sport the new look was Photoshop 4.0, followed by Illustrator 7.0. While now lauded by customers, the change was at first not well received.

THE VIRTUE OF CONSISTENCY

At a tech summit five years ago I got up and said, "Look, guys, we can't have a hollow arrow mean one thing in one application and something else in another. We need to make applications act the same and we need to be able to export files so that all applications can open a file created in another."

John Warnock

Adobe took a metaphor that worked for painting with a brush and shoehorned that metaphor onto Illustrator 7. There was a mass uprising in the Illustrator user community because of the intense rivalry between the Bézier folks and the pixel pushers. Six years or so later Adobe applications have come to a good place in terms of the consistent user interface. Fortunately it's not a foolish consistency, and in places where the applications should differ, they do.

Sandee Cohen, educator, author, and "VectorBabe"

"The decision to change the user interface so that it was consistent across applications was not popular. Now the unified interface is a reason for staying in the Adobe family."

— **Bryan Lamkin, senior vice president, graphics business unit**

One day I found myself having to teach a class in Illustrator, which I didn't know all that well. Someone asked which keyboard shortcut to use. I automatically gave a Photoshop answer—but I was right. They were the same.

Katrin Eismann, author, artist, and "Photoshop diva"

We create content. The type tools being consistent across applications has helped a lot in letting us do our work.

Chris Krueger, vice president and executive producer, eNature.com

Compatibility across applications has been a key component of Adobe's product strategy since 1995.

BizStats: 2000

No. of employees: 2,947

Revenue: $1.3 billion

Stock price range: $27 to $87 (adjusted for 2-for-1 stock split, September)

Acquisitions: Glassbook

Product releases:

FrameMaker 6.0 (+SGML)

InCopy 1.0

InDesign 1.5

LiveMotion 1.0

Illustrator 9.0

Adobe Type Manager 4.1 Deluxe/Windows

InScope 1.0

GoLive 5.0

Photoshop 6.0 (with ImageReady 3.0)

Other:

>> Patent #6,151,576 to John Warnock and Thiruvilwam Raman: a method to play back digitized speech when the corresponding textual component is unreliable

Patent #6,125,200 issued to John Warnock: a method for separating black from nonblack components of a scanned page of text, by which the text has better contrast definition from any smudge marks

Geschke retires as president, remains co-chairman of the board with Warnock

Warnock steps aside as CEO to become CTO

Bruce Chizen promoted to president and CEO

Network Publishing launched

Industry:

Dot-com boom hits highest point

Corel acquires MetaCreations' graphics products

of the media. The application had its work cut out for it, however, as it was pitted against Flash, Web animation software from rival developer Macromedia. Flash created files in its own proprietary (though nominally open) format, SWF. Adobe recognized the popularity of Flash, but hoped to transition the market to another standard, Scalable Vector Graphics (SVG), which was backed by the World Wide Web Consortium (W3C). So while Adobe included in LiveMotion 1.0 the ability to export animations in SWF as well as other Web standards, six months later, it incorporated SVG into Illustrator. Adobe had planned to include SVG in LiveMotion 2.0, but Flash continued to be ubiquitous on the Web, SVG did not catch on fast enough, and LiveMotion 2.0, which came out in February 2002, called out its Flash support as a selling tool.

Serving Up Content

If GoLive was the agent with which dynamic Web pages were authored, then a platform was needed from which to serve content. Adobe began work on a raft of new server technologies designed to facilitate various publishing workflows. Among them were Acrobat InProduction, for managing PDF files in a prepress environment; InCopy, for tracking documents in an editorial environment; and InScope, for administering the tasks and teams necessary for magazine production or corporate publishing. InProduction and InScope were short lived, although the concepts behind InScope were to reappear shortly under another guise. InProduction became redundant when Acrobat 5.0 shipped.

Content is more than just text, however. Images are essential to effective communication, but Adobe didn't have a mechanism in place to dynamically serve images into a Web-based publishing workflow. In fall 2001 it announced AlterCast, server software based on Photoshop and Illustrator, which instantly updates images for Web sites and Web-enabled mobile devices (it also connects to print publishing workflows). AlterCast is well suited for e-commerce Web sites such as online catalogs, in which the color of a garment can change or the availability of an item can cease and the corresponding image must be updated immediately.

The Virtual Studio

As Adobe developed the tools and embraced XML and XMP as standards, emphasis on the Web became a drumbeat echoing throughout the company. Now its internal Web strategy had to evolve, too. Instead of using its Web site merely as a promotional tool and corporate mouthpiece, Adobe transformed Adobe.com into a creative meeting place and online work environment. For Adobe and for other companies, the World Wide Web was becoming both a destination and a vehicle for communication.

In 1999 the company launched a redesigned Web site that not only sold Adobe software but also, like *Adobe* magazine before it, offered feature

LiveMotion gave designers the ability to animate graphics and add audio or video to Web pages, which appealed to a new generation of tech-savvy HTML jockeys.

articles, news briefs, and tips and techniques about Adobe tools and industry trends. In fall 2001 Adobe went one step further and announced Adobe Studio, a Web community where designers can share ideas, download software, and promote their work via online portfolios. A subset of Design Studio, Design Team offers collaboration tools and project management via the Web. Designers who subscribe to the Design Team can post files for review, invite clients to comment on them, and revise them, all through a secure Web connection. Design Team is the Web evolution of the server product InScope.

In spring 2002 Adobe Studio Exchange was added to the site. Exchange serves the community of independent developers who create add-on software for Adobe products. Such software includes plug-ins and automated scripts that boost productivity and improve the efficiency of certain tasks in Photoshop or Illustrator, for example.

The Web now infiltrates every aspect of Adobe. It is a communications medium, a publishing platform, an enabling technology. Even more, the Web is a giant network that links together content creators and information consumers. Even printers use the Internet to reach customers, transfer files, and produce publications.

With all that in mind, Adobe readied itself to unveil a vision for its third decade: Network Publishing.

SECOND STORY INTERACTIVE

Second Story Interactive believes that the World Wide Web is more than just a mechanism for retrieving information or a storefront for selling wares. It views the Web as a means of telling stories through the blending of imagery, narrative, and interactivity. Many of Second Story's projects—commissioned by institutions such as the National Geographic Society, PBS, and the Smithsonian—are designed to be educational and inspirational—but the result is always entertaining. (www.secondstory.com)

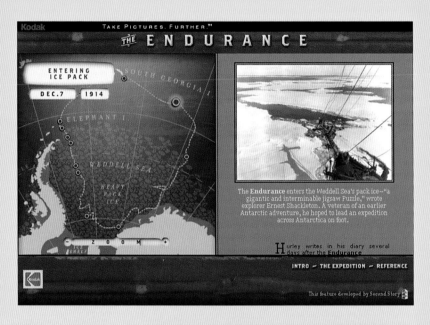

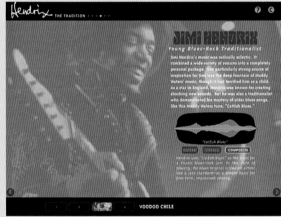

V
V

"When designing for the Web there's nothing to compare to Photoshop: it unleashes your imagination and focuses it into reality."

— Brad Johnson, cofounder,
Second Story Interactive

From left, John Warnock, Chuck
Geschke, Bruce Chizen

The Changing of the Guard

Although the term "Network Publishing" was not uttered publicly until fall 2000, the concept had been taking shape since late 1998. Adobe's management team understood that a cohesive product strategy was critical. Adobe was better known for its products—PostScript, Photoshop, Illustrator, PDF—than as a unified entity. The company needed to articulate a strategy that not only capitalized on the unique strengths of the individual products but also united them under a single umbrella.

Interestingly enough, Adobe's strategy echoed what was going on in the world of publishing, where print, Web, rich-media, and database-driven publishing had converged into a new buzzword: cross-media publishing. Adobe's message was that it could provide an integrated publishing solution that worked across all media and all display devices (printers, computers, hand-held devices, and so on). Whether documents were produced for corporate communications or creative design, whether destined for print or Web distribution, Adobe had the tools. From fonts to image editing to video effects to Web animation, Adobe's software helped you accomplish your goals. The strongest point in Adobe's favor was that most of its software looked and worked in pretty much the same way; the applications had common interface elements, and they shared key technology components—in fact, Adobe formed an engineering group dedicated to defining core technologies.

Adobe's message of an integrated publishing platform received a positive response. In New York in April 1999, Adobe rolled out its product strategy to financial analysts. During a 30-minute break, Adobe's stock price rose by several points as analysts made calls reporting what they had heard. "It was proof that this was what we needed," says Melissa Dyrdahl, senior vice president of corporate marketing and communications. "No one ever doubted that Adobe had great products, but we needed a strategy that they could point to."

With such favorable reactions in the marketplace, it seemed Adobe was heading in the right direction. The management team installed by Warnock and Geschke worked well together. The company the two men had built from scratch would be in good hands. It was time to move on.

"If anyone had told me 20 years ago that we would have a fundamental impact on the publishing industry, I wouldn't have believed them."

— John Warnock

From Mechanical to Digital

In the aftermath of 1998's management changes, Warnock and Geschke reasserted themselves at Adobe and righted a listing ship. But they also

ADOBE AND ITS LEGACY

I n the two decades since its founding, Adobe has had a lasting impact on the publishing and creative communities. As it moves into its third decade, the company will continue to evolve even as it strives to maintain its heritage.

FOUNDING FATHERS

John and Chuck put a human face on technology. I view them as distinguished, intelligent men who really accomplished something. In a young industry they were mature and confident, but they didn't need to boast about it to prove their worth. What defines Adobe is that these were scientists who took their craft very seriously.

Gene Gable, president, Seybold Seminars and Publications

There is a halo over the company because of John and Chuck's fundamental goodness.

Jonathan Seybold, digital convergence consultant and founder, Seybold Seminars

It all comes down to Warnock and Geschke. Their vision permeated the entire industry.

Frank Romano, Rochester Institute of Technology

ADOBE'S VISION

John put PostScript at the center of the universe and he was right.

Roger Black, chairman, Danilo Black USA

The language is PostScript, but essentially the language is Adobe.

Gene Gable

The Roman Empire created the roads, aqueducts, and infrastructure that became Europe. The empire disappeared but the infrastructure

remained. I think Adobe is creating the infrastructure for communication in this century.

Frank Romano

There is no continuity to this story other than Adobe. Second would be Apple, third would be Microsoft. There's enormous volatility in this industry. It's a very reassuring thing that Adobe has been here.

Roger Black

MARKET UNDERSTANDING

John's love of books and typography shows through everything Adobe does, from the programs themselves to the way they're marketed. They get the sophistication of their market, and it makes a difference in their products.

Gene Gable

The people in our market have taste; they care about design. Our saving grace is that Microsoft has no taste.

John Warnock

We helped a lot of start-ups go out of business.

Dan Putman, former senior vice president

The only company Adobe has to fear is Adobe.

Frank Romano

DESIGNING MINDS

We've always been in content, and Adobe has always helped us. Whether it's stories or moving pictures or audio or still graphics—we change the medium but we're using the same tools.

Chris Krueger, vice president, eNature.com

Adobe made it possible for artists to work, and even collaborate, in ways that were once inconceivable. Adobe put power in the hands of artists who wouldn't be able to do it otherwise.

Sharon Steuer, illustrator and author

I appreciate the fact that I don't need to be in the business of commercially producing material to actually produce creative material. All that it takes is to go over to my computer, sit down, and do it.

Gene Gable

The greatest impact you can have is when something is taken for granted. It's like electricity in the wall socket. I think today everybody takes the aesthetic marriage of computer and typography for granted. That was what we set out to do: on the screen, on the printed page, on the Internet eventually, all the way through the production process. I think that's a tremendous accomplishment. No one recognizes it and everyone takes it for granted. That is the best result anyone could ever hope for.

Steve Jobs, CEO, Apple Computer

CULTURAL SHIFTS

Sales and marketing had been an afterthought at Adobe. We had to infiltrate the culture with a marketing focus.

Melissa Dyrdahl, senior vice president of corporate marketing

Adobe has been a technology-oriented culture; it has more of a business orientation now. It's a good blend of both.

Fred Mitchell, vice president of venture development

Cultures are resistant to change. Keeping that culture going as you turn over people—especially founders—is hard, but it is going to change.

Jonathan Seybold

Warnock was allergic to processes. Long-term strategic planning? No way.

Linda Clarke, former vice president of marketing

MOVING AHEAD

If anyone had told me that that we'd have a fundamental impact on the publishing industry I wouldn't have believed it. If Adobe is here 20 years from now, then we'll have a legacy.

John Warnock

It's very special to work at a company with this history. We have an awesome responsibility to not screw it up.

Shantanu Narayen, executive vice president of worldwide product marketing and development

Our core competency is technology around rendering and imaging. As long as we stay close to our core competency, we'll be fine.

Bruce Chizen, president and CEO

Adobe tends to introduce technology 15 minutes ahead of the curve. They tend to invent the future.

Frank Romano

BizStats: 2001

No. of employees: 3,043

Revenue: $1.2 billion

Stock price range: $22 to $77

Acquisitions: Fotiva

Product releases:
 Premiere 6.0
 Photoshop Elements 1.0
 Acrobat 5.0
 Acrobat eBook Reader 2.1
 After Effects 5.0
 PageMaker 7.0
 Acrobat Approval 5.0
 Illustrator 10.0
 Adobe Studio and Adobe Design Team

Other:
>> Warnock retires as CTO, remains co-chairman
 of the board with Geschke

Industry:
 Economic slowdown hits technology industry
 in particular

knew it was a last hurrah of sorts. Both were nearing 60—Geschke is one year older than Warnock—and retirement loomed. (The difference in age is a long-standing joke between them. The two men were compensated exactly the same, but Geschke, given his "advanced age," received a few hundred dollars more per year to pay for medical insurance.)

On April 3, 2000, Chuck Geschke retired from Adobe Systems, but with Warnock he remains co-chairman of the board of directors. Even though he and Warnock walked away with tidy nest eggs, "we were never in this for financial gain," Geschke says. "We wanted to have an impact. We wanted to make a difference in the world." Yet even Geschke says he didn't anticipate the impact Adobe would have. "I'm most proud that Adobe transformed the printing and publishing industry from a mechanical process to a digital process," he says. "That's a huge accomplishment."

Geschke's pride is also more personal. His father was a color photo-engraver and an exacting craftsman. Like all other photoengravers of an earlier era, the senior Geschke had been exposed to cyanide, benzine, and other poisonous chemicals used in the trade ("stuff the Occupational Safety and Health Administration wouldn't let happen today," he says). After his father came to live with his family, Geschke routinely showed him PostScript output and then waited for his opinion. "My dad was extremely supportive," Geschke says. "The typography he liked, but he didn't care much for the color halftoning." One day Geschke brought home color output from a PostScript Level 2 device. "He takes out his loupe—even in his 90s, my dad always kept a loupe with him—and looks at it real close. He puts the loupe down and says, 'Charles, that's good.'" Geschke reflects on one more thing to be proud of: "Photoengravers don't need to use cyanide anymore."

On the day Geschke retired, Warnock announced that Bruce Chizen was the president of Adobe while Warnock retained the title of CEO.

Passing the Torch

On October 31, 2000, at the Tech Museum of Innovation in San Jose, Adobe unveiled Network Publishing, a singular concept that encompasses all of Adobe's products, technologies, and marketing efforts. Walking the few blocks to the museum from Adobe's high-rise headquarters, Warnock and Chizen got into a spirited debate about just what Network Publishing was. Warnock wanted to know the technology behind Network Publishing, while Chizen tried to explain that Network Publishing was not a technology but a "thought platform" or strategy. Warnock, ever the technologist, expressed skepticism that the concept would take hold, while Chizen, the salesman, insisted that market positioning was crucial. The clash of philosophies was telling.

"Good typography is something everyone sees but no one notices."

A perfect marriage
Creativity and technology enjoy a happy marriage in this poster. The design idea at Produce a portrait of Adobe co-founder John Warnock using the glyphs from the *Warnock® Pro* type family that he inspired. The code for the job included Adobe InDesign® software and the aforementioned Warnock Pro, a new member of the Adobe Originals line of OpenType® fonts. OpenType fonts from Adobe are among the most sophisticated typefaces ever offered, enabling designers and typographers to take better advantage of the power of the computer for digital design and typesetting. An OpenType face can incorporate all of the glyphs for a specific style and weight into a single font, eliminating the need for separate expert, alternate, swash, non-Latin, and related glyph sets. Plus, the same OpenType font file works on both Macintosh and Windows® computers, so designers no longer need to contend with font substitution when moving files across platforms. A savvy application like InDesign takes special advantage of OpenType features, streamlining how designers set and fine-tune text. For example, if a designer uses OpenType fonts in a layout, InDesign can instantly substitute discretionary ligatures, true fractions, ordinals, small capitals, and other typographic niceties. What's more, using OpenType fonts with the advanced typographic controls in InDesign produces optimal results. Together, InDesign and OpenType fonts offer enhanced typesetting features that deliver a new level of control and sophistication in modern typography.

John Warnock

Mucca Design created this poster entirely from characters of the font Warnock Pro.

"When John promoted me, I thought I'd be president forever. I thought he wouldn't leave," Chizen says. "But he kept giving me more to do. He was testing me, to see how I'd do." By the end of the year, Warnock was ready to relinquish control. He told Chizen he wanted to spend more time with his family. In December 2000, Chizen was named CEO, joining the board of directors. Warnock then took the title of chief technology officer (CTO).

With Warnock as CTO, Chizen assumed that nothing had really changed, that Warnock would come into the office every day just as he had before. "Three weeks go by and I don't see John. When I do, he tells me he doesn't want to be CTO anymore, either," Chizen says. "He stepped out and I was running the show."

Warnock announced his retirement on March 15, 2001. Geschke thinks Warnock's exit was in part inspired by his own departure. "After retiring I noticed that my shoulders were straighter and my gait was lighter. I think John's wife Marva noticed that, too," Geschke says.

That April saw a passing of the torch onstage at the Seybold Seminars publishing trade show in Boston. After receiving a memento from Seybold president Gene Gable, an emotional Warnock thanked the audience for allowing him to realize his dream of uniting technology and the creative arts. It was a fitting forum for his farewell: Nearly 20 years earlier Seybold had given Adobe a podium from which to trumpet PostScript and to foment a revolution. When Warnock left the stage, Chizen and Narayen appeared to explain Network Publishing.

"If anyone had told me 20 years ago that we would have a fundamental impact on the publishing industry, I wouldn't have believed them," Warnock says today. "We never expected it. It was a matter of being in the right place at the right time." But when asked about the impact of his company, Warnock says it was less about transforming the graphic arts and publishing industries than about changing how people communicate. "Adobe should always be tied to effective communication, about how we get ideas from point A to point B," he says.

Playing to Strengths

For his part, Chizen settled quickly into his new role. "Being CEO is easier for me than being head of products," he says. "I had to work hard to stay on top of the applications, especially the engineering," he says. "This job plays more to my strengths."

That said, Chizen knows he's competing with the legacy of Warnock and Geschke. "I need to maintain their culture and values, their integrity and honesty, their passion for results," he says. "But I'm tougher than John and Chuck. I hold people more accountable and responsible. I flush out the weaker performers." Chizen admitted to being anxious before a *Fortune* magazine article came out naming the best places to work in America as ranked by their employees. Adobe had traditionally scored in the top 100. Had it changed for the worse since he took over? The February 2002 list placed Adobe 27th out of 100—up three places from the previous year.

"There's a common thread of honesty and integrity that runs through John, Chuck, and Bruce," says Dyrdahl. "It's found in your values of how you treat people."

There's no doubt that Adobe will be a different company as it goes forward. For 20 years it was identified with men widely considered to be not only two of the nicest guys you'd ever meet but also astute businessmen, brilliant scientists, formidable competitors, and unshakable partners. Chizen brings different skills. "Bruce is an extrovert," Dyrdahl says. "He loves to sell. He's the guy in Brooklyn with the trunk of his car open just selling what he's got. He loves selling the opportunity."

Chizen has the backing of both Warnock and Geschke. "We couldn't find a clone of ourselves," Geschke says. "Bruce has a great sense of marketing and he knows how to carefully manage resources." Warnock adds: "Bruce is a straightforward guy. He has no agenda other than the success of the company."

In retirement, Warnock and Geschke remain close, but they don't see each other as much as they used to, even though they live a half-mile from each other in Los Altos, California. One reason: "I don't play golf," says Warnock, referring to Geschke's time on the links. Warnock owns a bed-and-breakfast in Utah and spends much of his time there, skiing in the winter, oil painting in the summer, and trying to educate his customers about fine wines. Geschke divides his time between his main residence and outposts in Indian Wells, California, and Nantucket Island, Massachusetts.

As co-chairmen of the board, both are still actively involved with Adobe. "Bruce is brilliant at execution," Warnock says. "Chuck and I have a tendency to think outside the box. Customers and employees like that out-of-the-box thinking. As long as we can be on the board of directors, we keep that spirit alive."

Adobe's new executive team includes: this page, top, Melissa Dyrdahl, bottom, Jim Stephens; opposite page, top, Bruce Chizen, bottom, Shantanu Narayen.

"Technology is changing so rapidly that it is impossible to assess the landscape ten or even five years from now."

— John Warnock

Into the Thic Third Decade

Just as the desktop and online publishing revolutions freed information from proprietary production systems, so publishing in the 21st century will liberate content from its means of distribution. Rapid advances in wireless communication mean that text, graphics, and even video can be delivered to cellular phones and other handheld equipment. Adobe refers to this new phase of communication as Network Publishing, in which the network that is the World Wide Web links together users all over the world and facilitates content distribution, whether that information is read on paper, accessed on a desktop computer, or received on a mobile device. Consistent with its PostScript origins, Adobe is working to establish new communication standards that make good on the promise of write once and deliver anywhere, anytime, and to any device.

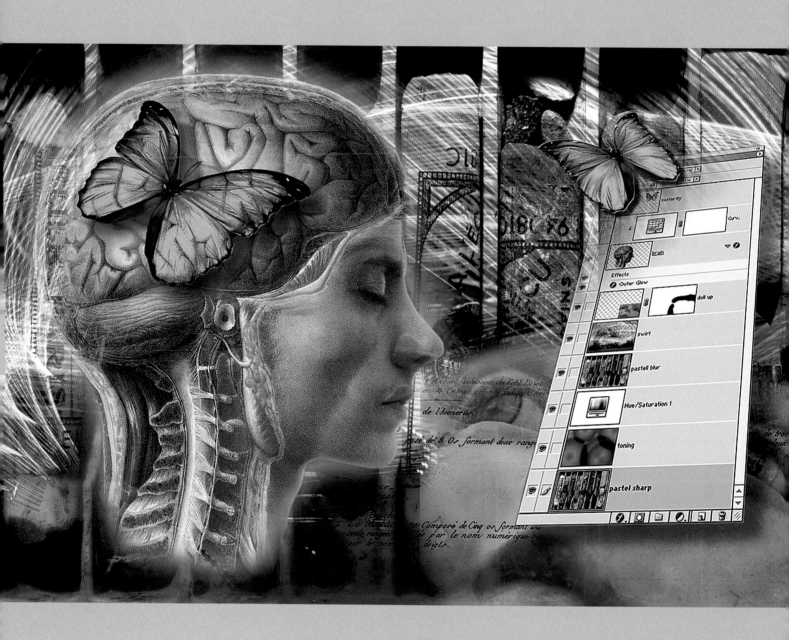

Everywhere You Look

Adobe enters its third decade a different company from the one founded by John Warnock and Chuck Geschke in 1982. Like the publishing industry itself, Adobe has transformed itself into a larger, more complex institution. In 20 years the company has grown from a handful of employees to more than 3,000, and moved from rented office space in Mountain View to a custom-built high-rise in San Jose. But as the company begins construction on its third office tower, Adobe's—and publishing's—biggest change is yet to come.

We've already seen the printing press joined by digital cousins of all sizes and scales, and paper documents augmented by the ability to broadcast (and target) information on the Web. We're now sending communications through wireless networks and moving toward distribution methods most of us haven't even pondered. The way we consume data has shifted, too, from reading general information to accessing pertinent information to subscribing to customized information. Finally, the apparatus through which communications are distributed have multiplied: printed paper has been joined by desktop computers and handheld equipment such as cellular phones, pagers, and personal digital assistants.

The nature of these progressions is remarkable itself, but what's even more astonishing is the pace at which publishing has evolved. The past 20 years witnessed not only the liberation of publishing but also the birth of a new medium in the World Wide Web. No sooner could you say "e-commerce" than another shift occurred: the Web went from boom to bust. Print's obituary was premature, it seems. Now the goal of the wise publisher is to leverage the best of both media—the confidence of print and the immediacy of the Web.

For a company like Adobe, whose foundation lies in developing tools and technologies that enable individuals and corporations to make well-designed, good-looking documents, the changes rippling through the publishing industry are profound. Adobe's worldview has always been that the appearance of a document is as important as its content: Type, color, imagery, and composition all contribute to a document's meaning. Adobe's products, from PostScript to Photoshop to Acrobat, are designed with that thought in mind. But in this new era of publishing, aesthetic intent takes a back seat to pure information, often because of technological limitations. Instead of the typographic richness we've come to expect after 20 years of PostScript, we may soon see the day, as designer Roger

"Adobe's future will rely on ideas and tools that may have no immediate markets or customers."

— John Warnock

Video art installations in Adobe's San Jose office lobby reflect the company's role in graphic arts and publishing.

Black has noted, when the only font that matters is the "AT&T font"—the generic one that appears on a cellular phone.

Adobe's challenge in the next decade will be to overcome these technological hurdles. The company still believes that visually rich documents are key, and that it can develop the tools to create and deliver content with impact regardless of the means of distribution. Its track record suggests it has a good chance of succeeding: With Acrobat and PDF, Adobe found an ingenious way to meld print and the Web, preserving the attributes of paper-based documents for electronic distribution. By making PDF available for the Web, Adobe also overcame the technical limitations of HTML. Now Adobe must do the same for a new generation of readers, a new breed of devices, and a new age of publishing in which every office—and many households—are publishers.

Ahead of the Curve

Throughout its history, Adobe anticipated the stages of the modern publishing revolution with surprising accuracy. The company concentrated first on systems, and then on applications; it focused first on print, then on the Web. "Adobe tends to introduce technology 15 minutes ahead of the curve," says Frank Romano, Fawcett professor of digital publishing at the Rochester Institute of Technology. "They tend to invent the future."

For John Warnock, the key to that future lies in the past. "Adobe's future will rely on heavy investment in basic ideas and tools that may have no evident immediate markets or customers," Warnock says. He cites the successes of PostScript, Illustrator, Photoshop, and Acrobat as examples of products and technologies that had a profound impact on communications, yet were developed well ahead of market demand. He ticks them off in order: "PostScript had no identifiable market or customer base when it was conceived. The potential customers for Illustrator did not use computers when Illustrator was invented. Photoshop was invented when machines were tiny by today's standards—the program was only marginally productive when it was created. Acrobat was invented four years before the explosion of the Internet, but found its home—and markets— when global communication became the norm." With such remarkable foresight, it's intriguing to consider what new technology Adobe might have up its sleeve.

But the company's immediate focus is to tackle the thorny issues of content authoring and distribution in this new world, where information is communicated through a variety of media and on a plethora of devices linked together by the World Wide Web, wireless networks, and more.

The problem is that each of these media types and distribution methods requires a different format. Content creators do not want to reinvent the

100-POINT LIGHT POSTER ITALIC

Original type development, once an Adobe cornerstone, continues with designs like Robert Slimbach's Brioso, a calligraphic typeface in the OpenType format.

ADOBE'S SAN JOSE OFFICE

Adobe's twin office towers, erected in the mid-1990s, are now a landmark of the San Jose skyline. The buildings' interiors reflect Adobe's commitment to and passion for graphics and communications. Window installations resemble color swatchbooks. Floors are studded with elegant typography. An "icon garden" sprouts in the lobby, revealing Adobe products and tools. The buildings are also designed to cater to the comfort of its employees, with outdoor patios, a gourmet cafeteria, and recreational equipment.

VV

"The company was founded on a set of core values based on trust, honesty, and treating people well. This results in a very nice working environment."

— Ed Taft

Senior vice presidents Bryan Lamkin (second from left) and Melissa Dyrdahl (third from left) drive Adobe's product marketing strategies. They are shown here with (far left) David Mills, senior director of research and planning, Mark Nichoson, senior marketing communications manager, and (far right) Mike Saviage, senior director of investor relations.

wheel every time they deploy information to a new medium. Instead, they want to scale content—words, pictures, audio, video—to fit the means of distribution. The solution is content that can be created once and then delivered to multiple devices in multiple ways with minimal manual intervention. With its suite of print and Web publishing tools, and its core technologies of PostScript and PDF, Adobe believes it has the tools that will allow content creators to "write once, deliver many."

The company has developed a brand strategy around that belief: Network Publishing. The concept itself is not new: it's Adobe's twist on what others have referred to as cross-media publishing. But for Adobe, Network Publishing is a unifying principle for the company's product line as well as its corporate image. By linking products such as Photoshop, Illustrator, and Acrobat together under the Network Publishing umbrella, Adobe brings cohesion to its brand identity. "Right now we have a collection of individual brands," says Melissa Dyrdahl, senior vice president of corporate marketing and communications. "We need to have a master brand, and that brand is Adobe."

Its position at the nexus of print and Web publishing makes Adobe uniquely qualified to make the transition to a new publishing model, according to Dyrdahl. "It's not about print or Web. It's about, how do I communicate?" she says.

"Cross-media publishing is the present and the future. It is doubtful that materials will ever be published or used in one medium only," says Romano. "What Adobe must address is the nature of the neutral file format that can be converted to every medium. They are building the conversion into all their programs, but there is still a need for the 'Switzerland' of file formats."

Adobe believes it has that neutral file format in PDF and its data-aware adjunct, XMP.

PDF Everywhere

Adobe proved PDF's versatility when the format evolved from its print origins to the Web, bringing with it such design integrity as complex page layout and font fidelity. Now the company has enhanced Acrobat so that PDF files can be read on handheld devices, not just desktop computers. On-the-go customers can download PDF files from a server or desktop computer, or have them mailed via wireless technology to Palm or Pocket PC personal digital assistants. Unlike text messaging on cellular phones and pagers, PDF files retain their page formatting and other appearance attributes that make for a more pleasant viewing and reading experience.

Adobe's electronic book, or eBook, initiative can be viewed as a microcosm of the company's overall publishing strategy for scalable content through PDF. The term *e-book* refers to content presented in electronic pages designed to resemble their paper counterparts and arranged according to tables of content and indexes. Displayed on either a computer monitor or a portable e-book reader, content can be flipped through, bookmarked, annotated, and so on, just like the pages of a regular book.

Under Adobe's integrated Network Publishing scenario, content designed in InDesign for print publication is exported in the PDF format. PDF files not only preserve the look of a page as it would appear in a book, but they can also contain bookmarks and other navigational elements that underscore their verisimilitude to the printed product. A PDF file destined for e-book distribution can be brought into Acrobat for final touching up, such as changing the page size to fit the intended output device or revising line breaks and other elements that make text easy to read. The e-book PDF file is then posted on a Web site with Adobe's Content Server, a Windows-based software package that allows publishers not only to manage and distribute PDF e-books but also to encrypt them as a safeguard against copyright infringement.

BizStats: 2002

Acquisitions: Accelio

Products released:
    After Effects 5.5
    AlterCast 1.0
    InCopy 2.0
    InDesign 2.0
    LiveMotion 2.0
    GoLive 6.0
    Photoshop and ImageReady 7.0

A customer then goes to a Web site that sells e-books, such as Amazon.com, to purchase and download the PDF file of the book. Using Acrobat eBook Reader, the customer can read the book on a desktop computer or on a dedicated eBook hardware device. (Adobe gained both the Acrobat eBook Reader and the Content Server through its acquisition of e-book software developer Glassbook in 2000.)

The e-book market has been slow to take off, in part due to customer resistance to reading large amounts of text onscreen, and in part due to the murky legal waters surrounding copyright and encryption. But the e-book publishing workflow can be applied to other types of content and devices. The ability to export PDF files is already incorporated into other graphics and content-creation applications such as PageMaker, FrameMaker, and Illustrator, in addition to InDesign.

And PDF is only part of the story. XMP, the eXtensible Metadata Platform, is the technological framework that makes PDF documents "smart," if you will. It allows publishers to add identifying labels and behavioral instructions into a document, so that rather than merely being a string of words, each document becomes almost a mini-database. The document "knows," for example, which pieces of data are appropriate for redeploying on which media. When you export it for viewing or output on a particular device, the suitable pieces of the document are exported in a suitable format. XMP documents are also far more accessible to the reader. In addition to reading it from start to finish, a reader can view and navigate through an XMP document in a number of ways—by topic, by heading, by index. And the document is far more accessible to Web searches or other external search engines.

Into the Enterprise

The promise of XMP documents is most interesting to the business world. With the possible exception of universities, it is corporations that will get the most out of being able to create and repurpose these smart documents. Which means that, in the coming decade, the definition of "publisher" will grow even broader. Graphic files, text files, animation files, and sound and video files are no longer relegated to a special "publishing" sector; they have become part of everyday work.

This broadening of what constitutes a publisher is why a key component of Adobe's strategy is to expand its traditional customer base beyond graphic arts professionals. Given Acrobat's success in the corporate, financial, and government markets, the company believes it has an opportunity to transform the enterprise environment, moving the emphasis away from the individual desktop application toward a more controlled client-server model. In such an environment, automation is key, as the server delivers information to smart PDF documents.

> *"As long as we stay close to our core competency— rendering and imaging technology—we'll be fine."*
>
> — Bruce Chizen

"The question is, how do you solve the problem of business automation for documents and forms?" says Shantanu Narayen, executive vice president. "With a variety of factors such as the government paper-elimination acts that are occurring worldwide, we need to find a way to move from paper to digital documents. We see forms and document automation as a good opportunity to extend the Acrobat franchise."

Adobe targeted the enterprise market once before in the early 1990s with Acrobat and withdrew somewhat bruised, concluding that the time had not yet come. This time, however, Acrobat has momentum, both due to the widespread adoption of the Acrobat Reader, and the ubiquitous presence of PDF documents throughout the business world.

Adobe took steps to bolster its presence in this unfamiliar arena by acquiring Accelio in 2002. An electronic-forms company with deep hooks in the enterprise market, Accelio not only employs an active sales force already working with enterprise customers, but also markets a raft of server technologies that automate the creation, routing, and output of secure electronic forms.

In 2002, Adobe broke ground on its third high-rise tower in San Jose.

"When you couple these server technologies with PDF, you start to get electronic distribution of forms. You can start to customize forms, make the forms intelligent, and personalize them with secure delivery," Narayen says. In one scenario, "smart" PDF forms are tagged for individual users, so certain data fields can be filled out only by the appropriate people, with privileges set by the form's creator and controlled by the server.

Adobe actually uses such a system in-house for its human resources and administrative forms. Expense reports, performance reports, bonus requests, and other such forms are entirely electronic and, backed by a server, route themselves through the company email system with certain text fields turned off or on, depending on the level of approval required. According to several employees, it works fairly painlessly.

"Adobe has the opportunity to revolutionize the enterprise just as Chuck and John did earlier with desktop publishing," says Narayen. "We can change the way people communicate."

To accomplish such a brand identity makeover, however, will require a concerted marketing effort on Adobe's part, given the company's reputation as a darling of independent creative professionals. "Our challenge is to move the business from our core customer base of creative professionals to business decisionmakers in the enterprise," Dyrdahl acknowledges. "Acrobat has to become core to the enterprise. It's a different customer and a different selling proposition. Right now Adobe's image is neutral in that space."

JOHN LUND

In 1991 photographer John Lund faced a slumping market and searched for a way to differentiate himself commercially. He quickly realized that Photoshop allowed him greater creative freedom and better economies than did traditional photography. Lund, whose work is available through stock agency Stone Images, recognized that Photoshop was a natural for the stock photography market, in which product labels have to be removed and images composited for editorial effect. "Flight of the Pigs" (1992) combined elements of two commercial shoots: one for a pig ear-tag company and one involving egrets in flight. These days Lund says he shoots images for their "parts," knowing that he will later manipulate them in Photoshop. (www.johnlund.com)

"The computer and Photoshop eliminate the barrier between imagination and execution. It's possible to make any vision into photographic reality."

It will be tricky for Adobe to maintain its traditional customer base and revenue stream as it courts new markets. "Adobe has done a great job of meeting the high-quality needs of creative professionals," says Gene Gable, president of Seybold Seminars and Publications. "Designers have their own fussy needs, and Adobe was successful at saying, 'We understand you.' But those qualities aren't as important in the IT world, which is more driven by hard-core commerce."

In addition, the new enterprise initiative puts the company in the cross-hairs of the world's largest software company. The challenge will be to avoid direct competition with Microsoft while making an impact in the corporate computing market. Warnock, who has run up against Microsoft in the past, says he advised Adobe president and CEO Bruce Chizen: "Don't ever play on Microsoft's turf or play by their rules."

Looking Ahead

It will be interesting to watch Adobe as it transforms itself once again. Interesting because, if history holds true, the rest of the publishing industry will soon be headed where Adobe is going.

Although the company will continue to develop such flagship products as Illustrator and Photoshop, the time will come when bolting new features onto the twentieth version of an application will fail to entice customers. Adobe's applications are so dominant in their fields that it's already difficult to attract new buyers. The vision of Network Publishing, along with the broader enterprise market, offers the opportunity to both further the Acrobat franchise and to add new life to Adobe's product line.

With the Accelio acquisition and its stated intent to conquer the enterprise, Adobe has set its sights high. No longer is it an interesting little company founded by two nice guys who licensed technology to others. Adobe is a powerhouse, with annual revenues in the $1 billion range and plans to reach $5 billion within five years. Its products and technologies reach into every corner of computing, and its dominance in the graphic arts arena has made the company plenty of enemies.

The company knows it's in for a balancing act. "Adobe wants to be loved and adored by the creative professional community, but analysts want Adobe to be known as an enterprise company that has this great other business," Chizen says. He is quick to point out that Network Publishing embraces both markets: it helps creative professionals produce high-quality graphics for print or online distribution, and lets corporate clients create good-looking documents that have the intelligence and flexibility to streamline internal and external workflows. "Network Publishing is as relevant to a small design shop as it is to a corporate environment," says Bryan Lamkin, senior vice president of the graphics business unit.

ADOBE AND ITS CORPORATE CULTURE

Adobe enjoys a reputation for providing a comfortable and supportive work environment that allows employees to excel in their jobs. In return, the company demands excellent performance. Adobe's corporate values have been committed to paper, but its culture thrives in personal interactions.

CARE AND CONCERN

One of the things that struck me over the years was that John and Chuck led by moral example. The integrity is palpable, and the consequence is that there's a level of respect that stems from them. People know they're good, caring people.

Jonathan Seybold, Seybold Seminars

There were times when John and Chuck had to deal with difficult situations with employees, and they did so with such care and concern. They'd pull people out of a project and give them down time. The attitude was, yes, what you're working on is important, but you're more important than that.

**Dan Putman, former senior vice president,
North American systems division**

At one of the Friday beer bashes, someone started a water gun fight. I'm watching all these executives in their t-shirts and shorts running around squirting each other. I remember that Chuck was particularly good at it.

Colleen Pouliot, former general counsel

John and Chuck were always true gentlemen and respectful of what one could go through in life.

**Fred Mitchell, vice president
of venture development**

People need to be reminded more frequently than informed.

Chuck Geschke

MANAGING WELL

To succeed in management, you should mentor your employees so that they can do your job as well as you can. Effectively replacing yourself is the most direct career path to a more senior management position in the company.

**Chuck Geschke, from a 1998 memo
to employees**

Adobe is quite clear that the major asset is in the heads of its employees.

**Dick Sweet, principal scientist,
Advanced Technology Group**

BEING SUCCESSFUL

On more than one occasion, an Adobe employee has remarked to me that our company stands out from the ordinary because its culture transcends the purely economic engines that characterize many other businesses. But, let us be perfectly clear—Adobe is a business. Maintaining a warm, supportive, caring culture is not the primary mission of this organization. To maintain the important components of our culture, we must commit to excellent, predictable financial performance.

Chuck Geschke, from the same memo

BE RESPONSIBLE

This is an inquisitive company. People ask a lot of questions. Marketing answers don't do well here.

Bruce Chizen, president and CEO

If you make good products, the finances will take care of themselves.

John Warnock

I [HEART] MY JOB

Many things have changed, but one thing has not: the Adobe culture. The company was founded on a set of core values based on trust, honesty, and treating people well. This results in a very nice working environment.

Ed Taft, ATG principal scientist

Adobe is a place we all loved to work. Everybody I worked with displayed caring, dedication, focus, energy, and vitality. It was innovation at a higher level, a way of looking at the world.

Colleen Pouliot

Even now, when you no longer work there, you become an evangelist for Adobe. You loved to go to work.

Dave Pratt, former co-COO

JOHN PAUL CAPONIGRO

John Paul Caponigro describes himself as having "one foot in painting and one foot in photography." In his evocative abstract landscapes, he combines a photographer's observation of place and time with a painter's sense of color and proportion. Caponigro uses Photoshop to strip images down to their bones while expanding their color and tonal ranges. Images like "Dangerous Passage" (top) and "Triple Goddess" (bottom) underscore Caponigro's realization that with Photoshop "taking elements out of pictures was more important than putting them in."

But the concept of Network Publishing alone isn't enough to propel Adobe into its next 20 years. It's a handy catch-phrase to describe Adobe's integrated communications strategy, but the future of publishing extends beyond a single slogan. "Technology is changing so rapidly that it is impossible to assess the technological landscape ten or even five years from now," says Warnock, who even in retirement plays the unofficial role of chief technologist. "Adobe cannot rely on today's markets for its future," he says. Network Publishing is a step toward erasing the boundaries between paper and electronic distribution, but Warnock for one says the vision goes much further.

"In my view the world is attempting to automate almost all aspects of the business process," he says. "There are the highly automated approaches that rely on computer programs for almost all aspects of their implementation, and there are manual processes that are founded, and rely, on hundreds of years of paper flow and human interaction to implement. Mixed in with this is a fundamental change in communication—both in the media that is used, and in the way information is delivered."

Adobe plans to supply the tools and technology to address "the collision between fully automated and traditional paper flows," as Warnock puts it, especially through Acrobat and Acrobat Capture, which translates paper files into searchable PDF documents. Future plans for Acrobat involve imbuing PDF with other properties of paper, such as the ability to enclose it in confidential envelopes or to make multiple sets of copies.

While its vision has yet to be tested, Adobe does have the means at hand to at least tackle that transition. First, it has the solid technological underpinnings of PDF and XMP. Second, it enjoys the market dominance of its tools of the trade, aided by cross-application integration. Thanks to a unified applications model, it's possible for anyone—whether creative professional or corporate communicator—to author and distribute content. And third, and perhaps most important, is the timing: Adobe, it seems, is once again in step with the evolution of publishing.

As it enters its third decade, Adobe believes that the publishing revolution continues—although the term "publishing" may be too quaint for today's hyper-connected, myriad-media markets. The next ten years will test the mettle of the company that twice before rose to the challenge of a new publishing model. Chizen sounds unfazed by the prospect: "There are few companies that can transform themselves into a new business," he says. "This is one of them."

index

Photoshop, 87, 112, 117–122, 124–126
  and Barneyscan XP, 118
  cult of, 125–126
  and Display (Knoll), 117
  first version of, 122, 124
  Magic Wand tool, 118
  new user interface for, 125
  revenue expectations for, 104
  for Windows, 124
  and the World Wide Web, 176–177
pixels, 85, 117
PostScript, 23, 27–29, 36–39,
  and "appearance problem," 36–37
  Bézier curves, 80, 83, 95
  and device-independent resolution, 23, 26, 56
  evolution of, 71
  and font legitimacy, 59, 63
  forging alliances for, 69–70, 73
  as glue for office publishing system, 48
  impact on commercial printing, 53–55
  JaM precursor to, 21–22
  in Japan, 74
  Jobs's pitch for, 33–34, 69
  key to breakthrough of, 29
  and Linotype leap of faith, 40
  and new typeface for computer world, 62
  opening up of, 97
  and OpenType format, 65
  and PageMaker, 49, 53–54
  as subsidizer of Adobe group, 103–104
  Type 1 font format, 89–91, 94, 96
  Type 3 font format, 89
Pouliot, Colleen, 78, 243
Pratt, David, 97, 112, 113, 199, 205, 243
  and Aldus PageMaker acquisition, 205
  as director of support-products division, 103–104
  on Frame acquisition, 159
Premiere, 104, 130–131, 134–135
Putman, Dan, 21–22, 27, 28, 34, 36, 37, 47, 51, 70, 72, 106, 222, 243

Q

QMS, 43
Quark Inc., 129, 183, 208
  proposal to buy Adobe Systems, 187–191

QuarkXPress, 129, 150, 205
  XTensions, 208
QuickDraw (Apple), 90
QuickTime (Apple), 129–130, 214

R

raster image processor (RIP), 54, 55, 90
Ricoh, 74
Rochester Institute of Technology (RIT), 40, 55, 232
Romano, Frank, 40, 50, 55, 84, 94, 95, 222, 232, 237
Rosenbaum, Sarah, 197, 203
Roth, Steve, 38
Royal font technology (Apple), 94, 96

S

SADIM. See Stanford Art Directors Invitational Master Class
San Jose, California, 126, 234–235, 239
Saviage, Mike, 236
Scalable Vector Graphics (SVG), 210, 216
Schewe, Jeff, 64, 120, 122, 126
Schuster, Mike, 80, 96, 97
Scull, John, 49
Sculley, John, 34, 48, 53, 90, 150
Seattle, 154, 155
Second Story Interactive, 212, 218–219
Securities and Exchange Commission (SEC), 78
Seibold, J. Otto, 109
Seybold, Jonathan, 28, 33, 40, 43, 47, 49, 50, 53–55, 89, 91, 94, 97, 174, 178, 223, 243
Seybold Seminars, 94, 96, 139, 144, 149, 187, 226, 242
SGML (Standard Generalized Markup Language), 158, 175
Shaken (Tokyo), 73
Siegel, David, 62
Silicon Beach Software, 162
Silicon Graphics workstation, 87
Slimbach, Robert, 57, 58, 59, 61–63, 233
Smith, Burrell, 37
Smith, David, 75
Sony, 74
Spiekermann, Erik, 63
Spindler, Michael, 150

ILLUSTRATION AND PHOTOGRAPHY

All photographs, graphics, and artwork appearing in *Inside the Publishing Revolution* is protected by the conventions of international copyright law and cannot be reproduced without the express written permission of the respective copyright holders. We thank the many contributors for their cooperation in making this publication possible:

Adobe Systems, Inc. Graphics courtesy Adobe Systems, Inc., pp. 4, 9, 13, 20, 23, 39, 40, 46, 47, 49, 52, 63, 66, 67, 70, 71, 75, 80, 83, 84, 85, 86, 91, 97, 102, 103, 105, 120, 130, 136, 137, 138, 139, 140, 141, 148, 149, 151, 153, 156, 157, 158, 162, 164, 174, 175, 176, 177 , 179, 188, 189, 192, 194, 196, 198, 203, 209, 210, 214, 217, 225, 228, 233.

Adobe Systems, Inc. Photographs courtesy Adobe Systems, Inc., pp. 4, 8, 11, 16, 17, 19, 22, 26, 27, 28, 29, 46, 53, 86, 102, 149, 153, 168, 171, 172, 173, 186, 190, 192, 194, 195, 220, 226, 227.

Assassi Productions Photograph by Assassi Productions for Adobe Systems, Inc., pp. 4, 154.

Birkenseer, Jim Graphics by Jim Birkenseer, p. 39.

Brown, Russell Graphics by Russell Brown for Adobe Systems, Inc., p. 83.

Burns, Diane Artwork by Diane Burns, TechArt, pp. 50, 74.

Caponigro, John Paul Artwork © John Paul Caponigro. Dangerous Passage © 1994, p. 244; Triple Goddess © 1996, p. 244.

Chan, Ron Artwork by Ron Chan, pp. 92, 93, 100.

Curtis, Hillman Artwork by Hillman Curtis, pp. 180, 181.

Eismann, Katrin Artwork by Katrin Eismann, www.photoshopdiva.com. Memories and Bits © 2002, p. 124; Repetition © 1997, Für mein Vater © 1991, and Memories of Asia © 1996, p. 127; In Progress 2002, p. 230.

Fishauf, Louis Artwork by Louis Fishauf, pp. 166, 167.

Graphic Arts Monthly Photograph courtesy *Graphic Arts Monthly*, p. 29.

Greiman, April Artwork by April Greiman / Made In Space. "Something From Nothing," text by Aris Janigian, Rotovision, United Kingdom, 2001, pp. 132, 133; Amgen Café, Thousand Oaks, California, environmental mural, p. 132; "Light Is Always Looking for a Body," Aspen Design Conference 2001, p. 133.

Guthrie, Stewart Photograph by Stewart Guthrie, "Riverside House," Georgie Road, Edinburgh, for Adobe Systems, Inc., p. 172.

Hobbs, Pamela Artwork by Pamela Hobbs, www.pamorama.com, pp. 200, 201.

Holtzman, Eliot Photograph by Eliot Holtzman, www.eliotholtzman.com, p. 145.

International Typeface Corporation Photograph courtesy International Typeface Corporation, p. 32.

Janssens, Glen Artwork courtesy Glen Janssens, eMotion studios, Inc., www.emotionstudios.com, pp. 128, 131.

Johnson, Brad Artwork courtesy Brad Johnson, Second Story Interactive, pp. 212, 218, 219.

Johnson, Stephen Photographs © 2002 Stephen Johnson. All rights reserved worldwide. pp. 30, 31.

Kashi, Ed Photograph by Ed Kashi, p. 48.

Kim, Scott Graphics courtesy Scott Kim, pp. 4, 20, 38.

Krueger, Chris Artwork by Chris Krueger for Adobe Systems, Inc., p. 106.

Lund, John Artwork © John Lund, www.johnlund.com, pp. 240, 241.

Mabry, Michael Artwork courtesy Michael Mabry, pp. 204, 207, 211. Design by Michael Mabry and Margie Chu, illustration and handlettering by Michael Mabry.

Mac Publishing, LLC Reprinted with permission of Mac Publishing, LLC, p. 88.

Menuez, Doug Photographs courtesy Doug Menuez © 2002, pp. 4, 6, 10, 18, 22, 24, 25, 34, 36, 42, 44, 46, 57, 62, 68, 72, 76, 78, 79, 81, 82, 98, 99, 102, 104, 105, 107, 108, 110, 111, 113, 125, 146, 160, 182, 185, 215, 222, 223.

Modern Dog Artwork by Modern Dog, p. 207.

Mok, Clement Artwork by Clement Mok, p. 53.

Monroy, Bert Artwork by Bert Monroy, pp. 87, 116, 123.

Mucca Design Artwork by Mucca Design for Adobe Systems, Inc., p. 225.

San Francisco Examiner Photograph courtesy *San Francisco Examiner*, p. 16.

San Jose Mercury News Photograph courtesy *San Jose Mercury News*, p. 14.

Schewe, Jeff Images © Jeff Schewe. All rights reserved. pp. 4, 64, 102, 118, 119, 120, 122, 192.

Seybold Publications Photograph courtesy Seybold Seminars and Publications, p. 54.

Smith, David Artwork by David Smith for Adobe Systems, Inc., p. 75.

Steuer, Sharon Artwork by Sharon Steuer, p. 126.

Stone, Sumner Photographs copyright Sumner Stone. All rights reserved. pp. 60, 61, 63, 67. Photograph courtesy Sumner Stone, p. 65. Artwork by Sumner Stone for Adobe Systems, Inc., p. 73.

Storey, John Photographs by John Storey Photography, pp. 39, 59, 86, 96, 139, 148, 152, 155, 159, 171, 197, 208, 214, 232, 234, 235, 236, 239, 242, 243.

Studer, Gordon Artwork by Gordon Studer, pp. 114, 115.

Trek 1 Artwork courtesy of Trek Bicycle Corporation. Tricia Burke, Designer, p. 206.

Wang, Min Artwork by Min Wang, Square Two Design, for Adobe Systems, Inc., pp. 4, 12, 60, 66, 67, 194.

Weinman, Lynda Artwork by Lynda Weinman, President, lynda.com, inc., p. 135.

Acknowledgments

This book could not be written without the kind assistance of many individuals. Some of their names appear in the text, others do not, but all lent their wisdom, insight, and talents.

The Content

Writing a book of this scope is a daunting prospect. Adobe Systems has touched the lives of millions of people during its 20-year history. If I had my druthers I would talk to every person influenced by Adobe, repeat every anecdote about the company's impact, show every piece of art ever created with an Adobe product, and so on. My greatest regret is that I could not do so in the time and space allowed. I did talk to many people whose experiences represent Adobe's history, people, culture, and inventions. I hope I have done justice to their stories. My deepest appreciation goes to:

Chuck Geschke and John Warnock, for sharing their ideas and insights, reflections of the past, and thoughts about the future. Being in the presence of these two men is a privilege I won't soon forget;

Bruce Chizen, Shantanu Narayen, Melissa Dyrdahl, and Bryan Lamkin, for making time in their extraordinarily busy schedules to talk to me about Adobe's future directions;

Steve Jobs, for giving me his views about Apple and Adobe's relationship and its impact on communications;

Paul Brainerd, for telling me about Aldus, Adobe, and the birth of desktop publishing;

Jonathan Seybold and Frank Romano, for providing thoughtful context and analysis about the modern publishing revolution and Adobe's place in the industry;

Doug Brotz, for explaining the inner workings of PostScript and PDF with patience and humor;

Doug Menuez, for allowing us to reproduce his wonderful photographs of Adobe from the early 1990s. As a complete photographic record of an important era for Adobe—and indeed Silicon Valley—his images have been invaluable;

Jeff Schewe, for letting me borrow from his comprehensive history of Photoshop;

Seybold Publications, for giving me access to its back issues, which are hands-down the single, most reliable written record of the early years of the publishing revolution;

The following artists, for lending their work for publication and giving me a window onto the creative process: John Paul Caponigro, Ron Chan, Katrin Eismann, Louis Fishauf, April Greiman, Pamela Hobbs, Glenn Janssens, Brad Johnson/Second Story Interactive, Stephen Johnson, John Lund, Michael Mabry, Modern Dog, Clement Mok, Bert Monroy, Jeff Schewe, Sharon Steuer, Gordon Studer, Trek, Lynda Weinman; and

Diane Burns, Luanne Seymour Cohen, Scott Kim, Sumner Stone, and Min Wang, for providing historical artwork from their personal collections.

In addition, I could not have written this book without the help of those who generously spent hours sharing memories with me, often skipping meetings and ignoring phone calls to do so. I am deeply indebted to: David Biedny, Jim Birkenseer, Roger Black, David Blatner, Steve Broback, Russell Preston Brown, Matthew Carter, Linda Clarke, Sandee Cohen, Janice Coley, Ed Fladung, Gene Gable, Al Gass, Allan Haley, Kim Isola, Jim King, Thomas Knoll, Chris Krueger, Olav Martin Kvern, Kathleen Lau, David Lemon, Steve MacDonald, Robin Maccan, Tom Malloy, Jill Merlin, Sam Merrell, Dan Mills, Fred Mitchell, Glenn Mitsui,

Clinton Nagy, Bruce Nakao, Colleen Pouliot, David Pratt, Dan Putman, Melvin Rivera, Sarah Rosenbaum, Steve Roth, Robert Slimbach, Dick Sweet, Ed Taft, Peter Truskier, Carol Twombly, Jen Van Deren, Chuck Weger, Bob Wulff, and David Zwang.

The Book

Producing a book of this complexity is truly a collaborative effort that demanded the talents of an exceptional cast. That my name alone is on the cover seems odd to me. For making this book a reality, my thanks go to:

Serena Herr, my smart, funny, and sure-footed editor, for displaying a level head and even temper throughout this process; she is an equal partner in this book in every way imaginable;

Andrew Faulkner, my fabulous art director, for creating an elegant design that not only illuminates its subject matter but shines bright on its own;

Kate Reber, my production manager, for keeping this very complicated project on track;

Karen Seriguchi, my copy editor and proof reader, for mending split infinitives and toiling day and night to make me look better than I deserve;

Christine Yarrow, publisher of Adobe Press, for entrusting me with the company "jewels," giving me the inside scoop, and making many helpful introductions;

Jeffrey Warnock, project manager for Adobe Press, for teaching me the secret Adobe handshake, wrangling art and humans, and excelling as an all-around go-to guy;

Anita Dennis, my designated hitter, for stepping in to help with many details, especially those nit-picky timelines and the masterful sidebar on PostScript printing;

Marjorie Baer, executive editor of Peachpit Press, for opening this door for me as another one closed; and

Nancy Aldrich Ruenzel, publisher of Peachpit Press, for having faith in the project from the beginning.

The Rest

Writing a book can be a solitary exercise, but thanks to the following folks, I'm never alone. I am grateful to:

Cindy Samco and Jeff Lalier, my partners in Creativepro.com and more importantly my friends, for keeping the site alive and clicking, and cutting me slack as I said "It's almost done" for months; and to Eric Stone, for pitching in on the site and videotaping the Olympic curling events for me;

Maggie Canon, Sandee Cohen, Rick LePage, Olav Martin Kvern, Janice Maloney, David Morgenstern, Margaret Richardson, and Scholle Sawyer McFarland, for offering necessary perspective, safe harbor, and emotional buoyancy;

Bruce Fraser, for being my Adobe co-conspirator during many of the years when these events took place;

The McLaughlin-Graham clan, for reminding me that there is more to life than this book; and

Nancy Williams and Sandy Morrison, for more than I can ever say or these pages could possibly hold.

Pamela Pfiffner, Portland, Oregon, June 2002

COLOPHON

Pamela Pfiffner wrote *Inside the Publishing Revolution: The Adobe Story* on an Apple Macintosh Titanium PowerBook and an Apple iMac DV Special Edition, using Microsoft Word and Adobe Acrobat, Illustrator, Premiere, Photoshop, and Photoshop Elements. She also made extensive use of her RadioShack microcassette recorder, an RCA cable modem, and Peachpit's sturdy FTP site, which housed the 5,000-plus image archive for this book.

The book team used Adobe's DesignTeam online collaboration tool for online reviews.

Designer Andrew Faulkner used several applications on his Macintosh G4 system, including Adobe Photoshop 7.0, Adobe Illustrator 10.0, InDesign 2.0, and Adobe Acrobat 5.0. He also used a Titanium PowerBook, an Epson 3000 color printer, and an Apple 17" flat-panel monitor.

Proofing was done on an Epson RIP station 5000 with a Fiery RIP.

Fonts used are Warnock Pro, Myriad MM, Adobe Garamond Pro, and Trajan, all from Adobe Systems, Incorporated, www.adobe.com.

This book was printed with computer-to-plate technology on 80-lb Influence Soft Gloss on a web press at Quebecor World Printing in Taunton, Massachusetts.